# Diversity's Child

# Diversity's Child

People of Color and the Politics of Identity

EFRÉN O. PÉREZ

The University of Chicago Press
Chicago and London

The University of Chicago Press, Chicago 60637
The University of Chicago Press, Ltd., London
© 2021 by The University of Chicago
All rights reserved. No part of this book may be used or reproduced in any manner whatsoever without written permission, except in the case of brief quotations in critical articles and reviews. For more information, contact the University of Chicago Press, 1427 E. 60th St., Chicago, IL 60637.
Published 2021
Printed in the United States of America

30  29  28  27  26  25  24  23  22  21      1  2  3  4  5

ISBN-13: 978-0-226-79976-6 (cloth)
ISBN-13: 978-0-226-80013-4 (paper)
ISBN-13: 978-0-226-79993-3 (e-book)
DOI: https://doi.org/10.7208/chicago/9780226799933.001.0001

Library of Congress Cataloging-in-Publication Data

Names: Pérez, Efrén Osvaldo, 1977– author.
Title: Diversity's child : people of color and the politics of identity / Efrén O. Pérez.
Description: Chicago ; London : The University of Chicago Press, 2021. |
    Includes bibliographical references and index.
Identifiers: LCCN 2020054612 | ISBN 9780226799766 (cloth) |
    ISBN 9780226800134 (paperback) | ISBN 9780226799933 (ebook)
Subjects: LCSH: Minorities—United States—Attitudes. | Group identity—
    United States—Public opinion. | Group identity—United States. | Group identity—
    Political aspects—United States. | Identity politics—United States. | Political
    psychology—United States. | United States—Ethnic relations—Political aspects.
Classification: LCC E184.A1 P388 2021 | DDC 305.800973—dc23
LC record available at https://lccn.loc.gov/2020054612

# Contents

Introduction: Marable's Forecast 1
1. The Elusive Quest for People of Color 14
2. People of Color, Unite! 23
3. The Many Faces of People of Color 33
4. New Wine in New Bottles 67
5. I Feel Your Pain, Brother 92
6. Galvanizing People of Color 122
7. Falling Apart 147
Conclusion: People of Color in a Diversifying World 179

*Acknowledgments 187*
*References 191*
*Index 207*

INTRODUCTION

# Marable's Forecast

In the year 2000, fully one-third of America's total population will consist of people of color—Latinos, Asian-Americans, Pacific-Americans, American Indians and African Americans. The fastest-growing groups in this country are people of color.
—MANNING MARABLE, *New York Amsterdam News* (1993)

Although 2000 has come and gone, Marable's prediction remains as prescient as ever. The US continues to diversify rapidly. When the renowned professor of African American Studies first wrote these words, he envisioned that demographic growth would be followed by greater solidarity among diverse minority communities. The latest estimates from the Census Bureau (2018) reveal that the first half of his vision has been fulfilled, with Blacks, Asian Americans, Latinos, and Native Americans now constituting 38.3% of the US population—a share that continues to rise. In fact, new figures suggest people of color will soon demographically overtake Whites, transforming the US into a majority-minority nation (Pew Research Center 2015).

This palpable sense of profound and imminent transformation hangs heavily in the air. Indeed, dispatches from several intellectual circles—Marable's included—alert us to some of the consequences this demographic reality has already produced. In particular, social scientists are discovering a White population that is hunkering down and lashing out against the growth of PoC (Craig and Richeson 2014; Danbold and Huo 2015; Jardina 2019). As the lone dominant racial group since the inception of the US, many Whites have grown accustomed to a relatively higher station in life that is attended by greater access to power, resources, and status (Carter and Pérez 2015; Sidanius et al. 1997; Sidanius and Pratto 1999). Yet the tide of PoC washing over America signals to Whites, in the starkest terms possible, that their privileged foothold is loosening, and fast (Jardina 2019)—hence, the resistance of some Whites to multicultural initiatives (cf. Danbold and Huo 2015; Pérez, Deichert, and Engelhardt 2019), the rightward shift of a substantial proportion of Whites toward conservativism and Republican allegiance (Abrajano and Hajnal 2015; Craig and Richeson 2014a, b); the resistance of many Whites to minority candidates for elected office (Fraga 2018; Hajnal 2007); the White opposition to Latino, Asian, and Muslim immigrants (Hainmueller and Hopkins 2014; Malhotra, Margalit, and Mo 2012; Newman 2012; Newman and Malhotra 2019; Oskooii, Lajevardi, and Collingwood 2019; Pérez 2016; Reny, Valenzuela, and Collingwood 2019); and some Whites' support for punitive policies that incarcerate unequal numbers of African Americans and Latinos (Ramirez 2013a, b; Weaver and Lerman 2010).

However, although people of color are profoundly shaping what Whites think of a shifting US society, research on what people of color themselves think about this sea change and how they are reacting to it is nearly absent. This omission is odd given the diversity of demographic trends among racial and ethnic minorities themselves. In the aggregate, African Americans (13.4%) and Latinos (18.3%) comprise the largest segments of non-Whites; whereas Blacks have held this distinction since times of slavery, Latinos have only assumed this role in the past 50 years, mainly due to immigration and robust fertility rates. In contrast, Native Americans (1.3%) and Asian Americans (6.1%) comprise smaller segments of the total US population. In addition, while demographic growth among Blacks has been anemic, Latinos are now considered the fastest-growing racial minority (Frey 2018; US Census Bureau 2018). This heterogeneity in population trends is further matched by the fractious political histories, goals, and aspirations of these groups, which many times weakly overlap with one another (Dawson 1994; García 2012; Kim 2003; Masuoka and Junn 2013; McClain and Johnson Carew 2017; Nagel 1996; Omi and Winant 1986; Vaca 2004; Wilkins and Kiiwetinepinesiik Stark 2018).

The very assumption, then, that racial and ethnic minorities see themselves as Marable called them—as *people of color*—is just that: mere assertion, speculation, and supposition, but not an established fact proper. In fact, many scholars (not a few of them minorities themselves) have threaded a rich tapestry of findings that teach us how and why distinct non-White groups, such as African Americans, Asian Americans, Latinos, and others, sometimes see themselves as economic and political competitors rather than allies (e.g., Benjamin 2017; Cutaia Wilkinson 2015; McClain et al. 2005; McClain and Karnig 1990). In many major cities across the US, groups such as African Americans and Latinos—who often share neighborhoods, schools, labor markets, and lower social status—display extremely hostile attitudes toward each other (Gay 2006; Telles, Sawyer, and Rivera-Salgado 2011; Vaca 2004; Zou and Cheryan 2017). Yet whether various minority groups can sometimes share a common identity and sense of solidarity as people of color is a lingering question that has largely escaped researchers' attention.

This is a mistake, I think, and one I hope to rectify in the subsequent chapters of this book. Accordingly, I aim to convince you that despite their unique identities as Black, Asian American, Latino, and so on, members of these distinct minority groups often share an identity as people of color, or what I call PoC ID. Although the precise origins of the label *people of color* remain largely shrouded in mystery (Yuen 1997), a close reading of the historical record suggests that Black Americans' struggle with slavery and its aftermath is a key source (Carter 2019; Franklin 1947). In the US republic's early days, for example, *free people of color* denoted individuals who were of African and European heritage, but not enslaved (Dunbar Nelson 1917). At the peak of Jim Crow, moreover, Black leaders used *colored* and *people* to christen the National Association for the Advancement of Colored People (NAACP), which still fights racial discrimination today (Sullivan 2009). Even Martin Luther King Jr. drew on this label to build the felicitous phrase "citizens of color" to highlight Black inequality in his iconic "I Have a Dream" speech (King 1963; Safire 1988). These scattered examples, and many others, suggest the term *people of color* has deep roots in the African American community, with the epigraph from Manning Marable—a Black academic—underscoring the label's origins among African Americans as well as its increasing application to non-Black minorities.

But *people of color* is more than a descriptor. It is, I hope to persuade you, a distinct attachment in the identity portfolios that racial and ethnic minorities possess. Similar to their respective identities as African American, Asian American, or Latino, I contend that racial and ethnic minorities have access to PoC ID: a new form of identification in their repertoires of group attachments. This is a different type of identity that, when made salient, encapsulates minorities' sense of being Black, Asian, Latino, and so on. In other words, PoC ID encourages racial and ethnic minorities to view themselves as largely interchangeable members of the same broad-based group, *people of color* (cf. Turner et al. 1987, 1994). This does not mean that individuals forget that they are Black, Asian, or Latino—or that they dismiss being Jamaican, Chinese, or Mexican—which are politically important identities in their own right (Abrajano and Alvarez 2010; Garcia 2012; Greer 2013; Lien, Conway, and Wong 2004; Pérez 2015a; Rogers 2006; White and Laird 2020; Wong et al. 2011). Instead, each of these categories becomes temporarily subsumed under the larger collective, *people of color*, much like individuals from various backgrounds and diverse groups can think of themselves as *American* when a foreign policy crisis or other contextual feature demands it (Kam and Ramos 2008; Transue 2007).

The social and political influence of PoC ID, I argue, hinges critically on its situational salience and relevance—two features that vary predictably with a setting's frame of reference (Tajfel 1981). Just as in social contexts, the political arena often highlights specific cleavages that divide "us" from "them" (Huddy and Virtanen 1995; Kinder and Kam 2009; Pérez and Tavits 2019; Turner et al. 1987, 1994). In the US, one of these axes arises from the racial hierarchy that places Whites at the apex and several non-White groups arrayed in varying degrees below (Carter and Pérez 2016; Kim 2003; Masuoka and Junn 2013; Sidanius and Petrocik 2001; Zou and Cheryan 2017). When this divide becomes salient, non-Whites are motivated to weight more heavily the many features (e.g., a sense of discrimination, inequality, marginalization) that they share in common, that distinguishes them from Whites, and that they use to combat their shared devaluation in society. My primary claim, then, is not that PoC ID supersedes or replaces other forms of group attachment among racial and ethnic minorities. Rather, I contend that PoC ID is a heretofore understudied form of identity that can illuminate our understanding of the demographic flux gripping the US and the political response to it as expressed by a growing cast of non-White protagonists.

But a new identity that spans *across* racial minority groups? Really? Given the social, economic, historical, and political differences present between various non-White communities, it is both reasonable and prudent to wonder just how prevalent and meaningful PoC ID is. The good news is that PoC ID stands on firm conceptual ground, as the study of racial and ethnic politics has already wrestled directly with comparable pan-ethnic and pan-racial categories, such as *Latino* and *Black* (Beltrán 2010; Garcia 2012; Greer 2013; Watts Smith 2014). The bad news is that confronting the cross-cutting nature of PoC ID head on is complicated by the lack of direct measures of this new attachment, which is one of this book's main contributions. Thus, to provide proof of concept, I present here three sources of data that, I hope, will convince skeptical readers that grappling further with PoC ID is a worthy scientific endeavor.

Consider the entries in table I.1. There we see average favorability ratings that Black, Latino, and Asian respondents to the 2016 American National Election Study (ANES) provided about three groups: African Americans, Asian Americans, and Latinos. Using what is called a "feeling thermometer," minority respondents in the ANES indicated, on a scale from 0 to 100, how positively or "warmly" they feel toward their own racial group as well as other racial minority out-groups. The entries in table I.1 underscore two basic facts. First, consistent with prior work, Black, Latino, and Asian respondents rate their own racial/ethnic group quite positively, and certainly more positively

TABLE 1.1. Average warmth ratings of Blacks, Asians, and Latinos by minority respondents in the 2016 American National Election Study

|  | Black respondents | Asian respondents | Latino respondents |
| --- | --- | --- | --- |
| Rating of African Americans | 83 | 62 | 68 |
| Rating of Asian Americans | 70 | 76 | 68 |
| Rating of Latinos | 68 | 64 | 78 |
| N | 333 | 113 | 351 |

Note: Warmth ratings occurred on a scale from 0 to 100, with higher values indicating greater warmth toward a group.

than other minority out-groups (Branscombe and Wann 1994; Kinder and Kam 2009). There is nothing quirky here. This pattern simply underlines the time-tested inclination of all humans—racial and ethnic minorities included—to express *in-group favoritism*: a behavioral and attitudinal bias toward one's more immediate group (Tajfel 1981; Tajfel et al. 1971). Second, and perhaps more revealing, is that Black, Latino, and Asian respondents all rate their racial in-group *and* other minority out-groups well above the middle of the scale (50 points), which reflects indifferent feelings. Indeed, racial and ethnic minorities seem to feel unmistakably positive toward their own group as well as other non-Whites, as evidenced by the robust degree of correlation between these ratings among Blacks (mean $r = .60$), Asians (mean $r = .59$), and Latinos (mean $r = .60$). These generally positive feelings seem to indicate a deeper and broader form of identity.

While positive feelings are one indication that racial and ethnic minorities might share a common form of attachment (Luhtanen and Crocker 1992; Shingles 1981), affect is not identity: one can feel positively toward a group without identifying with it (Leach et al. 2008). Consider, for example, how some Whites can feel sympathy toward Blacks, without necessarily identifying as African American (Chudy 2019). Thus, to wrestle with this prospect further, we require measures of PoC ID itself.

In September 2019, I administered three questions to measure PoC ID in a sample of Latino ($n = 137$) and Asian American ($n = 139$) undergraduates at a racially diverse flagship university in California. These three items resemble the ones that, later in this book, I will use to create a more extensive PoC ID measure for use in the US mass public. Using a seven-point scale (1 = "strongly disagree" to 7 = "strongly agree"), participants responded to the following statements: (1) "The fact that I am a person of color is an important part of my identity"; (2) "Being a person of color is *unimportant* to who I am as an individual" (reverse-coded); and (3) "I am glad to be a person of color."

Combined, these items form a reliable scale (α = .77), with higher values reflecting stronger PoC ID levels.

In April 2020, I recontacted these individuals to complete the same PoC ID items they answered in September 2019 (I analyze these responses in chapter 4, "New Wine in New Bottles"). In addition, I gauged their opinions of #BlackLivesMatter, an issue expressly focused on one racial minority group, but in which the opportunity for interminority solidarity exists (Merseth 2018). This latter item invited participants to indicate their degree of agreement, on a seven-point scale, with the statement "Limiting the protest activities of #BlackLivesMatter and other movements like it." I recoded responses so that higher values indicate greater support for #BlackLivesMatter. What do we learn from this particular source of data?

In the study of identity and politics, identities are activated by a variety of contextual stimuli, including the kinds of policies that individuals are asked to evaluate (Winter 2008). If, in fact, racial and ethnic minorities see themselves broadly as people of color under some circumstances, then one of those conditions should be the broaching of an issue such as #BlackLivesMatter, which implicates one of the major subgroups under this pan-racial umbrella. The key question here is whether minorities' opinions about this Black-centered movement are influenced by their level of PoC ID, measured months earlier.

Figure I.1 suggests they are. Specifically, a shift from the lowest to highest level of PoC ID, measured in September 2019, reliably increases Latino and Asian undergraduate support for #BlackLivesMatter, measured in April 2020, by nearly 20 percentage points. These results further hint that PoC ID is an important part of minorities' sense of self, although not necessarily the most important. These findings also suggest that the political world surrounding racial and ethnic minorities is likely responsible for whether and when minorities see themselves as people of color and that this broad attachment affects their political opinions.[1]

To further evaluate this prospect, I undertook a third data collection at the same flagship university in California. This study invited Black ($n = 36$), Latino ($n = 173$), and Asian American ($n = 114$) participants to indicate how important they considered five of their identities to be—namely,

---

[1]. This coefficient represents the association between both variables among participants who completed waves 1 and 2 (i.e., "compliers"). This estimate is robust to inclusion of wave 2 covariates (i.e., gender, nativity, liberal ideology, and Latino status). I draw the same conclusion if I analyze these data in a full information ML framework in Mplus, which is robust to missingness across waves.

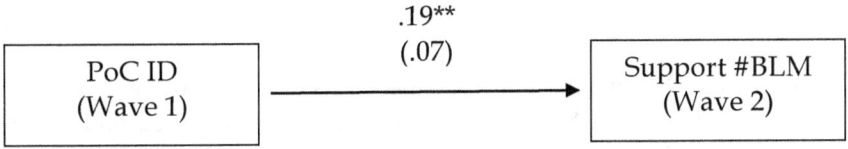

FIGURE I.1. PoC ID (wave 1) predicts support for #BlackLivesMatter (wave 2).
Note: Data are ordinary least squares estimates, with standard errors in parentheses. All variables range continuously on a 0–1 interval. $N = 109$. **$p < .05$, two-tailed.

TABLE I.2. People of color's rankings of PoC ID's importance to them in a portfolio of five identities

|  | Importance of my identity as a . . .<br>(1 = "least important," and 5 = "most important") |
|---|---|
| Family member | 3.74 |
| Member of my racial group | 3.44 |
| Person of color | 2.90 |
| Member of my academic major | 2.61 |
| Member of my university campus | 2.29 |
| N | 323 |

their identification (1) as a *family member*, (2) with their *academic major*, (3) with their *university campus*, (4) as a member of their *racial group*, and (5) as a *person of color*. More specifically, participants rated each identity on a five-point scale (1 = "least important" to 5 = "most important"). What do we learn here?

Several lessons, actually, as reflected in the findings displayed in table I.2. Given the absence of racial differences in these identity rankings, the entries reflect the average importance that people of color—that is, Black, Latino, and Asian participants, pooled together—assigned to an identity. There we see that within this portfolio of identities, individuals consider their family identity most important, while their university and major identities were ranked as the least important. In turn, one's sense of identity as a person of color registers in between these bookends, along with their racial identity. This pattern suggests that PoC ID is one key element in some minorities' portfolio of identities, but one that requires political stimuli—that is, policy issues, social movements, elite rhetoric, and the like—for it to become activated and politically influential. Pinpointing, isolating, and testing these political processes is the main focus of the rest of this book.

## What to Expect Next

The road from claiming that a new identity exists, to demonstrating that it actually does, to showing that it matters for politics, is a long and arduous one. It involves the wholesale development of a new concept; its appraisal through novel instrumentation; the assessment of its political effects; the isolation of conditions when it matters most; and, just as importantly, the pinpointing of circumstances when it matters less or hardly at all. I therefore start this journey in chapter 1 by investigating two major bodies of literature aimed to develop the concept of a people of color identity: research on interminority coalitions and politics (e.g., Benjamin 2017; Cortland et al. 2017; Cutaia Wilkinson 2015; McClain et al. 2005) and scholarship on racial and ethnic identities and politics (e.g., Dawson 1994; Junn and Masuoka 2008; Kuo, Malhotra, and Mo 2017; Michelson and Valenzuela 2016; Pérez 2015a,b; White and Laird 2020). My discussion reveals that there is plenty to learn and draw from these literature streams if we are interested in this new attachment. Yet neither body of work, I show subsequently, nails down this concept or its measurement. I therefore heed closely the lessons of these literatures to move a few steps closer toward establishing and appraising PoC ID.

Chapter 2 follows these leads to formally conceptualize PoC ID and develop a theoretical framework to shed light on its political effects. My thinking about this new identification is informed by social identity theory (SIT), a venerable research tradition that illuminates how group identities form and influence mass judgments and behavior (Tajfel and Turner 1986). Drawing on some of its most established tenets, I argue that while the expression of PoC ID is new, its emergence, operation, and influence as a broadly shared category is anything but. Just like other types of individuals, US racial and ethnic minorities juggle their membership in several groups (Pérez, Deichert, and Engelhardt 2019). In particular, as individual African Americans, Asian Americans, Latinos, and the like, they belong to their own unique racial ingroups. But as a collection of non-Whites, Blacks, Asians, Latinos, and other minorities also belong to a broader category that I and others call *people of color*. Social identity theory proposes that when a person sees their unique in-group reflected in a more broadly shared category, any benefits accruing to the larger group trickle down to the smaller groups nested below it (Gaertner et al. 1989, 1999; Transue 2007). This simple insight is the primary spark behind all of the hypotheses I derive and test across subsequent chapters. More specifically, I demonstrate that the fortunes of a pan-racial category like people of color depend critically on whether its diverse membership can perceive itself as one—and maintain that perception long enough for it to affect their politics. In generating this new knowledge about PoC ID, I then explain how a stronger grasp of this identity deepens our understanding of other larger-order attachments among racial minorities, including pan-ethnic and pan-racial identities like Latino and Asian American.

In chapter 3, I deepen my conceptualization of PoC ID by examining its origins and nature. I do this by drawing on 25 in-depth interviews with self-identified people of color who are African American, Asian American, or Latino, including some who describe themselves as multiracial. These rich conversations point out heretofore unknown qualities that make one a true person of color, including a shared sense of racial disadvantage that is experienced personally or vicariously, endorsement of progressive political views to remedy perceived racial injustices, and active distancing from European mannerisms and features (i.e., "looking" or "acting" White). This chapter also marshals evidence suggesting that part of the draw of identifying with the PoC category is its affirming and celebratory sense of the many attributes that mark one as non-White, especially compared with identifying with a category like *minority*. For example, whereas the term *minority* implies a diminutive sense of relative powerlessness, *people of color* infuses non-Whites with an affirming sense that the future is theirs, as evidenced by their growing demographic and political clout (e.g., Abrajano and Alvarez 2010; Anoll 2021; Fraga 2018; White and Laird 2020; Wong et al. 2011). I then demonstrate, using a psychological task known as the Implicit Association Test, that both non-Whites *and* Whites mentally associate—quite effortlessly, actually—different minority groups with the broader category *people of color*. Taken together, the evidence in this chapter supports and furthers my efforts to formally appraise the influence of PoC ID on US minority politics.

This is where chapter 4 comes in. I reason that PoC ID is an individual difference that all US racial and ethnic minorities display *to a degree*. In other words, it is not the case that a non-White individual is either a person of color or not, but instead that non-White minorities identify as PoC to a quantifiable extent. Those individual differences in PoC ID are what any measure of this identity should capture. And such a measure should do so without confusing PoC ID with other major attachments held by minorities, like their racial or national identity. Such a measure should also reflect PoC ID without conflating it with the very things this identity should explain, including solidarity with minorities, favorable feelings toward minorities, and a shared consciousness of being minorities.

I accomplish all this by drawing on SIT's concept of *identity centrality*: the notion that a category like *people of color* varies in how crucial it is to a person's self-definition. Seizing on this parsimonious conceptualization, I develop and validate a measure of PoC ID in three national samples of Black, Asian American, and Latino adults, which I call the "People of Color" surveys. This extensive original data collection yields evidence for three essential points: first, that PoC ID exists among a wide spectrum of non-White minorities; second, that we can reliably measure this new attachment; and third, that PoC ID is distinct from other major attachments that non-Whites possess, including their racial and national identity.

Chapter 5 then uses a series of studies called the "I Feel Your Pain" experiments to provide initial evidence about the steadfast influence of PoC ID among distinct racial and ethnic minority groups. The aim of these studies is disarmingly simple: to demonstrate that minorities' reactions to racial affronts are just as strong and swift when their own racial in-group is involved as when other minority out-groups are entangled, which would provide a sincere testament to their sense of being people of color (cf. Mackie, Smith, and Ray 2008). To establish this, I designed studies in which Asian, Black, and Latino adults read a news story about an altercation between a minority couple and a White waiter who publicly reprimands them for their use of English when completing their food order. They then reported their sense of commonality, perceptions of similarity, and identification with people of color.

The pattern emerging from these studies is consistent and robust. More precisely, minorities' support for people of color depends very little on who the aggrieved minority is. Blacks, Asians, and Latinos all come to the support of people of color in equal measure when their own in-group is involved as when other minorities are embroiled. This pattern, I show, emerges because people of color construe the altercation they read about between the White waiter and minority couple as racially insensitive rather than simply rude. Moreover, these effects arise even when the response is forced under short time constraints, which further suggests that this is how they really feel, rather than how they think they should feel. All this evidence firmly establishes a simple point: PoC ID is, in fact, a broadly inclusive, pan-racial category, in line with my theoretical reasoning and in-depth interviews.

Chapter 6 continues the presentation of experimental evidence to shed light on the circumstances under which PoC ID is politicized. That is, how much does it take for PoC ID—a form of social identity—to manifest *political* consequences? Social identity theory teaches us that one reliable trigger to such politicization is the presence of threat to an in-group (cf. Danbold and Huo 2015; Doosje, Ellemers, and Spears 1995; Ellemers, Spears, and Doosje 1997; Pérez 2015a, b; Pérez, Deichert, and Engelhardt 2019), which can manifest as a threat to the distinctiveness of an in-group in relation to an out-group, to the value of an in-group relative to an out-group, or to the very existence of an in-group in relation to out-groups. The generic prediction flowing from this work is that in the absence of threat, a particular social identity lies dormant or is weakly influential, but when a threat occurs, that identity is activated, with more highly identified group members affirming their membership in the embattled category.

Building on these insights, I undertook three parallel experiments with Black, Asian, and Latino adults to assess the conditions under which PoC ID is politically activated, what I call the "PoC Unity" experiments. Participants in each study were randomly assigned to a control group with no information or one of two treatments. In the first treatment, a minority spokesperson (matched to one's race) communicates a threat to people of color, specifically, that people of color are collectively targets of racial intimidation, vandalism, and violence—challenges that require all people of color to unite. In the second treatment, a White nationalist communicates a threat against people of color—that they are the perpetrators of racial intimidation, vandalism, and violence against White people—and that Whites must unite to push back against people of color. Following this manipulation, all participants answered questions related to their feelings about various racial minorities and political parties, as well as support for policies that broadly and narrowly impact people of color.

The goal of this experiment is to clarify when a threat to people of color galvanizes their PoC ID. Thus, if the question is "How much does it take for PoC ID to become politicized?" this trio of experiments suggests "not much." Consider that in the control, in which no threat is present, higher-identifying people of color express greater favorability toward various racial minority groups relative to Whites, as well as more positive feelings toward Democrats in relation to Republicans. Higher-identifying people of color in the control group also strongly endorse policies that broadly impact minorities—such as efforts at improving the reporting of hate crimes and initiatives to curb police brutality—as well as policies that are more narrowly associated with specific minority groups—such as increasing the number of visas for high-skill immigrants.

How do high-identifiers behave in the two treatment conditions, when a threat to people of color is actually present? Pretty much in the same way. Whether the threat to people of color is communicated by a racial/ethnic minority or a White nationalist, highly identified people of color continue to express these feelings and policy views at comparable levels to the control group. The answer to our question, then, is that it takes very little to politicize PoC ID among people of color because this attachment is already highly politicized for those who more strongly identify with this pan-racial group.

Chapter 7 shifts gears from showing when PoC ID matters politically to when it hardly matters at all. My theoretical discussion from chapter 2 suggests that the glue that holds a pan-racial group like *people of color* together consists of Blacks, Asians, Latinos, and other minorities seeing themselves as one—which is to say, underemphasizing the fact that they belong to distinct racial and ethnic in-groups. Yet social identity theory also teaches us that one of the most powerful threats to an in-group involves undermining its distinctiveness—that is, how coherent and special it is perceived to be. In the case of *people of color*, this undermining would entail reminding Blacks, Asians, Latinos, and other minorities about the unique struggles and aspirations of their respective racial and ethnic in-groups.

Seizing on these insights, I undertook the "Distinct Stations" and the "Distinct Experiences" experiments. In the first of these studies, college undergraduates from varied racial/ethnic minority groups (e.g., Asian Americans, Latinos) were randomly assigned to read information about demographic diversity on their campus. In the control, participants read about the regional diversity of their student body, noting how most students are from California. In the "Asians Predominate" condition, participants read about the racial diversity of their campus and that Asian Americans comprise the largest group of people of color on campus. In the "Latinos Ascending" condition, participants read about the same racial diversity on campus and but that Latinos are a rapidly growing segment of people of color at their school. This simple study establishes an important fact: individual perceptions about which groups count as people of color are sensitive to the social position of one's group. For example, relative to the control, Latino participants who read about their in-group's demographic ascendance were less likely to rate African Americans and Asian Americans as prototypical people of color.

The "Distinct Experiences" experiment builds on and extends this insight by administering another manipulation, this time, in national samples of Black, Asian American, and Latino adults. In one condition, adults from each minority group read census projections about the continued increase in people of color, noting in particular some of the many ways that this pan-racial group encounters and experiences common disadvantages, such as White hostility toward all minorities. In the other condition, adults from each minority group read the same census projections, but this time, the unique experiences and aspirations of their own racial in-group were highlighted. Accordingly, Blacks read that their group's struggle with slavery and its aftermath is incomparable to the trials and tribulations of being immigrants (like Latinos and Asian Americans), while Latinos and Asians read about how the legacies of immigration are incomparable with the generational consequences of descending from slaves.

What happens to PoC ID across these conditions? In the baseline condition, in which the shared disadvantages and experiences of people of color are affirmed, higher PoC ID levels sharpen perceptions of discrimination toward a broad swath of minority groups, increase participants' positive feelings toward these groups, decrease their sense of competition between minorities, and boost support for policies that implicate specific racial minorities. In sharp contrast, exposure to information underscoring the uniquely distinct experiences and aspirations of one's own racial group undercuts or eliminates PoC ID's effect on most of these outcomes. The lesson from this study is this: the degree to which people of color see themselves as one, politically, depends in large measure on whether they are encouraged to see the similarities between their subgroups or the differences that separate them.

In the conclusion, I then turn to reviewing and integrating the major empirical findings of my book. Specifically, I discuss their implications for political decision making among racial and ethnic minorities, paying special attention to how the presence and influence of PoC ID complicates and deepens our understanding of politics in a racially diversifying nation. Throughout my discussion, I wrestle with the normative implications raised by the presence of a pan-racial identity that can be bolstered or minimized simply on the basis of perceived commonality or difference.

Alas, this is a tall order of chapters to get through. Let us therefore begin by turning to the first, in which I search for PoC ID from the vantage point of two important literatures in the study of America's racial and ethnic minorities.

# 1

# The Elusive Quest for People of Color

The demographic explosion of racial and ethnic minority groups that characterizes the US is a trend at least five decades in the making. Surely, by now, scholars must have hit upon this new *people of color* identity (PoC ID) that I have been clamoring about?

Although it is easy to imagine this having happened already, the state of affairs surrounding PoC ID is far different and more complicated than accumulated research indicates. Scholars, especially those who focus on the study of race, ethnicity, and politics, have indeed grappled with America's teeming diversity and its implications for local, state, and national politics (e.g., Abrajano and Hajnal 2015; Barreto, Segura, and Woods 2003; Hajnal 2007; Jardina 2019; Masuoka and Junn 2013; Pantoja, Segura, and Ramirez 2001; Trounstine 2018). Yet their efforts have generally rubbed up against, hovered over, or skipped around the possibility of a PoC ID without formally conceptualizing and naming it as such. Two literatures, in particular, have engaged deeply with the political ramifications of racial and ethnic diversity, uncovering important insights about PoC ID but without formally identifying this concept: interminority coalitions and politics and racial and ethnic identities in politics.

In the pages that follow, I explain how each of these expansive literatures provides useful insights about what PoC ID might be, how it might operate, and whether it might plausibly exist; I also show that neither literature supplies the exact concept that forms the backbone of this book. Alas, the heavy lifting required to erect this new concept from scratch, situate it among related notions, distinguish it from these neighboring ideas, and clarify its operation is yet to be accomplished. This chapter's contribution, then, is to pull together the key layers of insight produced by previous scholarship with the aim of building a firm foundation for PoC ID to rest and grow on. Let us therefore begin this important work by taking a deep dive into the literature on coalition building among US racial and ethnic minorities and interrogating it for clues about PoC ID.

## Interminority Coalitions and Politics

One of the major literature streams that grapples with the political implications of racial diversity investigates the development of coalitions between various minority groups, and one of the chief protagonists in this arena is the political scientist Paula D. McClain. Throughout the 1970s and 1980s, major cities across the US became epicenters of growing racial and ethnic diversity, and McClain was one of the first social scientists to notice and appreciate what these trends entailed for minorities and political science. Working against the assumption that various racial/ethnic minorities are natural allies, she demonstrated in a series of seminal papers that little was instinctive about this intuition (McClain 1993; McClain and Karnig 1990; McClain and Tauber 1998; Meier et al. 2004). Whether it was labor markets, political representation, or educational resources, McClain's painstaking research consistently uncovered increasing conflict between racial and ethnic minority groups, finding that this competition sometimes manifested itself in zero-sum ways, with one group (e.g., Blacks) gaining at the expense of another (e.g., Latinos). Of course, some of these patterns arose from structural considerations rather than personal animosities (Trounstine 2018). For example, in electoral contexts with first-past-the-post rules, only one political seat can be won, which means that for every group that "captures" said seat, there will be a group that loses or, at the very least, gains nothing (Browning, Marshall, and Tabb 1984). Yet McClain's later work established that even in new contexts in which groups have little history with each other (e.g., Blacks and Latinos in the American South), the potential for conflict remained soberingly strong (McClain 2006; McClain et al. 2005, 2007, 2011).

In conversation with McClain's work, other scholars have rushed to inject some nuances into the general regularity she has documented by highlighting the influence of geographic context, history between groups, and the degree of contact between groups in modulating the intensity and scope of interminority conflict, especially between Blacks and Latinos (e.g., Barreto and Sanchez 2014; Carey et al. 2015; Cutaia Wilkinson 2015; Sawyer 2005). As one recent example, consider Benjamin's (2017) book-length treatment on interminority cooperation in local politics. Focusing on political races in a handful of major US cities, Benjamin demonstrates that political cooperation between Blacks and Latinos can be achieved through alliances cemented by cross-racial candidate endorsements, an electoral context in which racial issues predominate, and the promising viability of a minority candidate. Each of these extenuating factors, Benjamin shows, mitigates the strength of interminority conflict. Yet paradoxically, these limiting circumstances underscore the very power of McClain's original point: there is *little* that is natural about minority groups working in solidarity with each other. From the vantage point of PoC ID, then, these findings suggest a steep conceptual hill to climb.

Beyond political science, social psychologists like Jennifer Richeson and Maureen Craig have also investigated coalition building among minorities, this time, from a microlevel perspective. Unlike their political science colleagues, these scholars have focused intensely on the psychological forces that engender conflict or cooperation between minority groups, such as African Americans, Asian Americans, and Latinos. Their studies have reinvigorated this debate with a deeper appreciation for the psychological mechanisms responsible for interminority conflict and cooperation at the individual level— a much-needed intervention in a literature that generally elides these important factors.

The findings produced by Richeson, Craig, and their collaborators can be distilled into two varieties. In one strand of research, they find, consistent with the work of Paula McClain and other political scientists, that one's identification with a specific racial minority (e.g., African Americans, Asian Americans, Latinos) overwhelms any inclination to cooperate with minority out-groups who share a disadvantaged status. For example, akin to White Americans who have reacted to Latinos' rapid population growth by endorsing conservative beliefs and attitudes (Craig and Richeson 2014; Danbold and Huo 2015; Pérez, Deichert, and Engelhardt 2019; see also Abrajano and Hajnal 2015), many non-Whites, such as African and Asian Americans, have responded in comparable fashion (e.g., Craig and Richeson 2017; Craig, Rucker, and Richeson 2018; see also Abascal 2015; Shapiro and Neuberg 2008). Given the staying power of one's identification with a distinct racial minority, this work underscores how distant, even chimerical, a broad PoC ID might be.

Or does it? Other work by Richeson, Craig, and their collaborators shows some grounds for optimism on this front, suggesting there is plenty of room, psychologically at least, to maneuver racial and ethnic minorities into a shared sense of identity. Drawing on the influential Common Ingroup Identity Model first proposed by Samuel Gaertner and Jack Dovidio (Gaertner et al. 1989, 1999) and expanded by others (Transue 2007), the authors argue that shared experiences with discrimination and other disadvantages are key in whether distinct racial minorities perceive greater similarity between themselves—a core pillar of an identity held in common. Consistent with this thinking, Richeson, Craig, and their colleagues demonstrate in a series of path-breaking papers that highlighting shared experiences of discrimination between minority out-groups reduces conflict between them, an effect mediated by heightened perceptions of similarity with one another (Cortland et al. 2017; Craig and Richeson 2012; see also Kuo, Malhotra, and Ko 2017). Such a pattern is not singular to psychology. In political science, Sirin, Valentino, and Villalobos (2016a, b) find that some racial and ethnic minority groups express a strong sense of empathy for one another, prompting them to support policies that directly bear on the well-being of a minority out-group that is not necessarily their own. This is a huge step forward, conceptually and empirically. On the conceptual side, it lays some groundwork for thinking about what psychological foundations are needed to encourage a common sense of identity. On the empirical side, it demonstrates the reliability of these foundations. In the end, however, perceived similarity and a sense of empathy might be related to a PoC ID, but they do not constitute PoC ID proper. In this way, the concept that I am interested in remains a ghost in the machinery of interminority relations.

## Racial and Ethnic Identities in Politics

Whereas scholarship on coalition building largely skips around the shared sense of attachment that PoC ID is supposed to be, the booming literature on racial and ethnic identities offers more direct clues about this alleged new attachment (cf. Abrajano and Alvarez 2010; Allen, Dawson, and Brown 1989; Chong and Rogers 2005; Davis and Brown 2002; Garcia Bedolla 2005; Gurin, Miller, and Gurin 1980; Junn and Masuoka 2008; Lee 2008; McClain et al. 2009; Miller et al. 1981; Sanchez and Masuoka 2010; Silber Mohammed 2017). This research field shows that a person's degree of identification with a specific racial or ethnic group is a workhorse variable in the study of minority politics, shaping the political attitudes and behavior of members of various groups, including African Americans, Asian Americans, and Latinos (e.g., Block 2011; Kuo, Malhotra, and Mo 2017; Lien, Conway, and Wong 2004; Pérez, Deichert, and Engelhardt 2019; Sanchez 2006a). So, what is the challenge here? From where I sit, an embarrassment of riches that consists of many related concepts and measures all purporting to reflect the same thing. Alas, they cannot all be right.

Let us start with the influential concept of linked fate. First proposed by political scientist Michael Dawson to study Black political behavior (Dawson 1994), linked fate is the cognitive recognition that the fortunes of a group are a strong reflection of one's fortunes as an individual. For Dawson, this sense of a common fate serves individual African Americans as a heuristic—in other words, a cognitive shortcut that allows Black Americans to simplify their political choices by substituting their racial group's collective interest for their own self-interest, which is aptly reflected in a popular question measuring this concept: "Do you think what happens generally to Black people in this country will have something to do with what happens in your life?"

Understandably, linked fate has been a prolific concept, manifesting itself in a wide variety of studies investigating Black political behavior (Block 2011; Davis and Brown 2002; Dawson 1994; Tate 1991). However, critics have assailed this crucial concept on two grounds. The first concerns the scope conditions of this variable. As a concept that was developed with the case of African Americans in mind, does it travel much beyond this particular group of individuals (Gay, Hochschild, and White 2016)? Standing tall in the background is a towering layer of works on linked fate among other non-Black groups, like Latinos and Asian Americans, which reveals (for some) a disappointingly spotty record for linked fate's impact on the political opinions and behaviors of these groups. These works suggest the very real possibility that this concept is not as broadly universal as some scholars might hope (e.g., Junn 2005; Junn and Masuoka 2008; Lee 2008; McClain et al. 2009; Sanchez and Masuoka 2010).

Other work, in contrast, cuts against this concept in the other direction, suggesting that linked fate is too amorphous, applying to any and all types of social groups—not necessarily just racial or ethnic ones. For example, Gay, Hochschild, and White (2016) demonstrate that linked fate can be measured across different nonracial, nonminority groups (see also Carter and Pérez 2015) and is often weakly related to political outcomes, which, from their perspective, raises questions about whether linked fate is an inherently racial concept that is adequately measured with extant items (cf. Davis and Brown 2002). These and other findings led Gay, Hochschild, and White (2016: 140) to conclude that "the enormously fruitful concept of . . . linked fate is due for empirical, and perhaps, conceptual, re-examination."

This is a complicated set of findings. What should we make of them? I infer the following from this evidence. Linked fate is appealingly intuitive, but it is not identity per se. Rather, as the careful work of psychologist Colin Wayne Leach and his colleagues reveals (Leach et al. 2008: 147), linked fate appears to best represent a manifestation of in-group solidarity. Such solidarity is "a psychological bond with, and commitment to, fellow ingroup members," but it is not identity. Rather, it is a *by-product* of identity, resulting in the "investment of the self in coordinated activity with those to whom one feels committed"

(147). From this vantage point, the inability to consistently uncover political connections between linked fate and politics, and to establish these links across non-Black minorities (e.g., Asian Americans, Latinos) might simply be a function of looking for the wrong concept, in the wrong places, and at the wrong times (Elster 1989).

So, if linked fate is not identity, what does the latter concept consist of? Other scholars have answered this clarion call with the idea of *group consciousness*, which is best understood as "in-group identification *politicized* by a set of ideological beliefs about one's group's standing" (McClain et al. 2009: 476, emphasis in original). The idea here is that such beliefs give an identity its political spark. Thus, insofar as a researcher taps into these beliefs, they stand a better chance of witnessing the collective, political action undertaken by group members to enhance their status and reach their goals (cf. Chong and Rogers 2005; Conover 1984; Gurin, Miller, and Gurin 1980; Miller et al. 1981; Shingles 1981). This sounds reasonable. But the risk now is one of conflating the notion of identity with some of the very things that identity is supposed to explain.

Consider Sanchez's (2006a, b) measure of group consciousness among Latinos, which draws broadly and deeply on prior work. Group consciousness, he explains, involves three elements: "general identification with a group, an awareness of that group's relative position in society, and the desire to engage in collective activity that focuses on improving the situation of that group" (Sanchez 2006b: 439–40). To this end, he creates a scale out of a measure of perceived commonality between major Latino nationalities, a measure of perceived political commonality between major Latino groups, a measure of perceived discrimination against Latinos, and a measure of the desire to remedy Latinos' disadvantaged position via collective action.

These items are highly correlated, as scale items should be (Brown 2007). But it is unclear whether they are highly associated because they measure an underlying variable in common—group consciousness—or because they reflect a strong connection between a predictor(s) and an outcome(s). Most worrying here is the link between perceptions of discrimination and a desire for collective action. These constructs are folded into Sanchez's (2006a, b) scale of Latino group consciousness, as they are in other measures of group consciousness among other minority groups (Gurin, Miller, and Gurin 1980; McClain et al. 2009; Miller et al. 1981; Shingles 1981). Yet careful experimental work shows that perceived discrimination causally modulates a person's propensity to engage in collective action (Kuo, Malhotra, and Mo 2017). Thus, to appraise PoC ID—and only PoC ID—we need a measure that disentangles it from related constructs so that we can better establish when it becomes politicized, rather than baking this politicization into the measure itself (e.g., Pérez 2015b).

If the goal is to boil down identity to its fundamentals, then perhaps the answers about PoC ID rest within the concept of "group closeness" (Conover 1984). The notion behind this concept is that identity is strongly reflected in how close a person feels to a specific group. To assess this concept, researchers invite individuals to register how close they feel toward various groups—that is, individuals who are similar to oneself in their ideas, interests, and feelings about things (Huddy 2013). Such a concept and measure make sense and provide the type of parsimony that something like group consciousness cannot: "If *I* identify with a group, then it stands to reason that *I* also feel close to its members." However, this intuition is imprecise. The problem is not that closeness to a group is uncorrelated with attachment to it. Rather, the bigger challenge, as Wong (2010) points out, is that closeness is also conflated with sympathy for a group one might not belong to (Chudy 2019). In terms of PoC ID, a White progressive can feel "close to" other people of color, despite not formally belonging to a minority group. In this way, "closeness" reflects something akin to identification with a group, but not group identification proper (Huddy 2013).

One final research stream that provides important clues about PoC ID and its operation involves the literature on pan-racial and pan-ethnic identities (e.g., Abrajano and Alvarez 2010; de la Garza et al. 1992; García 2012; Lee 2008; Lien, Conway, and Wong 2004; Masuoka 2006; Mora 2014; Pérez, Deichert, and Engelhardt 2019; Wong et al. 2011), defined as attachments to broader categories that encompass a motley mix of subgroups (similar to PoC ID). One example of this is the category Latino, which encapsulates Mexicans, Puerto Ricans, Cubans, Salvadorans, Dominicans, and other groups with roots in Latin America (Beltrán 2010). Another example is the category Asian American, which covers Chinese, Koreans, Japanese, Indians, Filipinos, and a wide cast of other groups with roots in the Asian continent (Wong et al. 2011). Empirically, scholars have established that pan-group attachments like these are often associated with greater political participation and a host of political attitudes among members of these groups (Kuo, Malhotra, and Mo 2017; Pérez 2015a, b; Pérez, Deichert, and Engelhardt 2019). Yet conceptual and normative questions bedevil this concept.

On the conceptual side, scholars have raised important questions about how meaningful pan-racial identities are with respect to narrower forms of attachment. For example, scholars who study Latinos and Asian Americans often find that members of these pan-ethnic groups prioritize their national origin identities above their pan-ethnic identities (e.g., Alba and Nee 2003;

de la Garza et al. 1992; Portes and Rumbaut 2014; Wong et al. 2011), preferring, for example, to identify as Mexican rather than as Latino. The lingering question here, then, is how a broader group can have any meaning given the centrifugal force of national origin identities.

On the normative side of things, the penetrating insights of political theorists like Cristina Beltrán (2010) have sensitized many a political scientist to the homogenizing effects of these broad categories. As she explains in her incisive book, *The Trouble with Unity*, a pan-ethnic identity, such as Latino or Hispanic, tends to flatten, if not obliterate, the unique histories, legacies, aspirations, and pressures of component groups for the sake of the larger category's unity and coherence. Thus, in achieving Latino or Asian unity, the unique perspectives and needs of the smaller groups who contribute to the whole, such as Cubans or Koreans, are often lost.

Both points are crucial to acknowledge and consider; however, in the end, they do little to address how PoC ID can be a conceptual and empirical possibility. For instance, the relative prioritization of national origin versus pan-ethnic identity might simply reflect the absence of any specific contextual stimuli that encourages the subsuming of one under the other. What is needed is a way to explain the interface that exists between both types of identities. On the normative side of things, I readily acknowledge that everything Beltrán notes about pan-group identities is correct. The best of social and political psychology suggests this is exactly what any form of attachment does: it homogenizes to provide certainty and clarity about who belongs in a group, who is deemed a core member, and who is considered peripheral to a category (Doosje, Ellemers, and Spears 1995; Ellemers and Jetten 2012; McGarty et al. 1992; Reid and Hogg 2005; Turner et al. 1987). As an empirical political psychologist, then, I read Beltrán's criticism as a major part of what PoC ID needs to explain. In particular, the concerns she voices demand that I better explain why and how the trade-offs involved—uniqueness versus uniformity—might be worth the effort, at times, for members of broader groups, like people of color.

## Lessons Learned

This chapter has conveyed that the possibility of a PoC ID remains just that: a possibility. Nevertheless, four lessons emerge from consultation and interrogation of two literature streams that claim to speak to racial and ethnic identities among US minorities. The first lesson is a greater need for a parsimonious concept. Insofar as PoC ID exists, it should explain a lot with very little, especially with respect to competing concepts such as linked fate and group consciousness. The second lesson is that we must decouple PoC ID from its political effects; that is, we must measure this concept without contaminating it with the very things—political attitudes, evaluations, judgments, and behaviors—that it is supposed to explain. The third lesson is that any conceptualization of PoC ID must explain why and how a pan-racial group like this one makes cognitive sense for a class of highly heterogeneous subgroups that might face strong incentives to identify with smaller and more distinct groups (Brewer 1991). But perhaps the biggest lesson is that nailing down PoC ID is only half the story. The other half involves creating a theoretical framework that details *how*, *when*, and among *whom* PoC ID affects the political views, beliefs, and behaviors that racial and ethnic minorities express. The next chapter addresses this interplay between conceptualization, theory, and hypotheses.

# 2

# People of Color, Unite!

As the preceding chapters indicate, there is no shortage of intuition, speculation, and pontification about a people of color identity (PoC ID). What is in short supply, however, is a thorough conceptualization of this alleged new attachment among US racial and ethnic minorities. In particular, lacking is a keen sense of what a PoC ID is, how it relates to kindred concepts—like plain old racial identity—and how distinguishable it is from these close conceptual kin. Also sorely missing from the annals of political science and psychology is a strong grasp of the circumstances under which a PoC ID influences the political behavior of racial and ethnic minorities in the United States. And then there is simply the obvious absence of empirical evidence widely documenting that PoC ID even exists.

With a now firmer sense of what is at stake, my principal business here is to formulate a conceptualization and theory of PoC ID that can guide my exploration of this attachment in subsequent chapters. Toward these ends, I begin here by reviewing and drawing on a distinguished tradition of scholarship, known as social identity theory (SIT), which offers a generic set of psychological principles that I apply to explain the emergence, nature, and performance of PoC ID in US society and politics. I then turn to clarifying, with more precision than before, the exact relationship between PoC ID and one's racial ID, urging scholars to construe them as being nested—specifically, with PoC ID encapsulating one's racial ID. With matters of conceptualization cleared, I then turn to distilling a set of clear expectations about the conditions under which PoC ID matters for US minority politics, a conversation that will provide us answers to *when*, *how*, and among *whom* this attachment influences minority political behavior. Without further ado, then, let us take concrete action on this long research agenda by turning to SIT.

## SIT and the Psychology of Groups

Social identity theory is now considered by many an elegant framework for understanding, in a generic sense, how groups crystallize in people's minds and, consequently, how they structure individual behavior (Tajfel and Turner 1986). This elegance can be traced to SIT's parsimony: it explains a complex phenomenon like group formation with very few moving parts (Tajfel 1981). The origins of SIT, however, are rooted in humbler beginnings.

It was the late 1960s and budding social psychologist Henri Tajfel and his graduate students launched SIT through an imaginative platform of studies now known as the "minimal group experiments" (Brown 2020). These researchers recognized that real-world struggles between groups are often mired in politics, cultural differences, history, and other messy, seemingly intractable things. Thus, to uncover the basic cognitive principles suspected behind these conflicts, Tajfel and his associates reasoned that they had to start backwards, by obliterating all the messiness of the world and begin introducing, one by one, each of the complicating factors or conditions that ultimately produced intergroup conflict. This feature is what made their experiments so minimal.

The thrust of these bare-bones studies was to first categorize British adolescent boys into groups with no history with one another, on a purely random basis, and according to trivial criteria, like whether they overcounted or undercounted dots or whether they favored or disliked the paintings of certain artists (Billig and Tajfel 1973; Tajfel et al. 1971). Following this categorization, the researchers then waited and observed: how would these groups behave toward one another in a series of allotment tasks in which they could make awards to other participants as they saw fit? The expectation was that there was little basis here for collective ill will, thus providing a baseline against which complicating, real-world factors could be introduced to increase intergroup conflict. But the results were soberingly clear from this modest start: in this most minimal and artificial of settings, intergroup conflict was easily triggered, as evidenced by a consistent pattern of *in-group favoritism*: the behavioral tendency to privilege, at all cost, the group into which one was (randomly and trivially) categorized.

The grease behind the wheels of in-group favoritism is what we now know as *positive distinctiveness*, the third major principle offered by SIT. The idea here, first proposed by Tajfel and then refined by his acolytes, is that all individuals are motivated to maintain a robust sense of self-worth (Luhtanen and Crocker 1992; Tajfel and Turner 1986). As extensions of the self, groups are but one channel through which individuals can enhance their self-esteem.

Accordingly, this drive for self-worth means that in-group members are strongly motivated to put their group in the most positive light, which, in cognitive terms, entails a set of comparisons against an out-group that leads one to feel good about being in the in-group (Turner et al. 1987).

Two friendly amendments have been proposed to these otherwise generalizable regularities. The first one addresses who, within in-groups, propels these "groupy" tendencies. As Naomi Ellemers, Bertjan Doosje, Russell Spears, and others have demonstrated (Ellemers, Spears, and Doosje 1997, 2002; Leach et al. 2008, 2010), collective behavior in intergroup settings is often driven by high-identifying in-group members—that is, individuals for whom a given social category is central to who they are as an individual. For example, in the wake of xenophobic rhetoric against US Latinos, it is those individuals who most strongly identify with this ethnic group—rather than all co-ethnics—who respond politically to this discourse (Pérez 2015a, b). And they do so because being Latino is central to their sense of self. Hence, a threat to their ethnic group undermines their sense of who they are at their core.

The other amendment speaks to how a group becomes cognitively distinct and why it matters. Here, Marilynn Brewer, another distinguished social identity theorist, teaches that an in-group's distinctiveness is most optimal when the in-group is large enough that it infuses members with a strong sense of belonging, but not so large and amorphous that anyone can be a member. In Brewer's (1991: 475) own words, the more that an in-group enables one to be "the same and different at the same time," the more unique and special it feels to members. Key here is that when an in-group's distinctiveness is attained, identification with it is cemented via perceived similarity to the average in-group member (McGarty et al. 1992; Turner et al. 1987). That is, one internalizes an in-group's identity when "I" see myself as a strong and clear reflection of who "we" are as a group. As a prototype, one's main job turns to preserving this positive distinctiveness, which manifests as in-group favoritism.

## The Bond between Racial ID and PoC ID

From a generic standpoint, the principles of categorization, distinctiveness, and in-group favoritism are uncontroversial. But the proper nouns I am interested in—*African Americans, Asian Americans, Latinos,* and other minority groups—raise important questions about these SIT tenets. Indeed, as noted in the introductory chapter, US racial and ethnic minorities often find themselves locked in competition with one another, suggesting that the type of intergroup dynamics that consumed Tajfel's attention help explain why Blacks,

Asians, Latinos, and other minorities fail to come together under a common banner like PoC ID—the opposite of what I wish to explain.

Of course, someone could gently point out that as racial minorities, Blacks, Asians, Latinos, and other groups experience some degree of prejudice or discrimination because of their race. This should be enough to bond them together, right? The simple answer is no; SIT-based research suggests that when racial and ethnic minorities are reminded of disadvantages they face because of their race or ethnicity, their general reaction is to manifest greater in-group favoritism toward their distinct racial group, not to become more pro-minority (e.g., Branscombe, Schmitt, and Harvey 1999; Branscombe and Wann 1994; Huddy and Virtanen 1995; Pérez 2015a). In other words, in the presence of prejudice or discrimination toward one's racial in-group, Blacks become more pro-Black, Latinos become more pro-Latino, and Asians become more pro-Asian—not, as my intuition about PoC ID implies, more favorably disposed toward people of color writ large. Greater conceptual lifting is therefore needed to bridge this impasse.

Enter SIT-inspired work on intergroup cooperation. One of the virtues of the prodigious literature on SIT is that, even though most of its emphasis has been on documenting the emergence and persistence of conflict between groups, it has also covered other important terrain, including the production of cooperation between diverse out-groups. And the beauty here is that this has occurred with little need to develop new concepts or add new principles. Instead, intergroup cooperation arises on the basis of the same basic dynamics just discussed: categorization, distinctiveness, and in-group favoritism.

The specific model here, formally known as the Common Ingroup Identity Model (CIIM), was first developed by Samuel Gaertner, Jack Dovidio, and their associates (Gaertner et al. 1989, 1999; see also Hewstone and Brown 1986). As an SIT offshoot, the CIIM focuses on psychologically reducing, if not eliminating, intractable conflicts between groups. The model starts from the premise that it is difficult, if not impossible, for individuals to cease identifying with groups that conflict. For example, in the US, where Whites and non-Whites vie for prestige, power, and resources, Whites will find it exceedingly difficult to cease being White, while Blacks, Asian Americans, and Latinos will find it demonstrably hard to quit being Black, Asian, or Latino (Dawson 1994; Garcia 2012; Jardina 2019; Wong et al. 2011). It is much easier, claim Gaertner and his associates, to *recategorize* individuals on the basis of common groups that cut across a motley mix of out-groups (Levendusky 2018; Theiss-Morse 2009). By making salient a shared identity, this recategorization transforms what used to be out-groups into fellow in-group members, thus redirecting the benefits of in-group favoritism to all those who are thought of as included in the shared group. In one imaginative experiment, for example, Transue (2007) demonstrates that public support for a tax increase grows when a shared identity as Americans is primed relative to people's identification as Black or White, a finding that conceptually replicates the now classic result of the Sherif's Robbers Cave experiment, where the Rattlers and the Eagles—two conflicting groups at a boys' camp—overcame their differences when they shared an identity to solve workaday problems in a campground (Sherif et al. 1961).

What does this imply for the nature of *people of color*? Drawing on this work, I claim that for racial and ethnic minorities, their distinct identities as Black, Latino, Asian, and so on are nested under the broader category *people of color*. In other words, while these attachments are separable components, one's racial identity can be comfortably nested under one's PoC ID, which should make for a strong correspondence between the two. The observable implication here is that, insofar as this interface between PoC ID and racial ID exists, we should witness remarkably robust correlations between both attachments across distinct racial and ethnic groups. I call this the *nested identities hypothesis*.

If my reasoning about the interface between PoC ID and racial ID is correct, then when PoC ID is salient, members of distinct racial minorities should perceive narrower differences between themselves, while sensing larger differences between themselves and a respective out-group, like Whites. This internal homogenization and external differentiation will produce positive *distinctiveness*, which should help seal the bond of diverse minorities to the larger shared group. Indeed, with PoC ID as a common banner of identity, the benefits of in-group favoritism should be redirected toward all members of the broader in-group. Inasmuch as this is true, another straightforward prediction emerges for people of color: higher PoC ID levels should lead members of distinct racial and ethnic minorities to express attitudes, support policies, and endorse initiatives that are construed as benefiting specific minorities who are deemed people of color. I call this the *affirmation hypothesis*. And if it is correct, we should observe, among other patterns, Blacks opposing stricter immigration controls, Asians supporting measures to combat police brutality, Latinos supporting the #BlackLivesMatter movement—a reflection that PoC ID leads minorities to support one another's causes as "our own" cause.

## Hierarchy and the (De)Escalation of PoC ID's Effects

The insights produced by Tajfel's SIT and its offshoots are simple, arresting, and prognostic, leading to the nested identities and affirmation hypotheses outlined in the preceding section. Beyond this, however, SIT's insights are much easier to apply to, and more informative about, dominant groups in society than minority groups. Additional work is therefore needed for SIT to help predict the effects of PoC ID, an effort requiring acute sensitivity to racial hierarchy.

In the savanna of intergroup relations, clear pecking orders—or hierarchies—often arise and persist between social groups, with one group perched atop and its members enjoying better access to power, resources, privileges, and cachet (Carter and Pérez 2016; Haney López 1996; King 2000; Masuoka and Junn 2013; Sidanius et al. 1997; Sidanius and Kurzban 2013; Sidanius and Pratto 1999). When a person is a member of a valorized group like this, the tenets of SIT are pretty straightforward; indeed, how can one really go wrong with boosting one's sense of self-worth by affiliating with a powerful, dominant group? Tensions arise, however, when subordinate groups are involved. The challenge here is clarifying why one would stay with a lower-status group and, if one remains, how a devalued identity can propel behavior rather than paralyze it.

In response to this potential disjuncture, Henri Tajfel and his student John Turner proposed three identity management strategies geared toward defusing this tension in SIT (Tajfel and Turner 1986). The first is *individual mobility*, the notion that if intergroup boundaries are permeable, a person categorized into a subordinate group will dissociate from it and join the more prestigious dominant group. When permeability is off the table, however, members of a subordinate group have two other options. The first is *social creativity*, in which individuals from lower-status groups rearrange the terms of comparison that produce *positive distinctiveness* for the dominant group. This might leave the original hierarchy intact, but it provides an opportunity for members of subordinate groups to still draw that sense of self-worth that is so crucial. The second option is the rarest, but also the most conflictual and revolutionary: *social competition*. Here, the subordinate group does battle with the dominant group in an effort to wrest them from their perch. In other words, the subordinate group competes with the dominant group to objectively transform the hierarchy between groups.

To fully grasp the conditions under which PoC ID matters for politics, we must grapple with this notion of hierarchy and the identity management strategies available to minority groups nested under this broad category. This seems simple enough. Yet the incisive political scientist Michael Dawson (2000: 343) reminds us that the "American racial order is a phenomenon with which many researchers are loathe to deal." One reason for this dismal state of affairs involves how researchers construe the ordering of racial groups.

For SIT researchers, a status hierarchy is something that can, and often does, change between groups, as evidenced by short-term manipulations in laboratory studies (e.g., Doosje, Ellemers, and Spears 1995; Ellemers, Van Knippenberg, and Wilke 1990; Ellemers, Wilke, and Van Knoppenberg 1993; Spears, Doosje, and Ellemers 1997). For example, Doosje, Spears, and Ellemers (2002) demonstrate how anticipated changes in the status of one's in-group—here, in terms of how test performance could immediately shift the relative prestige of one's academic team—lead some individuals to cast their lot with a lower performing group only if their prospects for improvement seemed imminent in a subsequent task.

The world of racial and ethnic politics, however, is less amenable to such fleeting interventions. Hierarchies—or "racial formations," as Omi and Winant (1986) call them—are profoundly structural, stubbornly durable, and slow-changing, if they change at all. The social psychologist Jim Sidanius has made the study of these hierarchies a life mission, demonstrating repeatedly that racial orders reflect lasting inequities between groups in terms of wealth, education, and political representation—disparities that take a long time to accumulate and, by the same reasoning, take a very long time to undo (Sidanius et al. 1997; Sidanius and Pratto 1999; Sidanius and Petrocik 2001). Thus, in a world where racial orders are this "sticky," it is safe to say that *individual mobility* is generally off the table when you are a member of a minority group (Masuoka and Junn 2013).[1]

This is a fair characterization of the United States' racial order. Despite a discernible growth in multiracial individuals (Davenport 2018; Lee and Bean 2010; Masuoka 2017), the boundaries between Whites and racial and ethnic minorities are generally difficult to pierce, resulting in the reification and stability of groups like African Americans, Asian Americans, and Latinos (Ho et al. 2011). Thus, with the prospect of belonging to socially devalued group (with respect to Whites), minorities have an incentive to band together, for the purposes of both affirming themselves and increasing their cachet (*social creativity*), and improving, however modestly, their station in America's racial order (*social competition*).

---

1. To say "generally" is to admit to some exceptions to this claim. For example, within distinct racial groups, such as African Americans, Asian Americans, and Latinos, some individuals can—and do—dissociate from their in-group on the basis of attributes (e.g., lighter skin color, greater wealth, conservative beliefs) that enables them to pass into a higher status group (e.g., Garcia Bedolla 2005; Jiménez 2017; Zou and Cheryan 2017). Alas, these exceptions affirm the general rule of limited individual mobility for most members of racial and ethnic minority groups.

My claim is that PoC ID serves these purposes under very specific circumstances. As a broad-based attachment, PoC ID enables members of distinct racial minorities to attain *positive distinctiveness* by comparing themselves to the major out-group, Whites. This distinctiveness is not only positive, it is also, in the words of Marilynn Brewer (1991), "optimal." That is because as a racial or ethnic minority, "I" feel a sense of belonging with other racial or ethnic minorities, yet only racial or ethnic minorities can belong to this group. This sense of uniqueness operates only when individuals are encouraged to think of themselves on the basis of statuses, experiences, and histories that they *share* (Cortland et al. 2017). In other words, much like other pan-racial or pan-ethnic groups (e.g., Asian American, Latino), the category PoC works by mentally homogenizing the diversity of its internal membership—specifically, by minimizing cognitive and affective differences between minority groups and at the same time creating starker differences between racial minorities and Whites (Gaertner et al. 1989; Levendusky 2018; Transue 2007).

This coherence implies that when politics places an emphasis on PoC instead of specific minority groups, PoC ID will become activated, ready to structure minorities' political attitudes and behaviors. The signature mark here is not only the robust relation between PoC ID and related outcomes, but that this link should generally be invariant with respect to which minority group is implicated by said outcome (cf. Winter 2008). I call this the *solidarity hypothesis*, and I expect it to manifest itself in two forms. The first consists of judgments and feelings that indicate an affirmation of PoC, as in favorable evaluations of racial and ethnic minorities, which I construe as clear expressions of *social creativity* (Tajfel and Turner 1986). This means individual minorities will bolster PoC without necessarily remedying their lower station in the racial order. The second expression of this hypothesis involves public support for measures and initiatives that actually remedy, or intend to remedy, the objective station of racial and ethnic minorities in the US racial hierarchy. I consider such a pattern an indication of social competition (cf. Tajfel and Turner 1986), whereby minorities engage in politics aimed at modifying their lower rank in the racial order.

The other half of my theoretical framework concerns the deactivation of PoC ID's effects, that is, its weakening or elimination from politics. Clarifying this possibility involves a deeper appreciation for the vantage point that any one non-White individual possesses: do I see myself as a member of a distinct racial group, or do I see myself, more broadly, as a PoC? I contend that when the political arena emphasizes the uniqueness of a racial or ethnic group—e.g., the special histories, aspirations, and goals that make one Black, Latino, Asian, and so on—the influence of PoC ID will wane. I call this the *racial uniqueness hypothesis*. What is crucial for this prediction is not so much the specific comparison group, but whether an alternative category can, in principle, be nested under the broader PoC category. Hence, a sense of uniqueness can stem from not only one's pan-racial or pan-ethnic group (e.g., Black, Latino), but also one's national origin group (e.g., Jamaican, Mexican). I expect this uniqueness hypothesis to manifest in two ways. First, with the distinctiveness of one's particular racial or ethnic group highlighted, we should witness the effects of PoC ID on minority political behavior reduced to weakness, inconsistency, and many times, statistical insignificance. Second, in the presence of PoC ID's reduced influence, minorities' political opinions and evaluations should convey a degree of in-group favoritism narrowly wrapped around their particular racial in-group, rather than PoC more generally.[2]

## Implications and Next Steps

We started this chapter with two major blind spots to correct. The first one, involving conceptualization, demanded a clearer and more thorough sense about the nature of a PoC ID, especially with respect to other forms of attachment that minorities hold close to their chest. Now at the end of the chapter, we sit behind the wheel of a brand new and shiny concept, PoC ID, which I conceptualize as a shared form of identity that encapsulates the distinct identities of specific racial and ethnic minority groups in the United States. As a cross-cutting form of identity, PoC ID recategorizes minority out-groups under a common banner of identity, leading to a redirection and spreading of the benefits of in-group favoritism.

The second blind spot concerns the conditions under which we should (fail to) observe the influence of PoC ID on minority politics. I have dissipated some of this fog by reasoning that PoC ID matters politically when the salience of this broad-based attachment is heightened by one's political

---

2. Astute readers will note I treat the ethnic category Latino as conceptually equal to the racial categories African American and Asian American, even though the US Census Bureau distinguishes them (Mora 2014). I justify this choice on three grounds. First, my theory zeroes in on the relative marginalization of these groups based on prestige and power, which minimizes technical differences between race and ethnicity (e.g., Sidanius et al. 1997). Second, I conceptualize race and ethnicity as mental categories defined by contextually salient attributes, not as coarse government designations (Chandra 2012; Sen and Wasow 2016). Finally, I recognize that all minorities have race in their identity repertoires—for example, Latinos can have a specific race (e.g., Black Latinos vs. White Latinos). Whether race matters more than ethnicity for Latinos depends, per my theory, on situational cues. For example, it is plausible that Black Latinos will be more supportive of #BlackLivesMatter than White Latinos based on racial identity.

environment. Here, one's sense of identification with other non-White individuals should become mentally accessible, ready to color one's personal views and judgments about racial and ethnic politics. In contrast, I argue that the influence of PoC ID is most likely to wane when the distinctiveness of one's specific racial or ethnic group is underscored by one's political environment. When one is reminded about how unique one's own racial or ethnic group is with respect to other minorities, that common banner of PoC ID is expected to lose its political punch.

Having corrected these blind spots and put the concept of PoC ID into sharper relief, I am now more fully prepared to examine the origins and nature of this new attachment. Let us turn to this important work, which consumes most of our attention in the chapter that follows.

# 3

# The Many Faces of People of Color

> The problem of the twentieth century is the problem of the color line.
> —W. E. B. DUBOIS (1903)

More than a century has passed since the Black sociologist W. E. B. DuBois first penned these words. Professor DuBois originally made his observation against a backdrop marred by the widespread lynching of African Americans (Franklin 1947), the cementing of a Jim Crow system that brutally marginalized southern Blacks (McClain et al. 2005), and the rise of a new and expanded Ku Klux Klan that mixed hostility toward African Americans with nativist aggression toward foreigners (Higham 1955). This was an era of demographic flux, and many Whites responded with reactionary politics aimed at keeping America exclusively White (King 2000; Ngai 2004).

The passage of time has not eroded this color line as much as casual observers might first suspect or even wish. Racially motivated lynching is mostly a thing of the past, but in its wake, acute police violence against Black and Latino communities has taken root, with the massive incarceration of individuals from both groups, especially African American men (Walker 2020; Weaver 2007; Weaver and Lerman 2010, Lerman and Weaver 2014). Gone, too, is the overt disenfranchisement of Black communities, only to be replaced with new, technically legal, tactics that include photo identification laws, legislative gerrymandering, and felon disenfranchisement laws—all aimed at limiting the political power of Blacks, Asians, and Latinos (Anoll and Israel-Trummel 2019; Haynie 2019). Even the Ku Klux Klan has shriveled into a shadow of its former self (Southern Poverty and Law Center 2019), only to be replaced with smaller, more well-organized, and more intensely violent right-wing groups pushing back against Blacks, Latinos, Asians, and other racial minorities (Green et al. 1999; Parker and Barreto 2013).

One thing *has* changed about the color line, though. It has grown brighter and longer to encapsulate a growing slew of racial diversity. The US Census

Bureau (2018) estimates that nearly 40% of America's population is now comprised of non-Whites: Blacks, Asians, Latinos, and other racial minorities. This is a far cry from DuBois's time, when non-Whites largely consisted of Blacks and Native Americans and totaled 12% of the nation (Census Bureau 1903). Indeed, in direct recognition of this trend, a new label—*people of color* (PoC)—has emerged to informally classify this heterogeneous mass.

To whom does this label apply? What does it entail for individuals classified under it? And who is excluded—and why—from membership in this group? Answering these queries is about more than solving an ontological puzzle. Without firm answers to them, we risk categorizing a mix of individuals without this classification packing any real meaning for them. This chapter, then, provides additional evidence to confirm that subsequent chapters—each examining some aspect of PoC—are worth my time as a researcher and yours as a reader. Accordingly, this chapter draws on a cornucopia of in-depth interviews with minority individuals, all aimed to provide a better grasp of how PoC understand this label and what it means when they apply it to themselves and others. The lessons we learn from these conversations will serve as a foundation for later chapters, which formally define and appraise a *people of color* identity (PoC ID). Let us see, then, what the fruits of this labor reveal about this matter.

## Conversing with PoC

In early 2019, I conducted $N = 25$ in-depth interviews with self-identified PoC to deepen my conceptualization of this category. This sample is composed of individuals residing in Los Angeles, one of the United States' most racially and ethnically diverse municipalities (Bobo and Johnson 2000; Sawyer 2005). This highly localized focus comes with some caveats. What we are observing here are the views of individuals who inhabit a dense metropolitan area characterized by significant numbers of many non-White groups, with relations between these groups characterized by both conflict and cooperation (Sonenshein 1993; Vaca 2004). As of 2019, about 49% of Los Angeles residents were Latino, nearly 9% were African American, and nearly 12% were Asian American, which in combination makes PoC the majority of residents in this large city of nearly 4 million inhabitants (2019 American Community Survey). This means that the views of racial/ethnic minorities from rural areas are not represented in this small sample; neither are the views from other contexts where one minority group exclusively prevails (e.g., African Americans in Memphis, Tenn.; Mexican Americans in San Antonio, Tex.; Chinese Americans in Monterey Park, Calif.). These blind spots, however, are partly offset by the fact that a city like Los Angeles can be viewed as a harbinger of interminority relations in the very near future, with growing numbers of racial/ethnic minorities occupying the same general space in closer proximity to one another (e.g., Lee and Bean 2010). Ultimately, then, the sample of respondents here reflects a "most likely" case (Gerring 2001, 2004): a particular setting where the individual motivation to identify as a PoC is likely to be relatively higher than in other contexts.

Out of the 25 interviews I conducted, 8 were with Black individuals, 10 with Asian American individuals, and 7 with Latino individuals. Five of these interviewees noted they were mixed-race, with most emphasizing a stronger identification with one of their racial/ethnic groups. Two-thirds of these interviewees were students at the University of California, Los Angeles (UCLA), recruited via campus ads. The remainder were adults unaffiliated with the university whom I directly approached in public settings (e.g., malls) and asked for referrals upon completing an interview. These conversations lasted 30 to 90 minutes, and all participants received compensation ($25 Amazon gift card for UCLA affiliates; $50 for non-UCLA affiliates). All interviews were conducted in the UCLA Race, Ethnicity, Politics & Society Lab or at a location convenient to the respondent (e.g., their home). The appendix to this chapter provides fuller details on my sample and protocol.

In-depth interviews like these are incredibly useful for developing one's understanding of a new concept (cf. Hochschild 1981; Jiménez 2010; Parker 2009; Walsh 2016). In this case, they stand to reveal how the category PoC operates among racial minorities (Charmaz 2014; Weiss 1994). Yet there is nothing representative about this sample or the views emanating from it. I held these conversations with purposive sampling in mind (Rubin and Rubin 2012), which means I maximized the range of views expressed across key attributes to heighten my senses about how some PoC construe this label. Specifically, I conversed with individuals from three US minority groups. I also interviewed people (un)associated with UCLA to yield insight into how higher education impacts this category's meaning. Moreover, I interviewed people who (un)enthusiastically used the label to describe themselves and others. One should therefore view the insights that emerge from these conversations as exploratory, with the aim of theory building, rather than hypothesis testing (Gerring 2004).

So what do we discover from a purposive sample like this one? A lot, if our interest is PoC. I discipline my discussion of what I learned by organizing it into two themes: (1) What makes one a PoC? and (2) What excludes racial minorities from being PoC? Although I did not expect to hear all of the details that interviewees shared with me, the themes were part of a protocol

I used to steer each conversation (see the appendix to this chapter), which consisted of general discussion topics, making for open-ended yet revelatory conversations (Jiménez and Orozco 2019). Throughout, I attribute all words to specifically named individuals so that readers can keep track of who said what. All these names are aliases to ensure respondents' anonymity.

## What Makes One a PoC?

The question of what qualifies one for membership in any group, including PoC, has many answers. But from a psychological angle, part of the answer hinges on the category, its attendant attributes, and who—that is, what other group—the frame of reference in a setting is (Turner et al. 1987, 1994; see also Chandra 2012; Eberhardt 2019; Sen and Wasow 2016). America's racial hierarchy means that, many times, Whites are a point of comparison for PoC. Those attributes that distinguish PoC from Whites often serve as a foundation for self-definition: who is the average, or prototypical, PoC—and on what basis is there variance around this mean (Ellemers and Jetten 2012; Turner et al. 1987)? My conversations with PoC provide some clues about these attributes—attributes that, I hasten to add, are not set in stone, but rather, can shift with changing features of majority-minority relations in the US (Craig and Richeson 2012, 2018; Zou and Cheryan 2017).

### SKIN TONE

Any group like PoC has boundaries that distinguish members from outsiders (Brewer 1991). The PoC I spoke with suggested that skin tone is one such key marker of this group—which does not imply that it is the *only* way to define PoC or that skin color *always* defines this group. But for my respondents, it is a prominent trait that can clarify who is a typical PoC and who fits less well within its borders. When I asked interviewees how they would help someone unfamiliar with this term differentiate PoC from others, Jessica Garay (Black-Latina) informed me that "you look at the color of somebody's skin and that's a big indicator," a point affirmed by Josephine de la Cruz (Asian, Filipina), who suggested that "you can usually notice them by . . . skin color." This attribute seems to apply to all PoC, not just African Americans. As Isaiah Carter (Black) put it, a PoC is "anybody who's not White." Or, as Orlando Díaz (Latino, Mexican) pointedly told me: "Anyone that's beyond this shade of White . . . is what I . . . consider a person of color, whether they are brown, more dark, [or] black."

To categorize PoC via skin color highlights America's color line. Yet part of why the term *PoC* resonates with some individuals is that the label envelops Black *and* non-Black minorities, something Linda Sánchez (Latina, Mexican) alluded to. When I asked her to tell me who counts as PoC based on skin tone, she said: "I . . . think Mexican, Black, Asian . . . basically people who aren't White." This was echoed by Christina Cheung (Asian, Vietnamese-Chinese), who added, "I . . . picture a coalition of . . . groups of African Americans, Latinx Americans, Asian Americans." These words reveal a key membership criterion. People of color are not White and display darker complexions, or as Mariana Espejo (Asian, Filipina) stated, "a person of color is someone who has . . . brownness, yellowness, or a shade deeper than whiteness in their skin."

### RACIAL DISADVANTAGES

But to focus simply on skin tone is to miss a larger point made by Brandon Phan (Asian, Vietnamese) and other interviewees: that PoC experience "inequality" and "hardships." In other words, skin tone differences often correspond with group-level disadvantages that entail less access to privileges, resources, and status—or as Cristina Cheung (Asian, Vietnamese-Chinese) suggested, being a PoC means "you're not in the majority and you are facing structural barriers that prevent you from . . . being on equal footing." Avery Wu (Asian, Chinese) expressed as much to me, saying that a PoC is "someone that has felt excluded or . . . unjustly treated," later adding, "regardless of how it manifests, it all goes back to the system . . . how does the system treat you?" David Santos (Asian, Filipino) expanded on this point:

> So, we're people with . . . dark skin, compared to others. And then . . . we're further categorized by certain . . . conditions, like the struggles . . . we face . . . I think that . . . if . . . someone . . . were to . . . ask what a person of color is, it's . . . people who are in the minority, who have faced a . . . degree of disadvantage because of their minority status.

David's view is well articulated but not unique. Consider Miriam Khoudry (Venezuelan-Lebanese), who described PoC as "nonwhite, . . . usually underprivileged communities." As she suggests, this status is collective, with entire communities at a disadvantage in relation to Whites. These inequalities are often personally felt by individual PoC, like José García (Latino, Guatemalan), who explained how "I can pretend that I am [White], and I can act, assimilate, acculturate, and act like I'm better, but at the end of the day, the color of my skin will define my experience."

This sense of racial disadvantage is something my conversations suggest is sharpened across one's life span, the accumulation of repeated reminders that one is different and, therefore, unequal. Consider here the insights of Sara Reyes (Asian, Filipina), who described her evolving sense of being a PoC like this:

> It evolved into me knowing, oh I'm not the same color as these [White] people. I don't have the same privileges as these [White] people. I don't have the same outlooks as these [White] people . . . I am different, I am a person of color.

Sara's words suggest the term *person of color* is more than a surface descriptor. Feeling different and excluded from mainstream society seems to sharpen one's attachment to this pan-racial group. But it is hard to miss from Sara's words how the definition of PoC occurs with respect to Whites—the group on the other side of the color line. Indeed, to be a PoC is to be non-White in terms of one's position in, acceptance by, and ability to maneuver in society. This is not to say that all racial and ethnic minorities are similarly disadvantaged with respect to Whites. As Zou and Cheryan (2017) remind us, the terms on which specific minority groups are marginalized with respect to Whites varies, sometimes dramatically. For example, while African Americans are denigrated for their alleged inferiority with respect to Whites, Asian Americans are deemed relatively superior to Black Americans, but still foreign with respect to Whites (Kim 2003; Masuoka and Junn 2013).

Notwithstanding these nuances, however, the PoC I spoke with seemed to understand that, on average, racial and ethnic minorities are marginalized with respect to Whites. This marginalization, more importantly, can occur directly or vicariously. As Iris Pierce (Black-Indian) highlighted: "I am very dark . . . I am a person of color. But I haven't experienced as much [discrimination]"; however, she noted, "I still identify with it." Thus, although directly experiencing racial disadvantage is a surefire way to encourage identification wither other PoC, more critical is the recognition that racial and ethnic minorities bear the brunt of such disparities.

## A SENSE OF BELONGING, PRIDE, AND SOLIDARITY

This self-definition of PoC based on what we do not possess might seem counterproductive. Why identify with PoC if they are underprivileged and socially devalued? Part of the answer is that many minorities have little choice, given that the boundaries between (non-)Whites (i.e., America's color line) are hard to penetrate (Haney López 1996; Ho et al. 2011; Jacobson 1998). As we learned in chapter 2, in this circumstance, members of an out-group, like PoC, will often engage in social creativity; that is, they shift the terms of comparison with the in-group (here, Whites) in order to gain positive distinctiveness and the benefits that flow from it, including a stronger sense of belonging, pride, and community.

Consider here the words of Alyssa Davis (Black-White), who described PoC as "a haven for me . . . it's been something that I can easily identify with . . . that I . . . fit into unquestionably." In these comments, Alyssa reveals how PoC provide personal security by affirming her sense of belonging to a mix of individuals who are not White and relatively disadvantaged. David Santos (Asian, Filipino) echoed this:

> The awareness [of being PoC] definitely sets up a lot of pride. And that comes directly from the disadvantages that we've had. So I have my grandfather, he was born in the Philippines, he was a fisherman back in the 30s. . . . He came to America and he worked in insurance, but he had disadvantages all the time. . . . There are inherent disadvantages that he faced because he was a minority and Filipino. But it makes me proud that he worked through it and was able to succeed despite those disadvantages. So, I do feel a sense of pride, that . . . we face struggle, . . . we have disadvantages, and it sucks, but we make it.

This personal sense of security through a larger community is one spark behind individuals' engagement in collective action on behalf of others (Fowler and Kam 2007; Olson 1965; Pérez 2015b). Consider here the insight of Josephine de la Cruz (Asian, Filipina), who explained why identifying as a PoC yields collective action: "My identity as a person of color has helped me . . . build community with other people who have shared similar struggles because we were able to share in these experiences"; she later added that "what matters is we're all suffering and if we want the suffering to end, there's only one thing that we can all do, which is work together."

Alyssa's, David's, and Josephine's observations strongly imply a sense of solidarity among PoC—a hodgepodge of disparate racial minorities who, to paraphrase Anderson's (1983) famous words, will never know each other yet still share a sense of communion. That sense of communion among PoC, my interviews revealed, rests on the view that racial minorities have undergone parallel experiences in the US. This orientation toward broad perspective taking is illustrated by the comments of Nadia Maddox (Black), who suggested a shared ability among minorities "to be able to look at the other race and understand that they too are having to get ugly and dirty and sweat and bleed before other people, in order to get to a place where our dream is." Avery Wu (Asian, Chinese) added to this view, explaining that "you wouldn't identify with a community unless . . . empathy was increased because you also experience similarities." What kind of similarities? Karina Bello (Latina, Guatemalan) suggested that "when I think of people of color, I think of struggles, and I think our struggles are what makes us what we are." Isaiah Carter (Black) put it even more colorfully. When I asked him why he sees Blacks, Mexicans, and other groups as "apples and apples," rather than "apples and oranges," he said: "Well, they are apples and oranges, but it's still fruit . . . and I think . . . these fruit trees are still in the same . . . farm [of discrimination]."

I hasten to add, however, that this perceived similarity between PoC does not appear to come at the expense of a failure to appreciate the unique experiences of various groups. For example, Karina Bello (Latina, Guatemalan) showed an ability to juggle both perspectives: "there are those commonalities that make us a group, but there are also differences that you can't just erase." Her recognition of the "forest and trees" was also expressed by Linda Sánchez (Latina, Mexican), who said, "I think that . . . diversity brings in . . . different knowledge and experiences that can be shared within . . . different groups . . . it's something that . . . makes you more aware." James Aquino (Asian, Filipino) brought up something similar, noting: "PoC is . . . a term for solidarity. When I'm talking about solidarity, it's about acknowledging these differences, but not . . . in an aggressive light—rather, sharing and learning from each other."

If you pay close attention, there is a celebratory power flowing from acknowledging the differences displayed by PoC: nuances that manifest at the interpersonal, intergroup, and even historical level. This rich diversity seems to enable PoC to link their unique backgrounds to the pan-racial group they imagine. As Ngoc Nguyen (Asian, Vietnamese) explained, "I think . . . the fact that I come from . . . a refugee background helps me connect with a lot of other groups . . . if any group . . . suffered from American imperialism, it's . . . Vietnamese."

This broad sense of identifying as a PoC is further clarified by comparing interviewees' views about the labels *person of color* and *minority*. Here is Ngoc Nguyen, again, in her own words: "I think the term *people of color* . . . centers us, whereas the term *minorities* . . . comes with being minor to someone else." Indeed, as Avery Wu (Asian, Chinese) pointed out, "I think saying a *person of color* is a bit more empowering compared to the term *minority* just because I think *minority* seems very isolating . . . I feel like *person of color*, you imagine more groups with you." José García told me as much, stating, "when you say *minority*, it means less than—I see it as less than, I see it as smaller." Indeed, as Ingrid Winters (Black) expressed: "It seems a little downgraded . . . Just

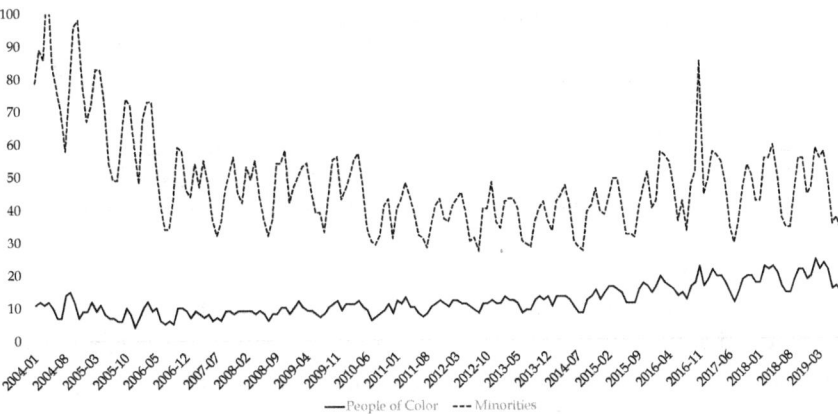

FIGURE 3.1. Monthly Google searches for "people of color" vs. "minorities," 2004–2019

*minority*? Ugh. I don't like that word." It is this downgrading that the term PoC pushes back against by giving one, in Linda Sánchez's view, "a sense of identity, something to stand for, believe in, a sense of being human."

This affirming sense of identity that Linda and other PoC describe manifests itself in other data I collected. Figure 3.1 displays two time series I created using Google searches from 2004 to 2019. The first series (solid) represents web searches for the term *people of color*, while the second series (dashes) reflects web searches for the term *minorities*. These data suggest a relative decline in the popularity of the term *minorities* during this time span, with a mild but discernible climb in the popularity of the phrase *people of color*. In fact, when I formally assess the association between these series, the correlation is negative and reliable ($-.167$, $p < .01$, two-tailed), suggesting the relative popularity of the term *people of color* coincides with decreases in the popularity of the label *minorities*, which aligns with the views shared by many of my interviewees.[1]

We can get further leverage over the affirming sense of PoC ID by turning to public opinion data I collected for this project. In three large online surveys of African American ($N = 1,200$), Asian American ($N = 1,200$), and Latino ($N = 1,200$) adults that I conducted in 2018, I asked four questions to directly gauge individual differences in PoC ID. I have more to say about these items

---

1. Both series display stationarity. The reported correlation reflects the relationship between current search levels for "people of color" and the previous month's search levels of "minorities," adjusted for the autocorrelation between current and previous search levels for "people of color." Mathematically, this distills to People of Color$_t$ = People of Color$_{t-1}$ + Minorities$_{t-1}$ + constant.

TABLE 3.1. PoC ID provides an affirming sense of attachment

|  | Black adults agree | Asian adults agree | Latino adults agree |
|---|---|---|---|
| "I am glad to be a *person of color*" | 90% | 60% | 58% |
| N | 1,200 | 1,200 | 1,200 |

Note: Percentages reflect individuals who somewhat agreed, agreed, or strongly agreed with the statement. Replies come from the "People of Color" surveys, which I analyze in detail in chapter 4.

in the next chapter, when I more fully examine and validate them; for now, I note here that one of these items asked all respondents to indicate their degree of agreement (on a seven-point scale) with the statement "I am glad to be a person of color." This item is designed to capture the emotional significance of a group to an individual (Tajfel 1981)—that is, the degree to which one is satisfied with membership in the category *people of color* (Leach et al. 2008). The adults answering this question replied in a way that aligns with the views of my in-depth interviews. As table 3.1 reveals, a majority of African American (90%), Asian American (60%), and Latino respondents (58%) somewhat agreed, agreed, or strongly agreed that they are glad to be a PoC, with Black Americans—the originators of this label—feeling especially positive about it. These patterns support my inference that PoC ID provides an affirming sense of group identity for many non-Whites. None of this, however, implies that PoC ID is more important for non-Whites than their specific racial ID. People's identity categories are stored in long-term memory (García-Ríos, Pedraza, and Wilcox-Archuleta 2019; Pérez 2015a, b; Turner et al. 1987), which we know is associatively organized (Collins and Loftus 1975; Lodge and Taber 2013; Pérez 2016). Hence, stimulating PoC ID is likely to activate racial ID to some degree, given their storage in close proximity to each other in long-term memory. This means that notwithstanding the relative importance of PoC ID and racial ID for an individual, what is crucial for politics is which of the two becomes relatively more salient in a given political moment.

## NESTING UNDER AN UMBRELLA

The ability of a group to impart a strong sense of dignity could hardly be clearer. And part of how this seems to operate among PoC is by enhancing what it means to be a member of a unique racial group. In other words, the category PoC seems to help racial minorities put their specific in-group in a more positive light. For example, Kisha Jackson (Black) explained to me, "White people are . . . put on a pedestal . . . already have money . . . I want to establish myself as a Black person that . . . has class," something the label *PoC* lets her accomplish. Kisha says this as a Black woman, but this link between one's racial in-group and PoC was also highlighted by non-Black PoC like Josephine de la Cruz (Asian, Filipina), who explained:

> I had ... very little ties to my cultural ... background. Once I got to college and ... started embracing that, it was more empowering ... I ... found a community [i.e., people of color] in which ... these experiences [as Filipino] are validated.

Mariana Espejo (Asian, Filipina) recalled something similar, but more painful:

> As a kid, my parents never told me I was Filipino ... Then I went to ... kindergarten and ... the second day ... someone chased me around the playground yelling, "Chinese, Chinese." and then I yelled back, "I'm not a food, I'm a human!"

Mariana later described this experience to me as helping her connect her personal sense of exclusion as Filipina to her broader sense of being a PoC.

This linkage between one's distinct racial identity (e.g., one's sense of being Black, Latino, or Asian) and one's membership in the pan-racial category PoC is something that chapter 2 foreshadowed. There, I explained that the interface between racial identity and one's identity as a PoC can be understood as a relation between a subordinate and superordinate identity, where narrower racial groups are nested below the broader PoC category. When this link is intact, one's distinct racial group is perceived as part of the larger whole, leading individuals to see more similarities between PoC. Evidence of this link emerged during my interviews of PoC. Consider the following three excerpts, each hovering around this basic point. First we have Lupe Ramírez (Latina, Mexican) who shared the following:

> I think it [the term *PoC*] was historically created to ... talk ... about Black individuals, and now it's become ... an umbrella term to talk about ... so many people where ... it takes away the emphasis on ... Black individuals.

What is revealing here is that despite Lupe's weak historical sense of PoC, she intuits that this label has evolved to include non-Black minorities, such as Latinos and Asians. What is also instructive is her description of PoC as an umbrella covering many racial minorities. Alyssa Davis (Black-White) described this symbiosis in the following way: "You know when kids have those massive tarps, and everybody hides underneath it ... ? That's what *people of color* is. Everybody coming under and sharing and we're all different people." Alyssa, then, also sees the inclusive nature of PoC. Or, as David Santos (Asian, Filipino) summarized for me: "We all face distinct things that are related because of the umbrella it comes from, but unique in their own ways."

This is the strength of a superordinate category, like PoC, but it can also be its Achilles' heel, as James Aquino (Asian, Filipino) and others remind us:

> I can see how the term PoC is . . . overshadowing my community's efforts . . . When I hear that some Black folks aren't really too crazy about the *PoC* term, I can . . . see that if I'm feeling this way about the term *PoC*, it probably . . . would also overshadow their own communities.

This overshadowing effect of PoC, where the broader category flattens the unique histories and aspirations varied minority groups, is one key to understanding when the category loses its political punch, a phenomenon I examine in more detail in chapter 7.

The last defining feature of PoC that my interviewees suggested is their progressive political views. When I asked PoC what kinds of outlooks or mannerisms make one a PoC, many interviewees described PoC as liberal, with progressive politics offering a blueprint for addressing the structural inequities that PoC face presently and have historically endured. As Alyssa Davis (Black-White) explained to me: "Central to left-of-center politics . . . is having a basic understanding that there [have] been historic challenges [that need] . . . rectification." Upon further probing, Alyssa said these needs include reparations for Blacks as atonement for the continuing legacies of slavery—something that she sees as highly consistent with progressive politics.

But it is not just Blacks who draw a connection between progressive politics and being a PoC. When I asked David Santos (Asian, Filipino) to describe the politics of PoC, he said: "I would say left-leaning . . . But then there is a heavy centralism toward the middle, towards the moderate. But I feel like it always leans towards the left." Of course, a skeptical reader might say that this progressive marker is nonsense given strong evidence that most people are ideologically innocent (Converse 1964; Kinder and Kalmoe 2017; but see Dawson 2001; Philpot 2017). But when I pressed David about how progressive politics speak to issues implicating PoC, he said:

> You should always strengthen voter rights. If you don't support that, it's a sham . . . I think that is one of the best ways for PoCs to have their voices heard, to end that idea that there is . . . discrimination, . . . disadvantage . . . If we want the hate crime to end, the police brutality to end, if we want to figure out the immigration problem, if we want to figure out anything, we need everyone's voice being spoken.

In just a few words, then, David names four areas—voter rights, hate crimes, police brutality, and immigration reform—that implicate PoC in some way and that progressive politics can address. Notice, too, that David's is a

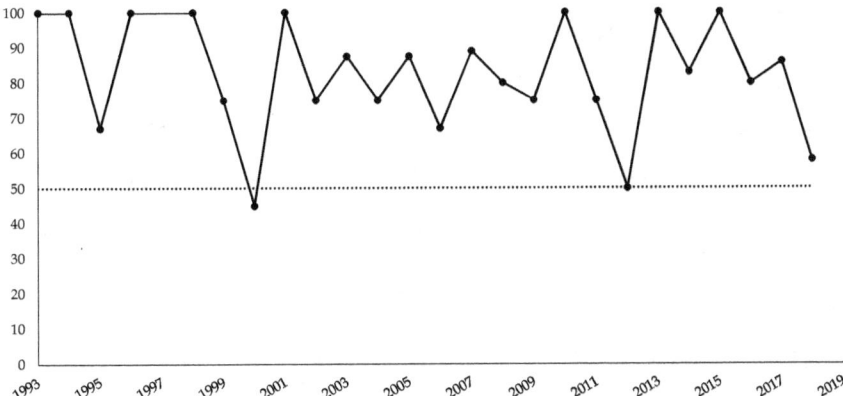

FIGURE 3.2. Percentage of mentions of "people of color" in the *Congressional Record* made by Democratic lawmakers, 1993–2018

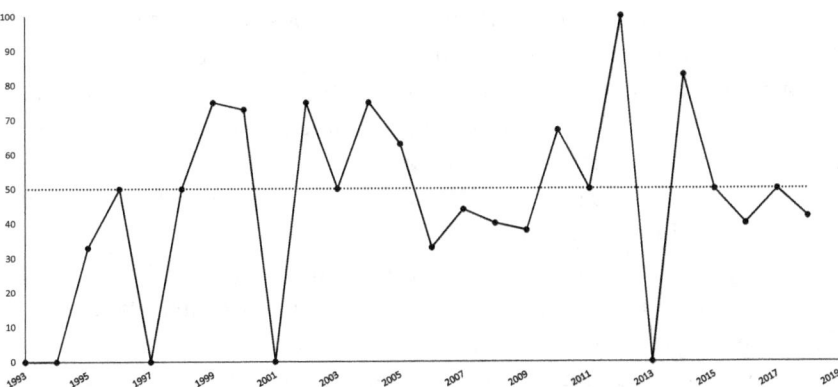

FIGURE 3.3. Percentage of mentions of "people of color" in the *Congressional Record* that were made by White lawmakers, 1993–2018

normative prescription. If, as a PoC, you do not support progressive views, then it is "a sham," for failure to support initiatives that affect any PoC is a failure to embody being a PoC.

This connection between PoC and progressive politics is corroborated by data from the *Congressional Record*, which registers the proceedings of America's legislative chamber. I coded a random 20% of all *Congressional Record* mentions of the term *people of color* from 1993 to 2018. These mentions arose in legislation, committee reports, and floor debates, with *people of color* mainly used in discussions of civil rights, health policy, and labor and employment. Figures 3.2–3.4 graphically illustrate this basic analysis.

In figure 3.2, we see the proportion of mentions of PoC by legislators, collapsed across chamber. It is clear that while Republicans sometimes invoke

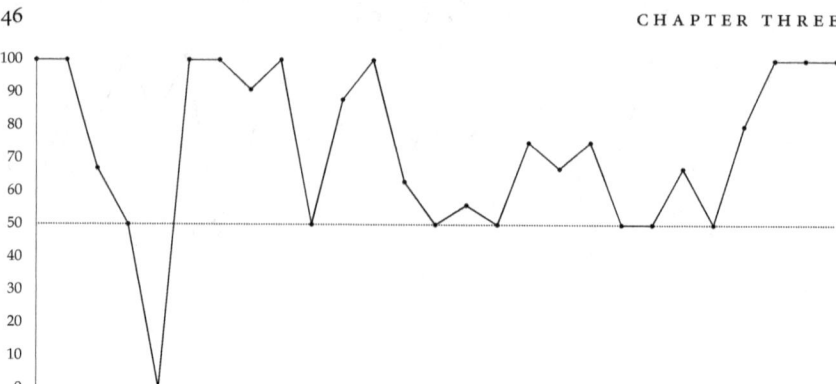

FIGURE 3.4. Percentage of mentions of "people of color" in the *Congressional Record* that referred to non-Black minorities, 1993–2018

the term *PoC*, it is Democratic lawmakers who mostly use this label in their discourse. In fact, save for two time points, Democrats employed this label in about 70% of legislative proceedings during this era. Figure 3.3 shows these mentions come from both non-White *and* White lawmakers. Pooling across parties, we can see that White lawmakers made about half of all mentions of the term *PoC* in the period under analysis. This pattern affirms that PoC is a meaningful category recognized by those inside and outside the group. Finally, figure 3.4 reveals that since the early 1990s, about half of all PoC mentions in the *Congressional Record* referred to non-Black minorities, such as Asians and Latinos, which affirms this label is a broad canopy encapsulating Black and non-Black minority groups. Taken as a whole, these data affirm the conclusion that part of what defines a PoC is a liberal political outlook, something that is even recognized by individuals who are not PoC.

## What Excludes Racial and Ethnic Minorities from the PoC Group?

### LIGHTER SKIN, MAYBE

These interviews illuminate the contours of PoC and some of the characteristics that provide access to membership in this pan-racial group. But all groups—even PoC—limit who can belong in order to infuse individuals with that sense of distinction that is so crucial to drawing self-worth from group membership. Indeed, as chapter 2 demonstrates, all individuals are motivated to join groups that provide a sense of belonging *and* distinctiveness (Brewer 1991). Distinctiveness, however, often emerges from the enforcement of in-group boundaries. How does this happen among PoC?

We learned earlier that skin tone is a major feature defining one's classification as PoC. As Aliyah Brown (Black) stated, "Well, me personally, I don't think people of color have a group. I don't think they have a group. I think [White] people put them in that group . . . because their skin is darker." But even that darker skin comes in various shades, with a range running from lighter to darker. As Sara Reyes (Asian, Filipina) clarified during our conversation, "if you see someone who . . . is . . . browner . . . that's a person of color."

Having a lighter skin tone, then, would seem to place some PoC outside the category *people of color*. Yet my conversations revealed that lighter skin tone is, at best, a crude indicator of worthiness in the group, for both those PoC who recognize themselves to be lighter skinned and those who see themselves as darker skinned. As Karina Bello (Latina, Guatemalan) explained "appearance-wise, I feel . . . that [makes] a big difference [in distinguishing PoC], so, like, blonde, blue eyes, very pale [skin] . . . you can have all of the attributes and still be a person of color."

The key thing here is that lighter-skinned PoC sense this, too, as evidenced by doubts concerning their self-classification as PoC. As Lupe Ramírez (Latina, Mexican) shared with me, "that's another reason why I find it hard to identify as a . . . [PoC] . . . because I don't see myself as just being . . . Spanish." As a fair-skinned Latina, Lupe acknowledges she is a blend of Indian and European ancestry. Yet her lighter skin tone complicates her claim to being a PoC.

This tension was also acknowledged by Miriam Khoudry (Venezuelan-Lebanese). When discussing the link between skin tone and identifying as a PoC, Miriam confided, "I have . . . trouble with that question . . . because I'm . . . Lebanese, but also Venezuelan . . . I'm Lebanese . . . [but] . . . Arab is White, you know." Miriam's reply stresses how hard it can be for lighter-skinned PoC to situate themselves in this broader group. And yet, many of them still self-identify as PoC, despite these tensions. Indeed, when asked directly whether they identify as PoC, both Lupe and Miriam stated, unequivocally, "yes."

### ACTING WHITE—DEFINITELY

It is safe to conclude, then, that lighter skin is neither sufficient nor necessary for exclusion from the category PoC. More definitive here is whether a PoC actively dissociates themselves from racial minorities and ingratiates themselves with Whites, or as Orlando Díaz (Latino, Mexican) described them, individuals "that . . . reject their heritage, that . . . reject who they are." Kisha Jackson (Black) made a similar observation:

> Okay, I don't want to say . . . , but they [some Blacks] shut themselves out . . . from other Black people . . . They just change their sound. Remain very stiff. They may have money. They may be very snooty and look down upon [other Black] people. Like very judgmental . . . like, they lost who they are.

In Kisha's view, being Black is insufficient to qualify as a PoC. Instead, darker skin must be accompanied by mannerisms that qualify one as truly Black and truly a PoC. But there is more to it than just this. The "change in sound," the "stiffness" that Kisha mentions reflect an active effort by some Blacks to "act White." Furthermore, it is not just something that Black PoC do. Other racial minorities also engage in this behavior, which is perceived as unbecoming of authentic PoC. Here is Sara Reyes (Asian, Filipino):

> In my home . . . if you talk like a White person . . . , people are like, "Oh are you White now?" . . . But . . . if someone were to just come up to me like that, as a person of color, just . . . talk to me [like a White person] . . . I'd be a little bit like, "Okay. Whoa. One second."

What Sara suggests is that when PoC ingratiate themselves with Whites, it raises a red flag to other PoC, indicating they are not really one of *us*. But her comments also remind us that skin tone is only one way that such distancing is facilitated. Take the perspective of David Santos (Asian, Filipino). When I asked him whether being light skinned disqualifies one from being a PoC, he answered in a way that told me there are other features that more strongly call into question one's bona fides:

> The biggest attribute I can think of is, they [racial/ethnic minorities] forget, or disinherit their roots or culture. So as much as we're a stewpot of cultures, we're different, we're mixed, we're all these things. . . . If a minority in the big spectrum actively decides to forget, or . . . is disingenuous to their roots that are inherent to them. They don't have to like it, they don't have to celebrate it, but if they choose to completely leave it behind, choose that "this is not a part of me anymore," that's when you're no longer PoC.

For David, then, the active distancing from PoC is what merits exclusion from this group. Indeed, in some sense, there is a "if you don't want us, then we don't want you" mentality to David's views and the views of other PoC. But part of why such active distancing grates on other PoC is because it undermines the collective spirit of this group: just like in other groups, there is no *I* in *We*. Here is David again:

> There are a lot of people, especially in the media, or the market, who just slap on the title *PoC*: "We have an actor here who is a PoC, so come watch our movie." And it seems like using the title in a disingenuous way for self-profit,

self-advertisement, whatever it may be. But taking advantage of it in a way that is tainting the purity and the pride that people have in what it is.... That's when you lose your "PoC card." Because you know your culture, but now you're taking advantage of it in a way that's not good.

David's comments segue into a related attribute that excludes minorities from PoC status: how individual minorities exercise any privileges they enjoy with respect to other PoC. This characteristic is best summarized by Jessica Garay (Black-Latina), who told me that there are many "White-passing" individuals who are technically PoC but prefer not to be categorized this way. As Ngoc Nguyen (Asian, Vietnamese) explained:

> But I think, like, some people who are . . . a little more White-passing, they can increase or decrease . . . others' perception of them as a person of color through . . . their political stances, whether or not they themselves identify with the term, . . . how much they identify with their . . . cultural . . . background . . . So if they didn't identify with their cultural background . . . , I think that would be [grounds for exclusion from the category PoC].

What does this White-passing behavior look like in practice? Ngoc offers an example:

> I feel . . . a name has a lot to do with it. If you're . . . a White-passing Latino, but you have a Latino name, . . . no one would ever think that you're just White. . . . I have a friend who is half Mexican, but his mom is White-passing and his dad is White and his last name is Greg. So . . . you would never know [that he is a PoC].

But sometimes, some PoC can be excluded simply on the basis of privileges they or their group enjoy relative to other racial minorities (Kim 2003; Zou and Cheryan 2017). On this point, Sara Reyes (Asian, Filipina) acknowledged, almost apologetically, "Okay, there's definitely a sense of, I will admit, privilege for Asian American groups because we are given this status of the model minority, which is in itself toxic, but it does give us a leg up, like in a sense of socioeconomic status."

Having a "leg up" can lead to the dissociation of a group like Asian Americans from the larger PoC category. On this delicate point, consider the words of Nadia Maddox (African American):

> I feel . . . unless you are . . . White or Chinese or some kind of other Asian, you are going to have a harder time. So if all of the people, besides the ones . . . I just mentioned, had to come together and say we don't like how America is treating us, I feel . . . we all have valid reasons because we just don't have certain gates open to privileges on the other side of that door. They are not wide open, they are not wide open for a lot of people.

But, again, privilege is not an automatic disqualifier from being a PoC. It all depends on one's outlook, as Alyssa Davis (Black-White) vigorously asserted:

> Socioeconomic status is not race . . . Being rich doesn't change the way your skin looks, the way . . . the world treats you. Oprah . . . is worth near a billion dollars . . . but gets followed into stores. . . . So, to me, . . . that's not the point. And when you start trying to separate people, you start trying to weaken them . . . that's not the game I play.

Indeed, as she explained in a different part of our conversation:

> It's not even like an oppression Olympics . . . here. That's just not it. The term *people of color* is supposed to unite us in that experience . . . not shy away from the differences.

Alyssa teaches us that despite PoC's diversity, unity is attainable by focusing on the shared oppression *we* face as PoC. How is this possible? Because, as Christina Cheung (Asian, Chinese) told me, "even if you do kind of move up in . . . economic status, you can still be discriminated against."

## POLITICAL CONSERVATISM

The words of these two women stress the commonalities between PoC and how this emphasis demands a worldview that justifies why disparate groups belong together and addresses how their different plights can be collectively addressed. This outlook is expressly left of center, which means another way that PoC can tell apart true members of the group from fair-weather friends is through conservative viewpoints. Indeed, the PoC I spoke with let me know that if you are a racial minority and you practice conservative politics, you are considered a persona non grata by other PoC. Why? Because there seems to be a wide recognition, underscored by Karina Bello (Latina, Guatemalan), that "most minorities tend to be more liberal and progressive for the most part" and that "there are always those odd ones that are very conservative, but it's very rare, so they're, like, outliers."

Notice how Karina views conservative PoC. They are exceptional because they stand several arms' length distance from what is seen as the norm for PoC, or as she later stated: "I think it's just the beliefs in very far right conservatives are very anti-minorities . . . almost every aspect of . . . conservative ideology is against minorities." But why is it so odd for a PoC to be politically conservative? Here is an incisive answer from Ebony Carter (Black-Japanese): "I . . . generally associate conservative people with . . . White Americans or

White people so I feel . . . if you have conservative views then you're . . . on . . . White people's agenda," a point driven home by Ngoc Nguyen (Asian, Vietnamese), who characterized Republicans as "the party of White supremacy."

To be a conservative, then, is a paradox for some PoC, because US conservatism appears to be anti-PoC. In the words of David Santos, "if you don't support immigration and you are a person of color, you're doing something wrong." Lupe Ramírez suggested as much, when she stated: "I would disqualify anyone that . . . supports Trump . . . I think for me, personally, I would want to disqualify a person that . . . doesn't want to . . . support other people of color."

Still, despite this readiness of some PoC to marginalize other PoC based on political views, some nuances peeked through my conversations. In particular, it is not that all conservative elements are antithetical to minorities. As Ngoc Nguyen taught me:

> I think in this country . . . we throw a lot of different things into . . . two baskets for the parties and in the Republican basket it's about . . . privileging White folks. So even if certain people of color . . . don't believe in that part, they believe in . . . other parts of conservatism, like . . . having lower taxes or . . . they don't believe in . . . abortion.

Given that Americans, including PoC, have only two political parties to represent them, it is not unnatural for some PoC to gravitate toward conservativism, especially if Republicans speak to other aspects of the minority experience among some PoC—for example, a sense of fiscal or social conservativism (cf. Dawson 2001; de la Garza et al. 1992; McClain and Johnson Carew 2017; Philpot 2017). But as other interviewees noted, a central tendency among Republicans is their hostility or passive indifference to PoC and their political preferences. Hence, being a conservative PoC is quirky because conservative politics these days are overshadowed by racialized politics.

### Are Some PoC More Worthy of the Designation?

We have learned about some of the attributes that distinguish true PoC from those who are not. But what about PoC themselves: do they distinguish who is a worthier group member? The answer is yes, and there is nothing unique about this. Social identity theory demonstrates that all groups can be generically thought of as normal distributions of attributes, complete with a central tendency and dispersion around that average (cf. Ellemers and Jetten 2012). The challenge at hand, then, is clarifying who that "average" PoC might be and how much variance exists around them.

My interviews shed some light on this. In particular, my conversations suggest that African Americans are the prototypical group that comes to mind for many PoC. Consider my exchange here with Isaiah Carter (Black):

INTERVIEWER. What kinds of groups are you willing to include [as PoC]?
ISAIAH. Obviously, Black and African.
INTERVIEWER. And then after that?
ISAIAH. Mexican and Latino.
INTERVIEWER. Okay.
ISAIAH. And then I would go Indians. And then I think I would stop . . .
INTERVIEWER. Really? . . . what is it about those three?
ISAIAH. The color of their skin.

Isaiah's insights return us to skin color's role in defining PoC. For him, Blacks are the quintessential members of this pan-racial category because they are darker than other minorities. He was not the only PoC who felt this way. When I asked Kisha Jackson (Black) who she thinks of when she hears the term *people of color*, she said: "I would say, mostly . . . Black people and maybe . . . some Mexicans . . . Or even . . . Indians. . . . That's who I would say the people of color are. Because our skin tends to get tanned." In a similar spirit, but more emphatically, Aliyah Brown (Black) asserted, "people of color are the Black people. They are the people of color. And that's just the way it has been forever."

But it is not just skin tone that makes Blacks the prototypical PoC. It is also their unique history and struggles in the US, as Nadia Maddox (Black) explained to me:

> The word *people of color*, . . . it originated from a place in history that doesn't suit why [other minorities] would be called that. . . . I very much disagree with how America handled things with a lot of countries, including . . . Mexico and all of that. But, due to the tone of your skin, that is not the reason why you'd be considered [PoC].

This sense that some African Americans might feel some degree of "ownership" over the group *people of color* is hard to miss. In fact, in my interviews with some of these individual African Americans, I sometimes found myself having to clarify that when I use the label *people of color*, I was referring, broadly, to racial and ethnic minorities. For example, during my conversation with her, Kisha Jackson asked me directly: "Why are you saying *people of color*? Why aren't you just saying like a Black person?" In another interview with one Ingrid Winters (Black), here is how our conversation unfolded:

# THE MANY FACES OF PEOPLE OF COLOR 53

INGRID. Yeah, I have heard of *people of color*.
INTERVIEWER. So when you hear it, what do you think it means?
INGRID. I just think it means, just Black people.
INTERVIEWER. So, what other groups might fall under there?
INGRID. Just Black people.

This strong mental association between one's racial in-group and PoC is a reflection of what Amélie Mummendey and her colleagues call *in-group projection*: the notion that in broadly diverse categories, members of one subgroup project their characteristics onto the larger category to define it and take cognitive ownership of it (Wenzel, Mummendey, and Waldzus 2007). In-group projection is what seems to be going on with some of these Black interviewees, who, like Ingrid Winters (Black), lay greater claim to PoC because: "I just feel . . . way back in the day . . . we went through more." Yet even some non-Black minorities recognize African Americans as the more prototypical PoC. For example, when I separately asked Sara Reyes and Josephine de la Cruz who they immediately think of when they hear the term *people of color*, they responded, respectively, and without hesitation, "Black people" and "definitely . . . Black, African American would be . . . the first." Indeed, in my conversation with Brandon Phan (Asian, Vietnamese), he shared how he associates Blacks with PoC because he perceives them as being even more disadvantaged than other racial minorities:

> Black people are . . . underprivileged because there's a long history when they got . . . sold. . as slaves. . . . So, that makes it . . . easier for me to consider them as . . . more disadvantaged. And so I associate that word [*Black*] with . . . *people of color*.

This broad notion of African Americans as an original PoC is corroborated by data from Black and mainstream newspapers that I collected. To further clarify the origins of the label PoC, I gathered all digitally available articles in major Black (*Chicago Defender*, *Los Angeles Sentinel*, and *New York Amsterdam News*) and mainstream (*Chicago Tribune*, *Los Angeles Times*, *New York Times*, and *Washington Post*) US newspapers that have used this term in their reporting from 1960 to 2017. Using these data, I build two series spanning this period that capture the average yearly number of stories in Black and mainstream papers using the term *people of color*. (Fuller details of this construction are in the appendix to this chapter.)

Figure 3.5 graphs these series against each other. First, it is evidently clear that Black papers have been invoking the term *people of color* for a longer

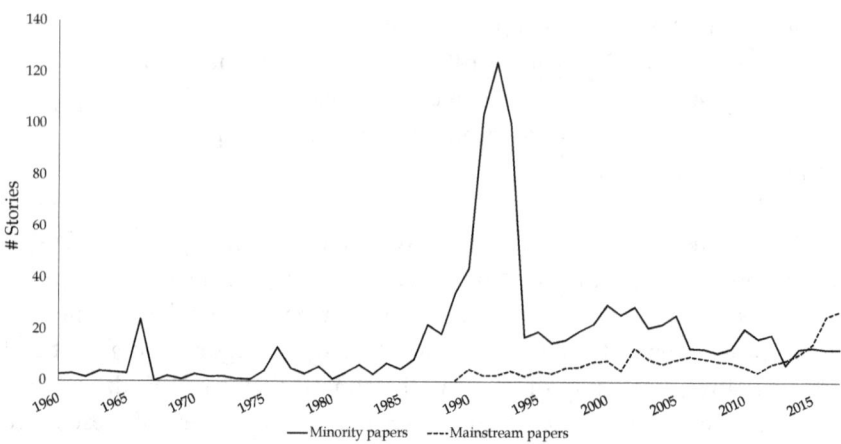

FIGURE 3.5. Stories in minority and mainstream papers mentioning "people of color," 1960–2017

stretch than mainstream papers. In fact, the latter series does not begin using this label until 1989. Even when both newspaper types use the label during a shared period, however, the correlation between the series is small and unreliable ($r = .07$, $p < .37$, one-tailed; $N = 28$), suggesting these aggregate news patterns are distinct from each other.

Figure 3.5 also reveals a surge of stories in Black newspapers in the late 1980s. As scholars of race and politics will note, several minority-related events transpired at this time: Jesse Jackson's 1988 presidential run; 1991's Rodney King beating; 1992's Los Angeles Riots; and 1994's Proposition 187, California's infamous anti-immigrant bill, among others (Bobo and Johnson 2000; Pantoja, Ramirez, and Segura. 2001; Tate 1991). This trend seems to reflect a rush to cover such events in a way that reflects the diversity of the stories' antagonists, with figure 3.6 providing visual support for this contention. There we see graphed a new series (based on Black newspapers) capturing the yearly percentage of stories using the phrase *people of color* with exclusive reference to Blacks. This lets us see the expansion of the term *people of color* from a strict focus on Blacks to a broader one on non-Whites. It is clear that in approximately the late 1980s, Black papers began shifting from using *people of color* to exclusively refer to Blacks to using it to refer to Blacks *and* other minorities, such as Asians and Latinos. This is underscored by the stabilization of this series around 50% during those years, which implies that from this period onward, about half of all articles in Black papers used the phrase *people of color* to refer to (non-)Black minorities.

But if the central tendency of some PoC is to define *people of color* as African Americans, then how might we characterize the variance around this mean? The general consensus arising from my interviews is simply "brown."

More specifically, the further removed from Black Americans, the lighter a PoC is likely to be. In turn, the closer one is to the Black prototype, the darker one's skin tone. Consider the words of Aliyah Brown (Black). During our talk, she shared that she views Blacks and Mexicans as belonging to a common team at work, calling them "Blaxicans." When I asked her to tell me more about why she sees a tight bond between them, she immediately stated, "Because everyone, everybody always is downgrading us. . . . Like in trying to get jobs or positions in jobs. They prefer us to work for little and do a lot. Not only that, we get attacked by the police more than others." This view is highly consistent with Kisha Jackson's (Black) insights, who said during our talk: "There's Mexicans and Black people kind of integrated together. And just as I got older, knowing how even sometimes the Hispanic people are treated really bad as well. That's how I guess I could distinguish the color part. Because they experience [discrimination]."

This general point appears to be recognized by non-Black minorities as well. For instance, Sara Reyes (Asian, Filipino) revealed that when she thinks of the phrase *people of color*, she thinks of "different racial groups," adding that "if you said *people of color*, my first immediate thought would be brown." David Santos (Asian, Filipino) was even more precise, noting that besides Blacks, "when you first said *person of color*, I thought of the ones who are brown, the ones who are dark," which in David's mind are "Mexicans . . . and . . . Central American ethnicities . . ." but also inclusive of "South East Asian, . . . Polynesian ethnicities."

But even this broad range of perspectives has limits. In particular, these interviews suggest that some PoC are deemed "core" members of the group, while others are considered "peripheral," having an ever so tenuous claim

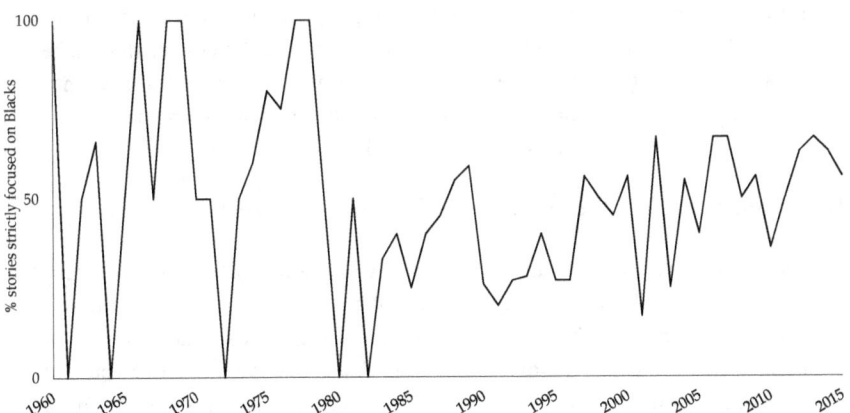

FIGURE 3.6. Percentage of stories mentioning "people of color" that referred to Blacks only, 1960–2017

on membership to the group (Ellemers and Jetten 2012). When it comes to PoC, Asian Americans seem to exemplify the "peripheral" PoC, a point recognized by both Asian and non-Asian minorities. For example, when I asked Aliyah Brown (Black) whether she considers Asian Americans to be people of color, she told me, plainly, "No, due to the fact that they look down on us as well.... They look down on us." In turn, Isaiah Carter (Black) suggested that "if you're Asian it is much easier to become a millionaire than if you are Black or Latino," adding that "Asians, they still have ... a much better chance [at economic success]."

But these are only one set of perspectives. Other PoC I interviewed see Asian Americans as more firmly within the category PoC because, as Josephine de la Cruz (Asian, Filipina) explained at length:

> I think that there are different ranges of what disadvantage can look like and it either could be ... the lack of social mobility ... [or] ... language barriers, which ... doesn't allow them to take on certain positions in society because they just can't communicate with the dominant language.... Or it could be ... lack of social mobility in terms of where they live ... But it can also range from ... very small microaggressions. Like, it could even be ... someone making a comment about ... an Asian person's eyes that could also be seen as ... a disadvantage because they're ... seen as ... a foreigner.

And it is not just Asian Americans who see this range of experience. When I asked Alyssa Davis (Black-White) about the spectrum of socioeconomic differences among PoC, she also explained to me in detail:

> There's this myth of the model minority ... about how Asian people get better education, whatever. We're all pushed in the different kind of jobs and groups and economic statuses. I mean, you go to certain communities, poor communities, and you see Latino people and Black people there, almost exclusively. It's hard to deny that. Then there are ... some Chinese Americans that make on average more than White people. There are Cambodian people that fit into the category of Asian that ... live in ghettos like everybody else does.... I mean, there are also incredibly wealthy Black people.

In a similar vein, Iris Pierce (Black-Indian) observed that

> Asian people can be fair skinned, and so, in a skin tone sense, they're not people of color.... But I think we have kind of grouped people of color and oppressed minorities, we've kind of swirled them together, so that's why Asian people are kind of on the outskirts of that [category PoC] ... But you still include them in the group if you're considering minority groups that have been oppressed.

The bottom line to these comments is that there is a clear pecking order of groups within PoC, with the relative station of one's group being structured by skin tone and relative disadvantage(s). Going forward, the question is whether this relative positioning of groups influences one's support for and identification with PoC, which I address in the next chapter. But first, one last point about these interviews.

### How Much Does Education Have to Do with Being a PoC?

We have heard from various PoC about what they think about this category: who it includes, who it excludes, and on what basis. Many of these perspectives, however, come from individuals who are actively studying at an institution of higher learning, while others already have their degrees in hand. Consider the words of Avery Wu (Asian, Chinese), who, like many of her UCLA peers, acknowledged the role of higher education in heightening her own sense of being a PoC: "I really only started resonating with it when I learned more about the way the United States works," adding, "I think it's because I've really only started learning about the significance about being Asian and a person of color and how the Asian community was treated historically, in the past two years [at UCLA]." Similarly, Mariana Espejo (Asian, Filipina) shared that "now," during her time at UCLA, is the "wokest I've ever been in my lifetime [about] who I am . . . and who you are and the privilege you have as a White person." Given these insights, how much of what we have heard from various PoC is a reflection of highly educated individuals?

Although many of my interviews were with PoC at UCLA, about a third of them were not. This was by design. I wanted to hear how individuals who do not possess a college education construe PoC. What I heard from them was more similar than dissimilar from what their more educated counterparts shared with me. Both interview sets generally hovered around the themes of skin color and disadvantage as criteria for inclusion as PoC. Both respondent types also identified similar characteristics that make one a less worthy PoC, including conservative views and Republican allegiance. The differences I see boil down to nuances in language and knowledge to articulate one's views about PoC. In particular, PoC with a college education expressed polished viewpoints, often drawing on history to bolster their comments. For example, here is Alejandra Ramos (Asian, Filipina), who provided a broad historical overview to explain the color line between Whites and PoC:

> Okay, just because of history surrounding . . . White supremacy . . . them being the ones who have risen up above people with darker skin, or people with

colored skin. They've just risen to the top. . . . [They] have this preconceived notion that they are superior and that their race, or their group, has control over—or should have the highest control over everyone else. Just from there, the colonization of different places where we do categorize people of color, such as Africa, Asia, even down in South America, and in America—or North America—just, everywhere from there on, they have colonized the indigenous people of each lands and have forced their values on to them.

In contrast, individuals who do not possess a college education expressed insights that were as revealing, but more often compact and commonsensical, rather than based on books or historical knowledge. For example, when Aliyah Brown (African American) shared with me her thoughts about why America's color line is so robust, she told me it is due to Whites lumping together all "because their skin is darker than theirs."

This educational difference signifies, to me, that universities are a socializing agent that brings together disparate racial minorities into contact with each other. As Iris Pierce (Black-White) explained her gravitation toward PoC: "I think it was probably higher education for me." Yet despite the greater depth of opinion that more educated PoC might have, Iris's comments also suggest that universities are no magic elixir to erase America's color line. On the contrary, they seem to underscore it.

### People of Color in Their Minds?

I believe the conversations I had with these individuals reveal a trove of conceptual riches: lessons I can use as I move to formally assess whether something like PoC ID even exists, out there, in the mass minority public. But before investing more deeply in that effort, can I further validate what I've heard so far from these PoC?

I think I can. One crucial basis of any identity is the associations we carry about it in our head (Devos and Banaji 2005). In the case of PoC, this means, at minimum, the associations that members of various racial and ethnic minority groups have between their specific racial in-group and PoC. Do they strongly associate their specific in-group with this pan-racial category? And, just as importantly, do they associate other racial out-groups with this superordinate group? Both things should be true if PoC is as meaningful a group as my interviews indicate it is.

To provide some evidence for these assertions, I administered an original Implicit Association Test (IAT; this test consists of speeded sorting tasks completed on a computer; Pérez 2016) to a diverse sample of UCLA under-

TABLE 3.2. Sample stimuli in *People of color | White people* Implicit Association Test

| IAT version | IAT schemes | Sample IAT stimuli |
| --- | --- | --- |
| 1. People of color = African Americans | *Matched*: People of color | Africa; White people | Europe<br>*Mismatched*: People of color | Europe; White people | Africa | Black names: *Jamal, Ebony*<br>White names: *Brad, Emily*<br>African nations: *Kenya, Ghana*<br>European nations: *England, Norway* |
| 2. People of color = Latinos | *Matched*: People of color | Latin America; White people | Europe<br>*Mismatched*: People of color | Europe; White people | Latin America | Latino(a) names: *José, María*<br>White names: *Brad, Emily*<br>Latin American nations: *México, Cuba*<br>European nations: *England, Norway* |
| 3. People of color = Asian Americans | *Matched*: People of color | Asia; White people | Europe<br>*Mismatched*: People of color | Europe; White people | Asia | Asian names: *Cheng, Mei*<br>White names: *Brad, Emily*<br>Asian nations: *China, India*<br>European nations: *England, Norway* |

graduates during winter 2019 ($n$ Blacks = 45; $n$ Latinos = 207; $n$ Asians = 98; $n$ Whites = 22). These tasks assess how quickly—on the order of milliseconds—individuals sort stimuli using two classification schemes. In this case:

1. a *matched scheme*, where the term PoC is associated with a specific minority (e.g., Black, Latino, Asian) and the term White people is associated with a variety of European groups (e.g., Irish, Italian, British).
2. a *mismatched scheme*, where the term PoC is associated with European groups (e.g., Irish, Italian, British) and the term White people is associated with specific minorities (e.g., Black, Latino, Asian).

These schemes are randomly ordered, making the IAT a within-subject experiment (Shadish, Cook, and Campbell 2002). In each scheme, subjects complete 40 trials, where each one is a single stimulus appearing randomly on a screen that subjects must sort. This IAT's stimuli reflect the categories in table 3.2. And, since the specific minority paired with PoC is also manipulated, there are three versions of this IAT.

The question at hand, then, is this: to what extent do individuals associate PoC with various minority groups rather than with various European groups? One of the IAT's virtues is that we can answer this without asking people about it. Instead, we infer their associations from their response times; and since these reactions are occurring in milliseconds, we can be sure they

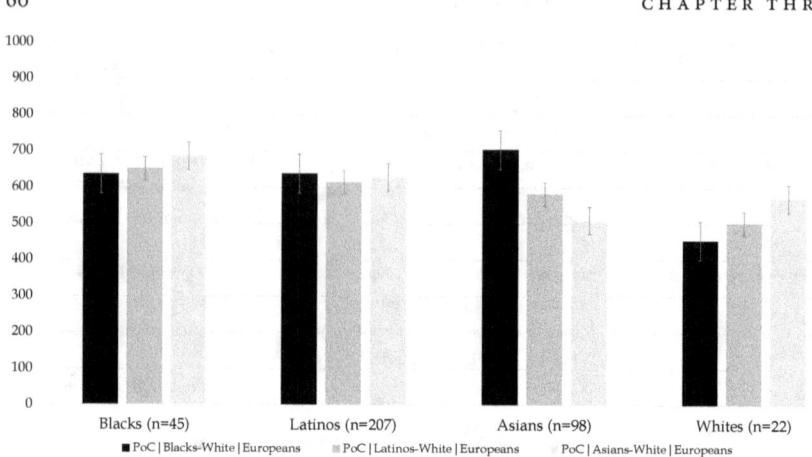

FIGURE 3.7. IAT effect (millisecond gap) by participant race and PoC group

reflect the associations people really possess, rather than the ones they think they should report. What does this IAT reveal?

Figure 3.7 indicates two main takeaways. First, when we subtract a respondent's average response time to the matched scheme from the mismatched scheme, we arrive at a raw IAT effect, with positive values indicating a stronger mental association between PoC and specific racial minority groups than European groups. As the dark bars suggest, this IAT effect is quite hefty, with scores ranging from 455ms (White subjects) to 704ms (Asian American subjects). We can standardize these effects by simply taking each of these differences and dividing by their respective standard deviation, which yields Cohen's $d$ values. By convention, $d$ values of .20, .50, and .80 are deemed small, medium, and large, respectively. The mean $d$ value for my IAT, pooled across subjects, is $d = 1.69$, which is a massive effect: a difference of about 1.5 standard deviations.

Second, across subjects, the dark bars reflect the IAT effect in which the term PoC is associated with African Americans, with the remaining bars reflecting IATs when Latinos and Asians are respectively substituted for Blacks as the category associated with PoC. What is clear from comparing the lighter bars with a dark bar is that there are hardly any reliable differences in IAT effects, suggesting that the category PoC is strongly and comparably associated with African Americans, Asian Americans, and Latinos—an association that even White subjects make. The one exception here is Asian Americans, who display a significantly weaker IAT effect when their own in-group reflects the category PoC. This is consistent with some of my in-depth interviews, which suggest that some (non-)Asian minorities see this group as a peripheral member of the category PoC. Yet despite this nuance, the IAT effect among Asian Americans is still large in absolute size ($d = 1.69$), which means they strongly associate their in-group with PoC. Finally, what does not emerge in these data is a reliably strong sense of ownership over this category by Black participants. As the leftmost bars in figure 3.7 reveal, African Americans' association between their racial in-group and PoC is just as strong if the minority group in question is Latinos and Asians, which underlines the generally expansive nature of this category. One possibility for this disjuncture between the IAT results and my in-depth interviews is that the former captures one's automatic associations about PoC, while the words of Black interviewees capture their more controlled thoughts (Lodge and Taber 2013; Pérez 2016; Ranganath, Smith, and Nosek 2008). It is theoretically plausible, then, that a sense of ownership over the group PoC manifests itself only after one's deliberative capacities kick in, a possibility I revisit when I develop a more direct measure of PoC ID.

What I see in these data, then, is this: with minimal prompting and with the pressure of impression management defused, (non-)Whites taking this IAT display strong associations between PoC and a broad cross-section of racial and ethnic minorities that include Blacks, Latinos, and Asians. These patterns generally affirm the insights my interviews yielded about the meaningfulness of the category PoC.

## Next Steps

We are now at this chapter's end, having learned two major lessons we did not know before about PoC. The first one involves the many nuanced meanings that individual PoC assign to this category. Through a rich collection of in-depth interviews, we learned about the range of views that some PoC have about what qualifies one as a member of this pan-racial group, what disqualifies one from PoC status, and, finally, how individual PoC differentiate themselves. The key insights here, perhaps, are that being a PoC boils down to not being or acting White; experiencing racial disadvantages, either directly or vicariously; and having a progressive political outlook to improve the general welfare of PoC. These characteristics, my conversations suggest, are widely recognized by Black, Asian, and Latino individuals. That is, racial and ethnic minorities seem to broadly appreciate these distinguishing characteristics. Insofar as these kinds of attributes are part of PoC, in general, we might expect some of these traits to be associated with expressions of higher PoC ID levels. For instance, given the role that progressive politics seems to play in identifying as a PoC, we might expect Democratic partisanship and liberal ideology to both contribute to the strength of PoC ID. Similarly, insofar as a sense of PoC ID is grounded in a sense of being racialized and marginalized as the "other," then we might expect those minority individuals born in the US to display stronger PoC ID levels. The larger point, here, is not that we have identified all of the roots of PoC ID, but that we can now obtain a better sense of what some of its correlates might be—a point we revisit in the next chapter.

The second lesson, which is just as important, is that *PoC* is more than a label; it seems to be a well-formed group in people's minds. Indeed, as the results of my IAT revealed, Asian, Black, Latino—even White—individuals mentally associate various racial and ethnic minorities with the pan-racial category PoC. These associations are incredibly strong, reliable, and vary little with respect to which minority group is considered a PoC. This basic insight suggests that PoC is a meaningfully recognized social category, one that might serve as the basis of self-identification for various racial and ethnic minority groups.

Both of these lessons were necessary to learn. Ultimately, however, they are opening salvos to a pair of much larger aims before us: directly assessing whether PoC ID exists and appraising its political influence over US racial and ethnic minorities. I begin tackling these objectives in chapter 4, which I turn to next.

### APPENDIX

**In-Depth Interview Sample Characteristics and Interview Protocol**

As table 3.A1 describes in more detail, this sample of in-depth interviewees is highly heterogeneous in racial and ethnic terms, with robust representation of three major minority groups in the US: African Americans, Asian Americans, and Latinos. In the aggregate, most respondents were female PoC, who self-described themselves as politically liberal or left of center. Moreover, while nearly all interviewees were born in the United States, over half of them indicated that both of their parents were not native-born Americans, thus providing some variation in terms of immigrant status and generation. Finally, while most interviewees were UCLA students, one-fourth of the sample is comprised of adults who are unaffiliated with this university. Following

TABLE 3.A1. Basic demographics of in-depth interview sample ($N = 25$)

| Demographic | % of sample |
|---|---|
| *Race/Ethnicity* | |
| African American | 24% |
| Asian American | 40% |
| Latino | 20% |
| Mixed-race | 16% |
| *Gender* | |
| Female | 76% |
| Male | 24% |
| *US-born* | |
| Yes | 92% |
| No | 8% |
| *US-born parents* | |
| 0 US-born parents | 60% |
| 1 US-born parent | 12% |
| 2 US-born parents | 28% |
| *Party identification* | |
| Democrat | 84% |
| Independent | 8% |
| Republican | 0% |
| No party | 8% |
| *Ideology* | |
| Liberal | 68% |
| Moderate | 24% |
| Conservative | 4% |
| N/A | 4% |
| *UCLA affiliate* | |
| Yes | 72% |
| No | 28% |
| *Year at UCLA (of total UCLA affiliates)* | |
| Freshman | 33% |
| Sophomore | 27% |
| Junior | 22% |
| Senior | 18% |

table 3.A1, I describe and display the interviewing protocol used during the in-depth conversations with these participants.

## In-Depth Interview Protocol

I conducted most of these interviews, except five of them undertaken by a political science graduate student whom I trained and supervised for this project. During each of our interviews, we utilized the protocol described in the next subsection, which consists of a series of broad prompts intended generate deeper discussions over a fewer set of topics (cf. Jiménez and Orozco 2019). Any mentions of UCLA students or staff in the protocol were eliminated when the interviewee was unaffiliated with the university.

### PROTOCOL FOR IN-DEPTH INTERVIEWS WITH POC

My name is Efrén Pérez, and I am a professor of political science here at UCLA, where I direct this research lab. I'm conducting in-depth interviews with UCLA students and staff as part of a research project that seeks a greater understanding of what it means to be a person of color.

As part of this research, I have undertaken several public opinion surveys and conducted some experiments on this subject. But none of these data can provide me with the deeper understanding I seek about what it means to identify as a person of color. That kind of knowledge can only be obtained from speaking on a one-on-one basis with individuals like you, who may or may not consider themselves to be people of color.

Our conversation will be around a couple of topics I want your ideas on. I would like for you to speak openly and honestly about these topics—there are no right or wrong answers. Also, I don't have an agenda or a specific point to prove. I'm simply interested in hearing your own personal and genuine opinions about the topics we discuss. That is, I'm here to learn from you. And, you have all of the answers since the questions we talk about concern YOUR life and experiences. Any questions before we continue?

### INTERVIEW PROMPTS

1. How would you describe *people of color* to someone who is unfamiliar with this group of individuals?
   1a. Do you consider yourself to be a person of color?
2. I want you to imagine a hypothetical world with me, a world where the category *people of color* does not exist or is not used to describe individuals. What would things be like for folks like you in that kind of world?
   2a. What would things be like for folks who are different from you?
3. What examples come to mind when you hear the label *people of color*? In other words, what kinds of individuals do you think of when you or other people use the term *people of color*?
4. When you hear the label *people of color*, what types of individuals best reflect this group, in your mind? Why?
5. What does it mean to be a person of color? What kinds of attributes, characteristics, and mannerisms qualify one as a person of color?

6. What kinds of attributes, characteristics, and mannerisms *disqualify* an individual from being a person of color?
7. How would you describe any socioeconomic differences that may exist among people of color? That is, differences in terms of where they live, what kinds of jobs they work in, how much education they possess, and the like? Is it possible to talk of racial and ethnic minorities as *people of color* if these differences exist—why or why not?
8. How would you describe any political differences among people of color? That is, differences in terms of the politicians they support and the policy proposals they endorse. This could be at the local level, state level, or national level. Is it possible to talk of racial and ethnic minorities as *people of color* if these differences exist—why or why not?
9. How would you describe any historical differences among people of color? That is to say, differences in how various communities of color first arrived to the US, how they were treated here, how they are currently treated here, and their future well-being? Is it possible to talk of racial and ethnic minorities as *people of color* if these differences exist—why or why not?
10. How would you compare the category *minority* to the category *people of color*?
11. What kinds of things keep people of color from being more united? What encourages them to be more divided from each other?

## Construction of Aggregate Newspaper Series

The Black newspaper and mainstream newspaper measures reported in this chapter were created using several overlapping, yet incomplete, time series of single newspapers. The unit of analysis is the mention of PoC in a story published by a Black or mainstream newspaper. Drawing on Stimson (1991), I extracted the common variance that exists between the Black newspaper series and mainstream newspaper series to create these longitudinal measures.

TABLE 3.A2. Measurement analysis of aggregate newspaper time series

|  | Black newspapers (loading) | Mainstream newspapers (loading) |
|---|---|---|
| Chicago Defender ($n = 33$) | .206 | — |
| New York Amsterdam News ($n = 53$) | .942 | — |
| Los Angeles Sentinel ($n = 50$) | .660 | — |
| % variance explained | 52% | — |
| Chicago Tribune ($n = 19$) | — | .103 |
| Los Angeles Times ($n = 25$) | — | .743 |
| New York Times ($n = 28$) | — | .920 |
| Washington Post ($n = 20$) | — | .622 |
| % variance explained | — | 49% |

This approach is akin to principal components analysis of time series with missing data.

Table 3.A2 reports the loadings of each series on their intended variable, as well as the estimated variance held in common by a set of series. By all indications, the resulting scales reflect valid measures of Black and mainstream newspaper mentions of PoC over time.

# 4

# New Wine in New Bottles

Thus far, you have leafed through an argument concerning a novel form of identity among US racial and ethnic minorities—what I have been calling a *people of color* identity (PoC ID). This new attachment, I claim, is distinct from other ones that minorities possess. I argue that PoC ID is not simply a synonym for one's attachment to a specific racial or ethnic group, such as being African American, Asian American, or Latino. Indeed, I reason that it encapsulates all of these distinct communities. I also contend that PoC ID has explanatory weight, shaping minorities' political views beyond the considerations borne by one's unique racial or ethnic identity. Last, but most important, I maintain that PoC ID is a powerful engine behind minority public opinion: a driver of the political attitudes these kinds of individuals express.

Each of these propositions, so far, has been light on evidence. In this chapter, I rectify this matter by formulating and validating a direct measure for this new identity.

Although the items on this specific research agenda are obvious enough, taking concrete steps to meet them is less than straightforward. Two challenges jut out sharply on the trail from developing a measure of PoC ID to establishing its empirical chops.

The first of these challenges is conceptual. To say that one identifies as a PoC is to claim that non-White individuals recognize the significance of a new group comprised of racial and ethnic minorities writ large. But what *is* the best way to tap into these perceptions, especially in an intellectual marketplace saturated with a plethora of group-related constructs like group closeness, group consciousness, and linked fate (McClain et al. 2009)? I resolve this tension by offering a parsimonious conceptualization of PoC ID as nothing more, and nothing less, than an individual difference in how central the category PoC is to one's sense of self (Ellemers, Spears, and Doosje 1997; Leach et al. 2008; Pérez 2015a). The virtue of this stripped-down definition is that it lends itself to a direct measure that captures PoC ID without being contaminated by the very things—social and political evaluations—that PoC ID should explain.

The second challenge is to empirically distinguish PoC ID from its conceptual kin. So much of what scholars know about the political behavior of various racial and ethnic minority groups in the United States rests on our understanding of their *racial* and *ethnic* identities (Barreto 2005; Dawson 1994; Greer 2013; Junn 2005; Lee 2008; Lien, Conway, and Wong 2004; Rogers 2006; Watts Smith 2014). This tapestry of findings means that PoC ID has its work cut out empirically, for it is simply insufficient to show that I can measure it. I also must establish, in painstakingly clear terms, that PoC ID is related to kindred constructs such as racial and ethnic identity, but not so related that I fail to disentangle it from these conceptual cousins. The objective, then, is to demonstrate, not that PoC ID surpasses racial and ethnic IDs, but that PoC ID applies explanatory power toward minorities' political opinions, beyond what their specific racial/ethnic identities already contribute. Nowhere is this more critical than in establishing PoC ID's unique predictive power over minorities' political opinions. Failure here would call into question the entire enterprise I aspire to undertake in the chapters that follow.

Alas, this is an impressive series of hurdles to leap over. To avoid stumbling over them from the start, I train my sights on what is perhaps the most essential one to clear first: defining the very thing I am interested in appraising.

## What Is—and Is Not—PoC ID?

In the study of racial and ethnic politics in the United States, scholarship on the role of identity is one of the most extensive and lively areas (McClain et al. 2009). Given this expansive collection of research on this topic, one would think there is enough information to say, precisely, what PoC ID is. Yet one would be wrong. As chapter 2 clarifies, scholars interested in this new attachment among racial and ethnic minorities face two critical impasses on the road toward its conceptualization. The first one is a matter of omission. For all of the accumulated findings on racial and ethnic identities in the US, none have examined the possibility of what I am calling a PoC ID. There are volumes written on Black identity (cf. Cohen 1999; Davis and Brown 2002; Dawson 1994; Greer 2013; Rogers 2006; Tate 1991; Watts Smith 2014; White 2007; White, Laird, and Allen 2014); Latino identity (cf. Garcia Bedolla 2005; García-Ríos and Barreto 2016; Pérez 2015a, b; Pérez, Deichert, and Engelhardt

2019); Asian American identity (cf. Junn and Masuoka 2008; Lien, Conway, and Wong 2004; Wong et al. 2011); and the identities of other distinct minority communities (cf. Dana, Wilcox-Archuleta, and Barreto 2017; Nagel 1996; Ocampo, Dana, and Barreto 2018). Yet systematic examination of an attachment that broadly encapsulates these groups—PoC ID—is simply missing, not only in political science, but in social psychology as well (cf. Cortland et al. 2017; Craig and Richeson 2012; Craig, Rucker, and Richeson 2018).

The second reason for our difficulty in delineating PoC ID is what I see as an embarrassment of riches. The frontiers of scholarship on minorities' racial and ethnic identities are littered with publications, not just on specific attachments held by minorities (cf. Carter 2019; Carter and Pérez 2015; Dawson 1994; de la Garza, Falcon, and Garcia 1996; Greer 2013; Lien, Conway, and Wong 2004; Rogers 2006; Silber Mohammed 2017; Watts Smith 2014), but on concepts that closely resemble group identities, such as group closeness, group consciousness, and—the most popular of all—linked fate (McClain et al. 2009), all of which we discuss in chapter 1. On the one hand, this breadth of accumulated work signals a vibrant research field: an indicator that other scholars, too, are fascinated with minorities' inter- and intragroup dynamics the way that I am. On the other hand, this growing thicket of research makes it challenging to determine which concept is doing what work in theories about identity effects among racial minorities, particularly considering these constructs are often empirically related, loosely defined, and interchangeably used (Leach et al. 2008).

There are many reasons political scientists and psychologists should care about all this, but herein I focus on two. The first has to do with the development of statistical models of minority political attitudes and behavior. If, for example, linked fate is more a consequence of intra- and intergroup processes, then its use as a *predictor* of minority political activity is a bit unorthodox. "But it's a good proxy for identity," I hear potential critics reply. "And what's the harm, really, if linked fate and identity are positively and robustly correlated?" These are reasonable points. But even reasonable views can produce undesirable complications. For example, consider the number of times that, in published literature, linked fate fails to predict political outcomes of interest at the individual level (cf. Gay, Hochschild, and White 2016). Null findings like those can be a reflection of no relationship at all, implying that identity does not matter. Yet my discussion here suggests it can also be due to the unrealistic expectation for an outcome to display the predictive work of an independent variable. There are, in my view, no statistical fixes to conceptual errors like this one.

What we have, then, are several concepts related to group identity, but not a clear sense of identity itself—and certainly not a convincing sense of PoC

ID, in particular. In the next section, I offer and justify a parsimonious way to conceptualize PoC ID to define, delimit, and measure this new attachment.

## From Generic IDs to PoC ID

So, what is an identity, if it is not just a sense of closeness to similar others (Conover 1984), of collective grievance (Miller et al. 1981), or of camaraderie with group members (Dawson 1994)? Rather than add another layer to these influential definitions, I step back from them by defining identity as *an individual difference in how central a category is to one's self-definition.* This bare-bones conceptualization rests heavily on what an identity does, first and foremost, at a psychological level (Ellemers, Spears, and Doosje 1997, 2002; see also Tajfel 1981; Tajfel and Turner 1986; Turner et al. 1987). Drawing on social and political psychologists' notion of centrality (Leach et al. 2008; Luhtanen and Crocker 1992; Pérez 2015a, b), I stipulate identity to be the degree to which a social category is cognitively and affectively significant to a person's self-image. It is, simply put, the extent to which *I* see a category as crucial to how *I* define myself.

In this view, a group is nothing more than one of many categories stored in long-term memory (Collins and Loftus 1975; Lodge and Taber 2013; Pérez 2016; Tourangeau, Rips, and Rasinski 2000). What makes this category an identity is the extent to which a person attaches cognitive and affective significance to it by treating it as an important reflection of their sense of self. Viewed this way, an identity is an individual difference, rather than a type. It is not the case that a person either identifies with a group or does not: rather, they identify with a group to some degree. That is, they deem a specific category a part of their self-definition to *a certain extent.* This range typically runs from very low to very high. The higher, or more central, a category is to a person's sense of self, the more important that category is to how they define themselves with respect to others. In turn, the lower, or less central, a category is to an individual's view of themselves, the less important that category is to their self-image. Tied to PoC ID, this conceptualization leads us to expect a healthy distribution of this attachment among racial and ethnic minorities, with some individuals weakly identifying as PoC and others more strongly so.

But what does a compact conceptualization like this one purchase for us theoretically? One thing it accomplishes is that it places heavier emphasis on the *gradations* of identity that individuals manifest. As Leonie Huddy reminds us, "identities are adopted by degrees and represent something intermediate between an all-encompassing group identity and a distinctively unique persona" (Huddy 2001: 145; see also Brewer 1991). Such individual differences are key because the extent to which one identifies with a group produces clear and empirically supported predictions (Ellemers et al. 1997, 2002). Specifically, social identity theorists teach us that in-group members vary in their sensitivity to group-related stimuli, especially the negative variety (Leach et al. 2008, 2010).

Individual reactions to such stimuli are motivated by how central a category is to an in-group member's sense of self. In the wake of negative stimuli surrounding a group—say, a criticism, an insult, or an actual physical attack—higher-identifying group members are remarkably predictable. They steadfastly stand by their group, advocate for it, and engage in behaviors that repair any real or perceived damage caused by a negative stimulus directed at their group (Branscombe, Schmitt, and Harvey 1999; Doosje, Ellemers, and Spears 1995; Ellemers, Spears, and Doosje 1997). In two studies, for example, Pérez (2015a, b) demonstrates that in light of xenophobic rhetoric, high-identifying Latinos display stronger ethnocentrism, greater support for pro-Latino policies, and weaker trust in government—all with the aim of bolstering their co-ethnics in the face of anti-immigrant discourse.

What about lower-identifying group members—how resolute are they? Not very much, really. Their reactions are, in fact, more variable and difficult to anticipate than high-identifiers. Since a group is less central to the self-image of low-identifiers, they are less likely to stick around when a group is in crisis or under threat (Ellemers, Spears, and Doosje 1997, 2002). Indeed, they are the first to bolt when an in-group encounters criticisms, insults, or attacks, especially when nobody is monitoring their actions (Ethier and Deaux 1994). For instance, in the aforementioned Pérez (2015a, b) studies, low-identifying Latinos express *less* ethnocentrism and support for pro-Latino policies, as well as *greater* political trust, than their high-identifying co-ethnics in light of xenophobic rhetoric. Applied to PoC ID, these insights suggest that, instead of all minorities enlisting in this group, it is minority individuals who consider the category PoC a more crucial part of their self-image who engage in social and political efforts that collectively benefit all minorities.

A more parsimonious conceptualization of identity like the one I offer also has another benefit: it provides scholars wider berth to pinpoint the conditions under which an identity like PoC ID is politicized. Notice that in my rendition of identity, attachment to a group is stripped of explicit political content. This provides political scientists an incredibly rich opportunity to clarify how, when, and among whom an identity is politicized. In this regard, social identity theorists suggest that person × situation interactions are a promising way to understand when social identities are catapulted into politics (Ellemers, Spears, and Doosje 1997, 2002; Sniderman, Hagendoorn, and Prior 2004). That is, an individual's response to varied intergroup contexts depends on the degree to which they identify with a relevant in-group. Identifying and testing these reactions is a job for political scientists (and, for this political scientist, at least, it is a job I undertake in subsequent chapters). Applied to the case of PoC ID, these insights imply that when something about PoC is threatened (e.g., their distinctiveness in comparison to other out-groups, the positive worth that in-group members attach to it), we should observe differential reactions between low- and high-identifying PoC.

Finally, but no less importantly, a streamlined view of PoC ID allows scholars like me to clarify what the relationship of this broad attachment is to narrower forms of identity like racial and ethnic identity. One perspective is to view PoC ID and racial and ethnic identities as conceptually independent from each other. But another perspective, and the one I adopt here, is to treat the interface between these two attachments as theoretically meaningful and worthy of hypothesizing (Brewer 1991; Pérez, Deichert, and Engelhardt 2019).

Recall chapter 2's introduction of *super*ordinate versus *sub*ordinate identities (Gaertner et al. 1989, 1999; Transue 2007). These types of attachments, I explained, often display a nested relationship. Akin to Russian Matroyshka dolls, narrower identities—such as racial and ethnic IDs—are nested within a larger one—such as PoC ID. From this angle, PoC ID is a more capacious attachment that encapsulates one's narrower and more distinct racial or ethnic identity. That is, one's identity as Black, Asian, or Latino is psychologically accommodated by one's broader identity as a PoC. This conceptual setup yields two observable implications.

The first one, the *nested identities hypothesis*, is that insofar as PoC ID envelops racial and ethnic ID, minority individuals should treat the latter as a reflection of what it means to be a PoC. In other words, as a Latino individual, I will treat my Latino identity as an important reflection of what it means, to me, to be a PoC in the United States. Ditto for individuals who identify as African American, Asian American, or as part of any other unique minority group. This process will be partly shaped by the degree to which a minority individual deems their unique racial or ethnic group as a prototypical example of PoC. That is, the more I sense that being, say, Black, is reflective of what it means to be a PoC, the stronger the observed correlation between a person's racial ID and PoC ID should be. Here, the insights gleaned from my in-depth interviews in chapter 3 hint that Black Americans, in particular, see themselves (and are seen by other minorities) as prototypical PoC (Wenzel, Mummendey, and Waldzus 2007). Hence, we might anticipate a very strong correlation between Black identity and PoC identity, with weaker, but still robust correlations between PoC ID and the unique racial/ethnic IDs of Asian Americans and Latinos.

Second, the correspondence between PoC ID and racial and ethnic ID also implies that the benefits of in-group favoritism should shift from one's immediate racial group to minorities in general, insofar as PoC ID is situationally heightened. Since identities serve to delimit who, in an intergroup context, is worthy of trust, loyalty, and cooperation (Brewer 2007), a shift from a narrower identity—such as one's racial or ethnic ID—to a broader attachment—such as PoC ID—should recategorize one's sense of who the relevant in-group is and, thus, redefine who merits any benefits of in-group favoritism (Gaertner et al. 1989, 1999; Levendusky 2018; Transue 2007). This yields the *affirmation hypothesis*: minorities will treat other minorities as bona fide in-group members if their gaze is broadly focused on PoC.

### Building and Validating a PoC ID Measure: The "People of Color" Surveys

Armed with the preceding insights, I commissioned the "People of Color" Surveys to appraise my conceptualization of PoC ID. In partnership with Survey Sampling International (SSI), I fielded three parallel surveys of African American ($n$ = 1,200), Asian American ($n$ = 1,200), and Latino ($n$ = 1,200) adults in February 2018. SSI generated these samples with US Census benchmarks in mind for each group (i.e., age, education, and gender). Thus, while these opt-in samples are not strictly representative, they are highly heterogeneous, providing an important opportunity for rigorous hypothesis testing about PoC ID.[1]

After consenting to participate, respondents in my surveys completed a brief schedule collecting data on their age, gender, country of birth, partisanship, ideology, and so on. This was followed by batteries of three to four items appraising three specific identities: one's identification as a PoC; one's identity as a Black, Asian, or Latino individual; and one's identity as American (with battery order randomized). I appraised racial and national identity in

---

1. I stress two more points about these samples. First, all interviews were done in English. I decided this based on earlier work with SSI, which offered non-English interviews. Those efforts yielded trivial rates of non-English interviews, making their statistical analysis infeasible. Hence, my Latino and Asian American respondents are relatively more acculturated to the US, making these samples "most likely" cases (Gerring 2003): cases where PoC ID should be widely present. Indeed, failure to find PoC ID here undermines my endeavor. Second, Asian Americans here are from six national origin groups (i.e., Chinese, Indian, Filipino, Korean, Japanese, and Vietnamese) to ensure representation of these major communities.

order to gain empirical leverage over whether my proposed scale of PoC ID captures anything that is meaningfully distinct from these other two crucial forms of identity among racial and ethnic minorities (cf. Carter and Pérez 2016; Davis and Brown 2002; Greer 2013; Rogers 2006; Watts Smith 2014; Wong et al. 2011). Indeed, as I noted in chapter 3, many identities—such as PoC ID and racial ID—are likely stored in fairly close proximity to each other in long-term memory (Collins and Loftus 1975; Lodge and Taber 2013), which means that activation of one identity (e.g., PoC ID) will likely activate another attachment (e.g., racial ID) to some degree. Thus, my goal in the pending analyses is to establish the unique predictive effects of PoC ID, not to show that PoC ID supersedes racial ID or some other attachment.

I measured all three of these identities by using statements that were completed on Likert scales from 1 = "strongly disagree" to 7 = "strongly agree." To gauge PoC ID, specifically, the survey prompted respondents to express their degree of agreement with the following four declarations, administered in randomized order:

1. The fact that I am a person of color is an important part of my identity.
2. Being a person of color is a major part of how I see myself.
3. I often think about the fact that I am a person of color.
4. I am glad to be a person of color.

Notice the simplicity of these items. Each one, in its own unique way, seeks to capture the cognitive and emotional significance that minorities attach to this PoC ID. These are the individual differences that any measure of an identity worth its salt must capture. Notice, too, that there are four items, rather than just one. The idea here is that each item, on its own, imperfectly reflects the individual differences in PoC ID that I seek to appraise. The use of multiple items therefore allows me to observe whether, notwithstanding their blemishes, I can combine these four statements into a valid scale of PoC ID that reliably taps into this attachment (Bollen 1989; Brown 2007).

Using similar logic, the "People of Color" surveys also fielded three items to assess the racial/ethnic identity of its Black, Asian, and Latino respondents. Here, individuals completed statements probing their degree of identification as Black, Asian, or Latino, with each statement tailored to a person's self-reported racial/ethnic group:

1. Overall, being [Black/Asian/Latino] is important to my sense of what kind of person I am.
2. In general, identifying as [Black/Asian/Latino] is central to who I am as an individual.
3. I feel good about being [Black/Asian/Latino].

Finally, but no less importantly, Black, Asian, and Latino respondents each answered a set of three items designed to capture their degree of identification as American. Using the same Likert scale as before, respondents answered the following:

1. Generally, being American is important to who I am as an individual.
2. Identifying as American is crucial to my self-image.
3. Being American gives me a good feeling.

## Outcomes

The preceding items provide a stab at measuring PoC ID alongside some conceptual kin: a key step in establishing the empirical existence of this new attachment. But that is only half of the equation here. What about the social and political outcomes that PoC ID is supposed to explain? To test the link between PoC ID and individual judgments of social and public affairs, my surveys also appraised four outcomes that capture the effects of identifying as PoC: (1) solidarity with PoC, (2) affect toward social and political groups, (3) support for public policies broadly impacting minorities, and (4) support for public policies narrowly impacting minorities.

Remember, my framework anticipates that the effects of PoC ID (or any identity, for that matter) depend on the contextual salience of this attachment. These items, by design, broadly implicate many PoC. Thus, we should find evidence that higher levels of PoC ID are associated with support for these outcomes (again, independently of their association with specific racial/ethnic identities).

To assess solidarity with PoC, I administered two statements on seven-point Likert scales: "I feel solidarity with people of color" and "People of color have a lot in common with each other." Consistent with prior validation studies (cf. Leach et al. 2008), items like this pair capture one's behavioral commitment to an in-group; in this case, PoC. Insofar as my PoC ID scale captures what I say it captures, we should observe that higher levels of identification as a person of color correspond with higher levels of expressed solidarity with other racial and ethnic minority groups.

In addition, I gauged affect toward social and political groups via feeling thermometer ratings on a scale of 1 = "very unfavorable" to 7 = "very favorable." These evaluations are designed to capture the "fast and frugal" feelings one has about others, such as racial and political groups—feelings that serve as building blocks to one's more cognitively effortful opinions (Lodge and Taber 2013; Osgood 1962; Pérez 2016). The rated groups were Asians, Blacks,

Latinos, and Whites, plus Democrats and Republicans. I used the racial group ratings to create an index of positive affect toward racial minorities relative to Whites. To this end, I averaged respondents' ratings of Asians, Blacks, and Latinos, and subtracted from this average a respondent's rating of Whites. If my proposed measure of PoC ID has any validity to it, then we should observe that higher levels of PoC ID lead to reliably more positive feelings toward minorities *relative* to Whites—the primary out-group that PoC are supposed to distinguish themselves from (cf. Brewer 1999, 2007).

In addition, I constructed a similar relative measure of positive feelings toward Democrats relative to Republicans. Recent work suggests that members of distinct racial/ethnic minority groups in the United States develop an attachment toward one of the two political parties on the basis of which one is deemed friendlier toward minorities and their interests (Hajnal and Lee 2011; Kuo, Malhotra, and Mo 2017; White and Laird 2020). That is, insofar as one perceives Democrats or Republicans as doing a better job of symbolically and programmatically incorporating racial/ethnic minorities, one should manifest more positive affect toward this party. By this metric, then, greater identification as a PoC should lead to more favorable feelings toward Democrats relative to Republicans.

Building on these cognitive and affective outcomes, my PoC surveys also measured *support for policies broadly impacting minorities* in three domains: voting rights, police brutality, and hate crimes. These policies, rather than implicating specific minority groups, widely impact individuals from all these communities. To this end, Black, Asian, and Latino respondents used seven-point scales to express their degree of support for two proposals in each of these domains. Specifically, the two items for voting rights were "Strengthening federal laws to protect voting rights" and "Requiring all states to automatically register eligible adults to vote." In the realm of police brutality, the item pair was "Setting stricter criteria for the use of deadly force by police officers" and "Limiting police officers' ability to engage in racial profiling." Finally, in the domain of hate crimes, participants responded to the items "Providing harsher penalties for hate crimes" and "Improving hate crime reporting and data collection." Insofar as greater identification as a PoC activates a more panoramic view of racial/ethnic minorities, we should observe that higher levels of PoC ID generate reliably stronger support for these broad policy proposals.

Finally, I assessed individual support for *policies narrowly impacting some minorities*. These proposals more specifically implicate particular racial/ethnic minority groups (cf. Gilens 1999; Pérez 2016; Winter 2008), and they provide a stringent test of just how broad the spirit of generosity behind PoC

ID actually is. Here, respondents used seven-point scales to indicate support for "Limiting the protest activities of #BlackLivesMatter and other movements like it," which focuses on African Americans; "Renewing temporary relief from deportation for undocumented immigrants brought to the US as children," which zeroes in on Latinos; and "Increasing the number of visas available to legal immigrants," which strongly centers on Asian Americans (Citrin and Sears 2014). Insofar as PoC ID broadens minorities' perspective, higher levels of PoC ID should yield greater support for these narrower types of policy proposals.

## Differentiating PoC ID from Other IDs

To claim that PoC is a meaningful identity among minorities demands a measure that can reliably capture those individual differences: something that is currently unavailable to scholars. I therefore evaluate how well the items I administered in my PoC surveys capture this attachment. With a mean interitem correlation of $r = .60$ across all three racial groups, this high degree of association between my PoC ID items suggests they are tapping something in common, that is, a PoC ID.

To formally establish this, I conduct a confirmatory factor analysis (CFA) using my measures of PoC ID, racial ID, and American ID. The idea behind any CFA—including this one—is this. My argument implies a very specific pattern of correlations between these ten items, as indicated by a *hypothesized* variance-covariance matrix (Bollen 1989; Brown 2007). Specifically, by my reasoning, we expect three identities, or factors, to underlie my survey data: PoC ID, racial ID, and American ID. A CFA allows me to compare this hypothesized variance-covariance matrix to the one I actually *observe* in my dataset. The smaller the discrepancies between my *hypothesized* and *observed* matrices, the stronger the support for my claims about a three-factor model. Hence, for each minority group, I model each battery of items as reflections of their corresponding identity, while estimating the degree of correlation between all three attachments. Table 4.1 contains the relevant results.

Notice, first, that each model displays excellent fit, with comparative fit indexes (CFIs) and Tucker-Lewis indexes (TLIs) nearing their maximum of 1.0, and root mean square errors of approximation (RMSEAs) in the advised range of .05–.08 (Brown 2007). This fit assures us that my hypothesized model of three related, but distinct identities, closely approximates my data's underlying structure: my PoC ID items capture PoC ID, my racial ID items capture racial ID, and my American ID items capture American ID, with all three attachments displaying a degree of association, which I discuss below.

TABLE 4.1. Confirmatory factor analyses of identity items (Blacks, Asians, and Latinos)

|  | Blacks | Asians | Latinos |
|---|---|---|---|
| *PoC ID* | | | |
| The fact that I am a person of color is important | 1.08** (.05) | 1.27** (.05) | 1.64** (.05) |
| Being a person of color is a major part of me | 1.38** (.04) | 1.58** (.04) | 1.77** (.04) |
| I often think about being a person of color | .90** (.06) | 1.21** (.05) | 1.30** (.05) |
| I am glad to be a person of color | .42** (.06) | .89** (.07) | 1.12** (.12) |
| *Racial ID* | | | |
| Being [RACE] is important to my person | 1.28** (.04) | 1.01** (.05) | 1.33** (.04) |
| Identifying as [RACE] is central to me | 1.50** (.04) | 1.31** (.04) | 1.45** (.04) |
| I feel good about being [RACE] | .37** (.07) | .65** (.06) | .84** (.05) |
| *American ID* | | | |
| Being American is important to me | 1.27** (.06) | 1.11** (.05) | 1.14** (.04) |
| Identifying as American is crucial to self-image | 1.43** (.05) | 1.31** (.04) | 1.25** (.05) |
| Being American gives me a good feeling | 1.12** (.04) | 1.05** (.04) | 1.16** (.04) |
| *Correlations between identities* | | | |
| PoC ID with racial ID | .78** (.02) | .60** (.03) | .55** (.02) |
| PoC ID with American ID | .26** (.04) | .30** (.03) | .11** (.03) |
| Racial ID with American ID | .30** (.03) | .30** (.03) | .23** (.03) |
| Comparative fit index/Tucker-Lewis index | .98/.96 | .99/.98 | .98/.97 |
| Root mean square error of approximation | .06 | .05 | .06 |
| [90% confidence interval] | [.05, .07] | [.04, .06] | [.05, .07] |
| N | 1,200 | 1,200 | 1,200 |

Note: Confirmatory factor analyses estimated separately per group. Models are identified by setting factor variances to 1.0. Loadings are in standard deviation units. Black and Asian models include two method factors: one for items mentioning *important*; the other for affective items. The Latino model omits the former method factor due to low salience.

Second, notice that all indicators reliably and substantively reflect their target attachment. Since all items have a 1–7 metric, the item loadings indicate the shift in an observed item (i.e., survey question) generated by a 1-point increase in the underlying variable (i.e., an identity). A one-point increase in PoC ID, for example, yields a shift of roughly one point in the item "I often think about being a person of color" among Blacks (.90), Asians (1.21), and Latinos (1.30). By this yardstick, all items tap their intended identity very well, including PoC ID.

Third, notice all three identities are related to, but distinct from, each other. For instance, PoC ID and racial identity are positively and robustly associated, which is anticipated by my *nested identities* hypothesis. Since I claim that the former encapsulates the latter, a high degree of correlation between these two attachments aligns well with my reasoning. For example, consider the remarkably strong correlation ($r = .78$) between this pair of attachments among Blacks. This high degree of association resembles the pattern often observed between measures of patriotism and nationalism—two forms of national attachment that nest under a larger banner of identifying with one's nation (Carter and Pérez 2015; De Figuieredo and Elkins 2003; Huddy and Khatib 2007). In the case of PoC ID and racial ID, my results here suggest that insofar as Black Americans identify as Black, they also identify, strongly, as PoC: a pattern that is highly consistent with chapter 3's in-depth interviews with Black adults, which implied a sense of ownership over PoC, or what some scholars call *in-group projection* (Wenzel, Mummendey, and Waldzus 2007). Nonetheless, it is reassuring that while the correlation between PoC ID and racial ID is weaker among Asian Americans and Latinos, it is still robust and substantial ($r \sim .60$) among these other minority groups, which bolsters my claim about a nested relation between PoC ID and racial ID. In particular, this strong bond between PoC ID and racial ID among all three groups suggests that, on average, members of each community project their own specific racial or ethnic group onto this larger shared category. In other words, they cognitively share in the collective ownership of this in-group.

Finally, but no less importantly, notice that PoC ID is positively and reliably related to American ID. This nugget of insight implies that identifying as a *person of color* is quite compatible with identifying as American, rather than being antithetical to it. This also bolsters my view that identifying as a *person of color* is part and parcel of the American experience for minorities in the US. That is, distinct racial and ethnic minority groups are forged into PoC as part of their socialization in the United States. In addition, this bond between PoC ID and US ID supports the inference that identifying as *person of color* is, at a fundamental level, a celebratory affirmation of the diversity displayed by various minority groups, rather than a collective hostility to anything construed as American, which includes Whites.

Based on the preceding results, I create an additive scale for each identity, with the PoC ID's distribution displayed in figure 4.1 below. This histogram reveals what any scholar of identity would hope to find: rich variation across *all* levels of a group attachment. Indeed, on a 0 to 1 scale, the mean level of PoC ID across all three survey samples is .65, with a standard deviation of .24. What does this mean in plainer terms?

It suggests that members of these three distinct minority groups in the US possess, on average, a very robust sense of identifying as a *person of color*. This sentiment, however, is not universal. Some minority individuals clearly report a very high degree of PoC ID—more so than this average level. In particular, about 16% of minority respondents reported a level of PoC ID that is

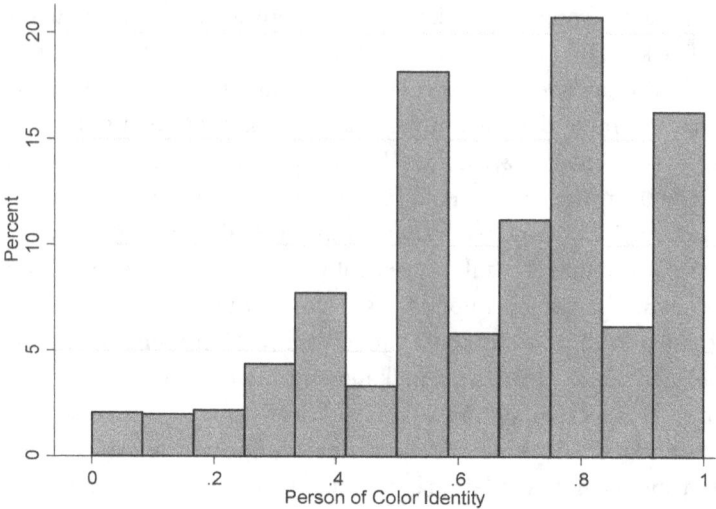

FIGURE 4.1. PoC ID distribution across minority groups in the PoC surveys

a full standard deviation above the observed mean of .64. Just as importantly, however, some minorities seem to attach a very low degree of importance to their sense of PoC ID, which means it is not a central part of how they define themselves. To be more precise, about 15% of survey respondents expressed a level of PoC ID that is a full standard deviation lower than the average level in these samples. By extension, this means that plenty of minority individuals possess a level of PoC ID falling somewhere in between these two extremes, suggesting my proposed scale of PoC ID captures the full range of individual differences in this construct that are necessary to test whether this new identity shapes minorities' political views in the ways I say it does.

But before evaluating whether individual differences in PoC ID impact minorities' political views, I validate its measurement in two other ways. First, I draw on ancillary data to address PoC ID's stability. One axiom in public opinion research is that individuals happily answer survey questions posed to them, even if they do not possess a crystallized opinion about a topic (Schwarz 2007; Zaller 1992). For PoC ID, this means that racial minorities answer items related to this new identity without really, or fully, holding this attachment to some degree. How can we tell if this is a problem here? The technology is simple but revealing. Formally known as a test-retest correlation (Brown 2007), the idea is to ask individuals to answer the same set of questions, spaced apart by days, weeks, months, or years. The stronger the correlation between measures of the same construct at two points in time, the more reliable the instrumentation and the more stable the underlying construct are considered.

In September 2019, I asked a sample of Latino and Asian American undergraduates at a flagship public university in California three questions about their level of PoC ID. These questions are similar in thrust and scope as the ones we just inspected.[2] Six months later, in April 2020, I re-administered these items to this sample of individuals. What is the degree of correlation between my scale of PoC ID in wave 1 ($\alpha$ = .77) and the same scale in wave 2 ($\alpha$ = .70)? Focusing on those who answered the items in both waves ($n$ = 109), the correlation is a robust $r$ = .76, $p$ < .001, two-tailed. This degree of association is well above the .50 level marking poor reliability (Brown 2007). Indeed, if we square this correlation, we learn that nearly 60% of the variance can be attributed to underlying PoC ID levels, with the remaining variance being unexplained (i.e., measurement error). This means that PoC ID is generally hard to shift, but that under some limited conditions, it can be moved by other forces. This aligns with the general construal of identities as predictors, rather than outcomes, of political stimuli.[3]

Having better established that PoC ID is a rather stable form of attachment, I then demonstrate its political influence on mass opinions. Specifically, I draw on the "People of Color" surveys to estimate ordinary least squares (OLS) regressions that assess the degree of association between each identity and several political and demographic covariates. This is meant to further establish that my PoC ID scale is tapping something meaningfully distinct from racial and American ID. I select most of these correlates based on chapter 3's insights and prior work on the internal heterogeneity of non-White communities (cf. McClain and Johnson Carew 2017). We know, for example, that racial minorities generally align themselves with the Democratic party to varying degrees (Hajnal and Lee 2012; Hopkins et al. 2019;

---

2. The three items were as follows: (1) "The fact that I am a person of color is an important part of my identity"; (2) "Being a person of color is *unimportant* to who I am as an individual"; and (3) "I am glad to be a person of color." All items were answered on scales running from 1 = "strongly disagree" to 7 = "strongly agree."

3. The stability coefficient reported in the text ($r$ = .76) is a lower bound estimate, since it reflects the degree of stability in a sample of "compliers," with minimal assumptions about possible biases introduced by those who did not answer wave 2 items. If I make stronger assumptions and impute missing values in a full information CFA (i.e., confirmatory factor analysis) (Brown 2007), the degree of stability increases to $r$ = . 93, $p$ < .001. This statistical wizardry does not change my underlying conclusion, namely, that PoC ID is a stable phenomenon that can be reliably measured with my family of items.

Kuo, Maalhotra, and Mo 2017; White and Laird 2020), which affirms chapter 3's view of PoC as rooted in progressive politics. Thus, I expect Democratic partisanship to be reliably associated with PoC ID. Similarly, we know that racial minorities acutely sense discrimination (Hopkins et al. 2019), which reflects the belief among chapter 3's interviewees that non-Whites are disadvantaged compared with Whites. I construe this belief as part of a broader worldview to explain inequalities (e.g., Reyna et al. 2005). Hence, I predict that those who report stronger liberal ideology will express higher PoC ID levels. We might also anticipate PoC ID to be correlated with higher education, since many of chapter 3's interviews hinted that universities provide historical grounding and formal language to express PoC ID. Finally, given their fuller socialization into America's racial hierarchy, I expect non-Whites born in the US to report higher PoC ID levels. Finally, I anticipate some variation by specific national origins. Specifically, it is plausible that within Latinos—a group that, like Asian Americans (Wong et al. 2011), contains enormous national origin variation—some national origin groups will endorse PoC ID more tepidly, especially where a stronger European influence prevails (García 2012). Thus, for example, I expect Cubans to more weakly identify as PoC than Mexicans and Puerto Ricans.

The results for each identity, by racial group, are displayed in table 4.2. Starting with the PoC ID results, one can see that across all three racial groups, reporting Democratic partisanship and a more liberal ideology are positively associated with higher PoC ID levels: a pattern aligning with the claim that this identity is partly rooted in progressive politics and worldviews. Second, higher education levels are generally tied to stronger reports of PoC ID, suggesting the realm of higher education might promote stronger identification as a person of color. This is consistent with some of the in-depth interviews reported in chapter 3, thus further underlining institutions of higher learning as one channel of socialization into this new identity. Moreover, among Asians and Latinos—the two groups containing substantial numbers of immigrants—those who were born in the US report higher PoC ID levels than those born abroad, suggesting this attachment also arises from being socialized in the US as a non-White individual (Skrentny 2002). Finally, national origins seem to matter for expressions of PoC ID. For example, Mexican Latinos and Puerto Rican Latinos report reliably higher PoC ID levels than their Cuban Latino counterparts.

When we turn to the results for racial and American identity, more differences than similarities arise. For example, although reporting Democratic partisanship is reliably associated with higher racial identity levels, expressing a more liberal ideology no longer packs the same punch across all three groups. And the influence of education on racial identity is not as consistently there as it was for PoC ID. Moreover, when we turn to American identity, we

TABLE 4.2. Correlates of PoC ID, racial ID, and American ID

| | PoC ID | | | Racial ID | | | American ID | | |
|---|---|---|---|---|---|---|---|---|---|
| | Blacks | Asians | Latinos | Blacks | Asians | Latinos | Blacks | Asians | Latinos |
| Democrat | .06** (.01) | .04** (.01) | .08** (.02) | .06** (.01) | .03** (.01) | .08** (.01) | .06** (.02) | .04** (.01) | .05** (.01) |
| Republican | -.07** (.02) | .01 (.02) | -.02 (.02) | -.05* (.03) | .02 (.02) | -.03 (.02) | .07** (.03) | .08** (.02) | .08** (.02) |
| Liberal ideology | .09** (.02) | .09* (.03) | .07** (.03) | .06** (.02) | .01 (.03) | .04 (.03) | -.10** (.03) | -.05* (.03) | -.07** (.03) |
| Education | .06** (.02) | .05* (.03) | -.00 (.02) | .03 (.02) | .03 (.02) | .02 (.02) | -.01 (.02) | .01 (.02) | .04** (.02) |
| Age | -.02 (.03) | .01 (.04) | -.21** (.04) | .03 (.03) | .03 (.03) | -.03 (.03) | .28** (.03) | .29** (.03) | .26** (.03) |
| Female | .00 (.01) | .01 (.01) | .01 (.02) | .00 (.01) | .01 (.01) | .04** (.01) | -.04** (.01) | -.03** (.01) | -.02 (.01) |
| US-born | — | .04** (.02) | .06** (.02) | — | .02 (.01) | -.03 (.02) | — | .09** (.01) | .03* (.02) |
| Foreign parents | — | .00 (.02) | .01 (.02) | — | .03* (.02) | .05** (.01) | — | -.02 (.02) | -.02 (.01) |
| One foreign and one native parent | — | .01 (.02) | .00 (.02) | — | .00 (.01) | .03 (.02) | — | -.05* (.02) | .00 (.02) |
| Chinese [Mexican] | — | -.02 (.02) | .03* (.02) | — | -.02 (.02) | .02 (.02) | — | -.03** (.02) | .03* (.01) |
| Indian [Puerto Rican] | — | -.09** (.02) | .04* (.02) | — | -.04** (.02) | .07** (.02) | — | -.03 (.02) | -.02 (.02) |
| Japanese [Cuban] | — | -.09** (.02) | -.08** (.03) | — | -.01 (.02) | -.04 (.03) | — | -.08** (.02) | .01 (.03) |
| Constant | .66** (.02) | .51** (.04) | .49** (.04) | .70** (.02) | .67** (.03) | .66** (.03) | .65** (.02) | .61** (.03) | .62** (.03) |
| Adj. $R^2$ | .07 | .04 | .11 | .04 | .09 | .09 | .09 | .16 | .11 |

Note: For all analyses, $N = 1{,}200$. Entries are ordinary least squares coefficients with standard errors in parentheses. All variables run on a 0–1 interval. **$p < .05$, *$p < .10$, two-tailed.

see that being Republican is now reliably associated with this attachment, while higher levels of liberal ideology are inversely related to it.

Finally, older individuals appear to report higher American identity levels and, among Asians and Latinos in this sample, those born in the US report reliably higher levels of this identity. All of these patterns can be distilled into a simple conclusion: PoC ID seems to be conceptually distinct from racial and American identity.

## PoC ID Influences Social and Political Views

The evidence, until now, is heavy on the measurement side of things, generally demonstrating that we can reliably capture PoC ID and meaningfully distinguish it from other important identities among racial minorities. But having cleared this major hurdle, can I also show that individual differences in PoC ID shape minorities' political opinions—that is, can I demonstrate that what I measure with my quartet of items matters, substantively, for our knowledge of US minority politics?

Although I find that PoC ID is a distinct attachment, it is hard to miss that it is robustly correlated with racial and national identity (especially the former). This degree of correlation and varied strength among these racial/ethnic groups is theoretically anticipated. Since PoC ID is a larger-order category that encapsulates distinct racial/ethnic identities, a robust degree of attachment is unsurprising between these two (Gaertner et al. 1999; Transue 2007). Moreover, the stronger interface between PoC ID and Black ID, in particular, is also a reflection of the genealogical origins of the label PoC among African Americans, which we have discussed before. All this is to suggest that any impact of PoC ID on political views might be due to minorities' more established racial/ethnic identities. It is also plausible that PoC ID is not as influential on minority opinions as other durable wellsprings of political opinion, such as ideology, especially given the link between PoC ID and progressive politics uncovered previously. That is, what we think is PoC ID at work might really be minorities' general left-of-center disposition. And, of course, there are the usual demographic suspects: individual differences in things like age, education, and gender which—when statistically accounted for—might snuff out any influence that PoC ID may have had on minorities' political views.

Rather than continue wondering about these possibilities, I formally assessed the association of PoC ID with the individual opinions about politics expressed by Blacks, Asians, and Latinos in my PoC surveys. To this end, I estimate a series of OLS regressions predicting the outcomes I described earlier on the basis of PoC ID, while holding constant individual differences in racial

ID, American ID, liberal ideology, and a suite of demographic attributes. This list of covariates is not meant to be exhaustive. Rather, the goal is to rule out, with some confidence, that what we have in hand is a PoC ID scale that is worthy of further scrutiny and testing in subsequent chapters. To make the evidence as plainly clear as possible, I rely on graphs of my main results, with the raw findings for each model embedded in table 4.A1 in the appendix to this chapter. I note here, however, that these raw results show, consistent with my reasoning, that other attachments are often also associated with people's expressed opinions. What we are observing in these graphs, then, is not the greater importance of PoC ID relative to other attachments, but rather, the unique predictive power of PoC ID relative to other established attachments, such as racial and national identity.

Let's begin with the influence of PoC ID on three sociopolitical evaluations: expressed solidarity with people of color, relative feelings toward minorities relative to Whites, and favorability toward Democrats relative to Republicans. Although these outcomes are more perceptual and affective than traditional opinion measures, they provide diagnostic insight into whether PoC ID yields the outlooks and sentiments that my affirmation hypothesis implies; that is, insofar as *I* identify as a person of color, *I* should express greater solidarity with other minorities (cf. Leach et al. 2008), more positive feelings toward minorities (cf. Osgood 1962), and more favorable views of Democrats (cf. Philpot 2007).

Figure 4.2 displays evidence that is highly consistent with this hypothesis. For example, panel A shows that across each minority group, a shift from the lowest to highest level on my PoC ID scale reliably increases expressed solidarity with PoC by 34 percentage points among Blacks, 31 percentage points among Asians, and 25 percentage points among Latinos. This implies that stronger identification as a PoC leads to a greater sense of unity and commonality with other racial minorities.

Indeed, consistent with this, figure 4.2, panel B, reveals that a similar unit shift in PoC ID also reliably increases pro-minority feelings by 12 percentage points among Blacks, 5 percentage points among Asians, and 6 percentage points among Latinos. Finally, these generally positive views and feelings toward minorities spill over into favorability toward Democrats. Here, a shift from the lowest to highest levels of PoC ID boosts Blacks,' Asians,' and Latinos' affect toward Democrats relative to Republicans by 9, 7, and 7 percentage points respectively—a pattern affirming the view that PoC ID is steeped in progressive politics. Again, these associations are independent of the influence that specific racial/ethnic identities sometimes display on these outcomes (see table 4.A1).

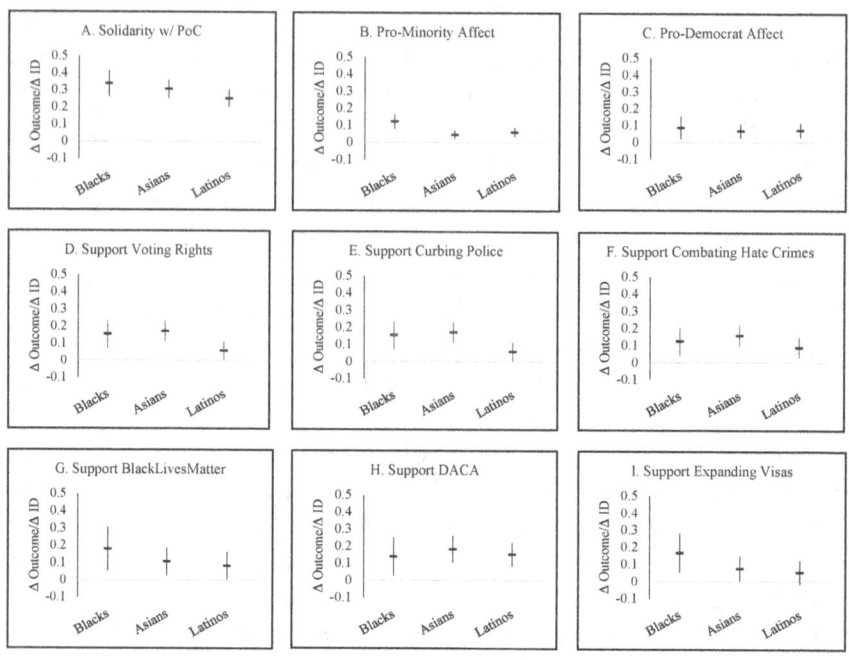

FIGURE 4.2. PoC ID substantively explains variation in social and political outcomes (with 95% confidence intervals)

We can observe parallel trends on policy proposals that broadly affect minorities, such as the strengthening of voting rights, the curbing of police brutality, and the combating of hate crimes. For example, figure 4.2, panel D, indicates that a shift from the lowest to highest PoC ID level boosts endorsement of strengthening voting rights by 16 percentage points among Blacks, 17 percentage points among Asians, and 6 percentage points among Latinos— all patterns that generally rival the impact of racial identity, American identity, and liberal ideology among these groups (see table 4.A1). Similarly, figure 4.2, panel E, shows that a unit shift in PoC ID heightens support for curbing police brutality by 13 percentage points among Blacks, 16 percentage points among Asians, and 9 percentage points among Latinos. Finally, figure 4.2, panel F, suggests that a unit shift in PoC ID increases backing for combating hate crimes by 18 percentage points among Blacks, 7 percentage points among Asians, and 5 percentage points among Latinos—again, all trends that are comparable to the impact of other identities and ideology (see table 4.A1).

We can draw similar inferences for policies that more narrowly affect certain minorities. As figure 4.2, panel G, shows, a unit shift in PoC ID heightens support for #BlackLivesMatter by 18 percentage points among Blacks,

11 percentage points among Asians, and 8 percentage points among Latinos, with these patterns emerging independently of racial and American identity, ideology, and other demographic traits. Moreover, figure 4.2, panel H, reveals that insofar as Deferred Action for Childhood Arrivals (DACA) support is concerned, a unit shift in PoC ID bolsters endorsement of this policy by 14 percentage points among Blacks, 18 percentage points among Asians, and 15 percentage points among Latinos—again, independently of other key covariates. And, finally, figure 4.2, panel I, indicates that a unit shift in PoC ID boosts support for increasing legal immigration visas by 17 percentage points among Blacks, 8 percentage points among Asians, and 5 percentage points among Latinos (this last trend is shy of statistical significance). Again, each of these patterns emerges independently of the contribution of one's specific racial/ethnic identity (see table 4.A1).

## Summary and Next Steps

This chapter started deep within two massive craters in the literature on US minority politics: namely, a muddled conceptualization of PoC ID and the complete absence of a valid measure to appraise this attachment. Across the preceding pages, I have done my best to get us out of this morass. To this end, I have endeavored to clarify what PoC ID is, both on its own and with respect to other common types of attachments possessed by racial and ethnic minorities in the US. This has produced a conceptualization of PoC ID as individual differences in the degree to which the category PoC is an important part of a person's self-definition. The more central this group is to a person's sense of who they are, the more it will shape their views related to inter- and intraminority affairs in politics.

Building on this conceptualization, I then proposed, validated, and empirically assessed a four-item scale to capture these individual differences in PoC ID. I found these four items to validly capture the range of PoC ID that, I claim, should exist among and across minority populations. With the help of this scale, we can now observe and distinguish between minorities who strongly identify as PoC, those who weakly identify as PoC, and those whose degree of attachment to other PoC falls somewhere in between. This measure, moreover, is related to other attachments in ways one would expect. In particular, higher levels of PoC ID correlate quite robustly with levels of racial and ethnic ID among Blacks, Latinos, and Asian Americans, with the correspondence between these attachments being strongest among Blacks—the group considered by Blacks and other minorities as the prototypical *people of color*. We also learned that PoC ID is compatible with American identity—a crucial clue suggesting that, one, this attachment is forged in the United States and, two, this identity is not based on antipathy toward other Americans.

But perhaps the most revealing piece of evidence in this chapter concerns the predictive power of PoC ID. Across a broad suite of outcomes I demonstrated, repeatedly, that higher levels of PoC ID produce stronger expressed solidarity with other people of color, more positive feelings toward minorities in general, greater favorability toward Democrats relative to Republicans, stronger support for policies that broadly impact minorities (e.g., strengthening voting rights), and stronger endorsement of policy proposals that more narrowly impact specific minority communities (e.g., #BlackLivesMatter). At minimum, I think this train of results suggests that PoC ID is deserving of a place in the pantheon of group identities that are politically relevant among US racial and ethnic minorities. It also strongly suggests, I believe, that PoC ID is worthy of further scrutiny and analysis.

In fact, this has been my goal in this chapter all along: to make readers and social scientists more comfortable with the empirical assessment of this new attachment I call PoC ID. Having met this objective, the following pages use my findings here as a springboard into key questions about *when* and among *whom* PoC ID matters politically. Let's turn to some of those questions now.

# APPENDIX

TABLE 4.A1. PoC identity and political evaluations and beliefs

| | Solidarity with PoC | | | Pro-minority affect | | | Pro-Democrat affect | | |
|---|---|---|---|---|---|---|---|---|---|
| | Blacks | Asians | Latinos | Blacks | Asians | Latinos | Blacks | Asians | Latinos |
| PoC ID | .339** (.040) | .306** (.027) | .252** (.026) | .122** (.021) | .045** (.012) | .060** (.013) | .087** (.033) | .068** (.022) | .072** (.022) |
| Racial ID | .208** (.036) | .144** (.032) | .181** (.031) | .057** (.020) | .055** (.014) | .070** (.016) | .063** (.031) | -.000 (.025) | .067** (.026) |
| American ID | .018 (.025) | .009 (.027) | .015 (.028) | -.127** (.013) | -.061** (.012) | -.074** (.015) | .006 (.021) | -.056 (.022) | -.037 (.024) |
| Liberal | .068** (.021) | .113** (.024) | .103** (.024) | .032** (.011) | .040** (.011) | .015 (.013) | .134** (.018) | .258** (.019) | .183** (.020) |
| Democrat | .005 (.013) | .034** (.012) | .045** (.013) | .007 (.007) | .010** (.005) | .012* (.007) | .136** (.011) | .132** (.009) | .161** (.011) |
| Republican | -.009 (.024) | -.026* (.015) | .004 (.017) | .001 (.013) | -.009 (.007) | -.032* (.009) | -.172** (.021) | -.104** (.012) | -.183** (.014) |
| US-born | — | .017 (.012) | -.066** (.017) | — | .024** (.006) | .019* (.009) | — | .012 (.010) | -.014 (.014) |
| Foreign parents | — | .009 (.015) | .013 (.014) | — | .007 (.007) | -.000 (.007) | — | .000 (.012) | -.002 (.012) |
| One foreign and one native parent | — | .021 (.018) | .007 (.016) | — | .001 (.008) | -.003 (.008) | — | .007 (.014) | .007 (.013) |
| Chinese [Mexican] | — | -.027* (.143) | -.005 (.014) | — | .012* (.006) | .014** (.007) | — | .010 (.011) | .005 (.012) |
| Indian [Puerto Rican] | — | .024 (.016) | .027 (.018) | — | -.009 (.007) | .016* (.009) | — | -.029** (.013) | .019 (.015) |
| Japanese [Cuban] | — | -.027 (.018) | .013 (.024) | — | .009 (.008) | .013 (.013) | — | -.011 (.015) | -.013 (.020) |
| Age | .024 (.027) | -.114** (.029) | .041 (.034) | -.027* (.015) | -.006 (.013) | -.019 (.018) | .108** (.023) | .007 (.023) | .103** (.028) |
| Female | -.019* (.011) | -.011 (.010) | -.007 (.012) | .002 (.006) | .002 (.005) | .010 (.006) | .040** (.009) | .002 (.008) | .013 (.010) |
| Education | -.008 (.020) | -.039* (.022) | -.005 (.019) | -.008 (.011) | -.007 (.010) | .004 (.010) | -.028* (.017) | .011 (.017) | .006 (.016) |
| Constant | .233** (.030) | .298** (.035) | .312** (.036) | .477** (.016) | .428** (.016) | .437** (.019) | .371** (.025) | .386** (.028) | .373** (.030) |
| R2 | .26 | .29 | .25 | .15 | .12 | .16 | .39 | .49 | .52 |

*continues*

TABLE 4.A1. (continued)

| | Strengthen voting rights | | | Curb police brutality | | | Combat hate crimes | | |
|---|---|---|---|---|---|---|---|---|---|
| | Blacks | Asians | Latinos | Blacks | Asians | Latinos | Blacks | Asians | Latinos |
| PoC ID | .155** (.041) | .172** (.030) | .058* (.027) | .125** (.041) | .158** (.032) | .088** (.030) | .180** (.042) | .074** (.026) | .051* (.026) |
| Racial ID | .079** (.038) | .065** (.035) | .159** (.033) | .125** (.038) | .054 (.037) | .165** (.036) | .043 (.038) | .107** (.031) | .188** (.032) |
| American ID | .116** (.026) | .034 (.030) | .033 (.030) | -.063* (.026) | .014 (.031) | -.079* (.033) | .033 (.026) | .147** (.026) | .091** (.029) |
| Liberal | .073** (.022) | .138** (.026) | .108** (.025) | .137** (.022) | .176** (.028) | .202** (.028) | .134** (.022) | .133** (.023) | .123** (.025) |
| Democrat | .055** (.013) | .042** (.013) | .078** (.014) | .030 (.013) | .075** (.013) | .061* (.015) | .020 (.014) | .021* (.011) | .040** (.013) |
| Republican | -.027 (.025) | .001 (.016) | .029 (.018) | -.034 (.025) | -.020 (.017) | -.057* (.020) | -.036 (.026) | -.016 (.014) | .007 (.017) |
| US-born | — | -.057* (.014) | -.028 (.018) | — | -.022 (.014) | -.001 (.020) | — | -.026** (.012) | -.017 (.017) |
| Foreign parents | — | .001 (.017) | .010 (.015) | — | .005 (.018) | .003 (.016) | — | .007 (.014) | -.004 (.014) |
| One foreign and one native parent | — | .027 (.020) | -.018 (.017) | — | .016 (.021) | .016 (.018) | — | .033* (.017) | -.013 (.016) |
| Chinese [Mexican] | — | .007 (.016) | -.012 (.015) | — | -.009 (.016) | -.010 (.016) | — | -.005 (.014) | -.007 (.014) |
| Indian [Puerto Rican] | — | .086* (.017) | .059** (.019) | — | -.035* (.018) | .028 (.021) | — | .014 (.015) | .042** (.018) |
| Japanese [Cuban] | — | -.012 (.020) | .009 (.025) | — | -.019 (.021) | -.051* (.028) | — | .025 (.018) | .039 (.025) |
| Age | .168** (.028) | .061* (.032) | .056 (.036) | .038 (.028) | -.040 (.034) | .041 (.039) | .153** (.029) | .091** (.028) | .147** (.034) |
| Female | -.015 (.011) | -.008 (.011) | -.037** (.013) | .023** (.011) | .016 (.012) | .005 (.014) | .018 (.011) | -.009 (.010) | .004 (.012) |
| Education | .036* (.020) | .021 (.024) | .012 (.021) | .034* (.020) | .038 (.025) | -.018 (.023) | .017 (.021) | .089** (.021) | .033* (.020) |
| Constant | .383** (.031) | .431** (.038) | .473** (.038) | .565** (.031) | .442** (.040) | .504** (.042) | .468** (.031) | .392** (.034) | .409** (.036) |
| R2 | .19 | .17 | .15 | .14 | .17 | .20 | .15 | .17 | .16 |

TABLE 4.A1. (continued)

| | Support #BlackLivesMatter | | | Increase visas | | | Support DACA | | |
|---|---|---|---|---|---|---|---|---|---|
| | Blacks | Asians | Latinos | Blacks | Asians | Latinos | Blacks | Asians | Latinos |
| PoC ID | .180** (.063) | .106** (.041) | .083** (.041) | .168** (.058) | .076** (.036) | .053 (.034) | .139** (.057) | .182** (.040) | .152** (.035) |
| Racial ID | .142** (.058) | -.075 (.047) | .032 (.050) | .088* (.053) | .159** (.042) | .285** (.041) | .086* (.053) | .061 (.046) | .230** (.042) |
| American ID | -.193** (.040) | -.150** (.040) | -.138** (.045) | -.108** (.036) | -.059 (.036) | -.086** (.038) | .000 (.036) | -.045 (.039) | -.100** (.038) |
| Liberal | .156** (.034) | .356** (.036) | .300** (.038) | .131** (.031) | .187** (.032) | .167** (.032) | .112** (.031) | .311** (.035) | .238** (.033) |
| Democrat | .059** (.021) | .043** (.017) | .025 (.021) | .031 (.019) | .049** (.016) | .038** (.017) | .017 (.018) | .083** (.017) | .061** (.018) |
| Republican | -.080** (.039) | -.071** (.022) | -.113** (.027) | -.051 (.036) | -.050** (.020) | -.082** (.023) | -.017** (.035) | -.022 (.021) | .099** (.023) |
| US-born | — | .079** (.019) | -.009 (.027) | — | -.020 (.016) | -.057** (.022) | — | .021 (.018) | -.045 (.023) |
| Foreign parents | — | .038* (.023) | .008 (.023) | — | .007 (.020) | .006 (.019) | — | -.011 (.022) | -.004 (.019) |
| One foreign and one native parent | — | .031 (.027) | .028 (.025) | — | .050* (.024) | -.000 (.021) | — | .027 (.026) | .005 (.021) |
| Chinese [Mexican] | — | -.044** (.021) | -.038* (.022) | — | -.026 (.019) | -.032* (.019) | — | -.029 (.021) | -.031 (.019) |
| Indian [Puerto Rican] | — | -.027 (.024) | .020 (.029) | — | .060** (.021) | -.030 (.024) | — | -.003 (.023) | -.046* (.024) |
| Japanese [Cuban] | — | -.020 (.027) | .028 (.039) | — | -.030 (.024) | -.056* (.032) | — | -.025 (.026) | -.038 (.033) |
| Age | .142** (.043) | .045 (.043) | .099* (.053) | -.158** (.040) | -.094** (.039) | -.147** (.045) | .079** (.039) | .104** (.042) | .078** (.046) |
| Female | .013 (.017) | -.019 (.015) | .010 (.019) | -.013 (.016) | -.010 (.013) | -.002 (.016) | .019 (.015) | .004 (.015) | .010 (.016) |
| Education | .087** (.032) | .111** (.033) | .077** (.031) | .084** (.029) | .051** (.029) | .001 (.026) | .087** (.028) | .004 (.031) | .011 (.026) |
| Constant | .360** (.047) | .284** (.052) | .369** (.057) | .451** (.043) | .437** (.046) | .530** (.047) | .399** (.043) | .314** (.051) | .433** (.048) |
| R2 | .13 | .20 | .15 | .08 | .17 | .20 | .09 | .19 | .24 |

Note: For all analyses, $N = 1{,}200$. Entries are ordinary least squares coefficients with standard errors in parentheses. All variables range from 0 to 1. **$p < .05$, *$p < .10$, two-tailed.

# 5

# I Feel Your Pain, Brother

There is a tendency among some individuals, both White and non-White, to view racial and ethnic minorities as sharing many commonalities. The intuition is not that all minorities are identical but rather that they possess more similarities than dissimilarities, which makes their description as PoC accurate on average.

Several facts bolster this sense. Consider that for every dollar of wealth that Whites amass, Blacks and Latinos accumulate less than 8 cents and 10 cents, respectively (Shapiro 2017). Politically, Asian, Black, and Latino voting rates lag substantially behind those of Whites, with the prevalence of young, unnaturalized immigrants especially blunting Asian and Latino vote shares (Anoll 2018; Fraga 2018). Moreover, while Blacks and Latinos make up nearly a third (32%) of the US population, they constitute more than half (56%) of all incarcerated individuals (NAACP 2018). These disparities and many others have led some observers to conclude that PoC are "similarly disadvantaged, even if their disadvantages are based on different variables" (Vidal-Ortiz 2008: 1037).

There is a natural feel to this notion—the idea that despite the unique circumstances of racial minority groups, all PoC understand and appreciate one another's struggles (e.g., Sirin, Valentino, and Villalobos 2016a, b). In fact, some of chapter 3's interviewees expressed this precise sentiment, like David Santos (Asian, Filipino), who mentioned that "even though I grew up not experiencing police brutality or stuff like that, I cannot discredit it. . . . I think even if you don't see it for yourself, you need to take the bigger picture into effect . . . because it affects all of us when we're the *other*." David was not the only one who made this point. In explaining her ability to identify with other PoC, Linda Sánchez (Latina, Mexican) suggested it stems from "just knowing that that's my group of people, that's my community," which she said gives her a "sense of empathy for them." This vicarious sensitivity to others' racial struggles, I argue, is rooted in a collective identity (Mackie, Smith, and Ray, 2008;). As Seger, Smith, and Mackie (2009) teach us, a person's favorable thoughts *and* feelings toward an in-group are activated the moment a sense of group identification is situationally sparked. It is these cognitions and affect that minimize one's perceived differences within an in-group and cement the bonds that allow it to mobilize, in unison, for the sake of larger goals (Sirin, Valentino, and Villalobos 2016a, b). As Ngoc Nguyen (Asian, Vietnamese), one of our in-depth interviewees, explained incisively to me, while "each ... minority group hasn't experienced the same thing, if we allow these differences to ... get in the way of a collective identity, then none of us will have any power." The implication from all this should be clear: shared disadvantages can forge strong bonds and an abiding sense of communion among distinct racial minorities.

But to say that racial and ethnic minorities are correspondingly disadvantaged is not to say that all minority individuals are similarly underprivileged. Nor is it synonymous with saying that all PoC are equally deprived. Indeed, despite shared inequities, minorities display sharp socioeconomic and political differences, raising doubts about whether they really see themselves, collectively, as PoC (McClain and Johnson Carew 2017). In 2016, for example, median household incomes for Blacks ($39,490) and Latinos ($47,675) paled in comparison to Whites ($65,041), with all three figures trailing Asian Americans ($81,431) (US Census Bureau 2018). Further, while Black, Asian, and Latino voters generally identify as Democrats (Abrajano and Alvarez 2010; Tate 1991; Wong et al. 2011), about a third of Asian (27%) and Latino (28%) voters report some degree of Republican partisanship, yet only 15% of Black voters do (Pew Research Center 2018). Minorities are also just as variegated within. While poverty rates for Mexican Latinos (23%), Cambodian Asians (19.1%), and Blacks (24.1%) are similar, Colombian Latinos (13%) and Filipino Asians (7.5%) are much less impoverished (Pew Research Center 2015). Perhaps, then, it is more unnatural than natural to view minorities as one bloc, as PoC.

These two distinct poles—and the complex histories, tensions, and lived experiences connecting them—point to the main question in this chapter. Namely, in light of so much internal diversity, do PoC really view themselves as a unified whole? The findings in chapter 4 suggest the answer is yes. When asked to report their degree of identification with other PoC, Black, Latino, and Asian adults report a robust sense of attachment to this broader category. But the breadth of this self-reported pattern might easily stem from the fact that it rests on self-reports. By this view, some minorities feel that, as minorities, they should express a high degree of attachment to other PoC, even though, deep down, they feel otherwise. This possibility is a common challenge to self-reports on sensitive topics like this one (Sniderman 2011). And it is also suggested by some PoC from chapter 3, like Nadia Maddox (African American), who told me point blank: "if it's two Black people and then two of [an]other race, . . . in my heart, I would . . . help the black people first because that is where my alliance is." The question for us is whether more PoC truly feel the way Nadia candidly expressed to me, but restrain themselves from publicly articulating this in a survey.

This chapter sheds new light on my claim that PoC ID is a meaningful form of attachment among members of distinct racial and ethnic minority groups. I accomplish this by drawing on a collection of survey experiments with more than 9,000 Black, Asian, and Latino adults. These original studies randomly assigned individuals to read a developing news story about an altercation between a couple and a White waiter at a celebrity-owned restaurant. This vivid report describes the waiter loudly, and publicly, upbraiding the couple for their English-speaking skill when ordering their food.

Unbeknownst to participants, they all read the same story with one major detail changed at random: whether the couple was from their own racial in-group or a minority out-group. This general design allows me to judge whether PoC are sensitive to one another's plight with racial offenses, regardless of whether the aggrieved individuals are from one's racial in-group. In line with my claims about PoC ID, I find that Blacks, Asians, and Latinos react similarly to this racial affront, regardless of whether the verbally abused couple is Black, Asian, or Latino. That is, PoC do seem to feel one another's pain. But before embarking further down this tour of evidence, let me first revisit the psychological principles fostering a sense of group coherence amidst diverse group membership: principles that explain the emergence of groups beyond just PoC.

## Group Unity amid Individual Diversity

One of the most productive and revealing corners of psychological research, we learned in chapter 2, is social identity theory (SIT): a body of work expressly dedicated to explaining how, cognitively, groups form in people's minds. And one of SIT's more lasting insights is that the forging of coherent groups against a backdrop of disparate humans is actually the rule, not the exception. In other words, a deep sense of collective unity in a choppy sea of diverse people is precisely what is at stake when individuals identify, psychologically, with a group (Tajfel 1981).

One key to understanding this process is the interface that connects smaller, distinct in-groups to larger, shared categories (cf. Gaertner et al. 1989; Transue 2007; Wenzel, Mummendey, and Waldzus 2007). As is the case with PoC, individuals sometimes belong to narrower in-groups that can be comfortably nested, in a cognitive sense, under a broader category. This relationship between a subordinate and superordinate in-group regulates the extent to which individuals in the former perceive themselves to be part of the latter. If this connection is firmly intact, then a superordinate category becomes the basis of a shared identity. Accordingly, individuals recognize their narrower community as a crisp reflection of the larger in-group held in common.

African Americans, for example, will perceive Blacks as a robust example of PoC, with Latinos and Asian Americans doing the same for their own in-groups. To the extent that this occurs, the benefits of in-group favoritism are redirected from one's narrower community to the larger superordinate category. In the case at hand, a PoC should treat Blacks, Latinos, Asians, or any other racial/ethnic minority as interchangeable parts of this larger, superordinate whole.

Insofar as this superordinate–subordinate connection is firmly in place, SIT leads us to expect the operation of three psychological processes, all reflecting one's affinity toward a shared in-group. The first is what researchers formally dub "self-stereotyping": a process through which individuals begin to cognitively see themselves as increasingly similar to fellow in-group members (Leach et al. 2010; Spears, Doosje, and Ellemers 1997; Turner et al. 1987). Although identifying with an in-group demands one's inclusion in a group, it does not guarantee a deep bond with fellow members (Tajfel 1978). For instance, one can be classified as a PoC by others yet never feel a strong connection with other minorities, for reasons we highlighted earlier. To foster this robust link, one must feel they reflect an in-group's prototype or average member—that is, they must sense that "I" resemble "them" (Ashmore, Deaux, and McLaughlin-Volpe 2004; Oakes, Haslam, and Turner 1994). This implies that when a Black, Asian, or Latino individual identifies as a PoC, they are cognitively affirming that "I am a clear reflection of what it means to be a PoC."

Self-stereotyping therefore provides individual group members with skin in the game, so to speak, for it is only in the wake of this process that people cognitively and emotionally participate in their in-group's successes, shortcomings, and misdeeds (Lewin 1948; Mackie, Smith, and Ray 2008; Seger, Smith, and Mackie 2009; Sirin, Valentino, and Villalobos 2016a, b). In fact, failure to engage individual group members in this way introduces the possibility that a nontrivial portion of them will refrain from acting on an in-group's behalf, especially when things get rough for the group. Hence, the bonds of unity among PoC should result in minorities self-stereotyping themselves as archetypes of this community. Insofar as individual minorities genuinely view themselves as PoC, they should consider themselves PoC despite the heterogeneous groups that are nested under this pan-racial category. In short, one's degree of self-stereotyping as a PoC should be insignificantly affected by which racial/ethnic minority groups comprise this larger category.

The second principle driving identification with a shared group is *in-group homogeneity*. This standard might be better viewed as a by-product of self-stereotyping. That is, insofar as a person characterizes themselves as an in-group's paragon, they should be more inclined to view fellow members as resembling each other. This perceived in-group homogeneity allows individuals to cognitively establish the in-group as a coherent social entity that can be clearly distinguished from relevant out-groups—a process that John Turner and his colleagues dub "meta-contrast" (Turner et al. 1987). The perceived in-group homogeneity generated by this meta-contrast principle is a strong function of group members' desire to maintain their in-group's positive distinctiveness, which is the main driver of identification with any group (Billig and Tajfel 1973; Tajfel et al. 1971). In the case of PoC, this generates a straightforward prediction. To the extent that individuals from assorted minority groups are nested under a larger category of PoC, they should perceive this pan-racial in-group as relatively homogeneous and widely sharing commonalities. That is, despite their inherent diversity, members of distinct minority groups should view PoC as a unified whole with many parallels. One important implication that follows is that such perceptions of in-group homogeneity should, on average, be relatively robust to who the particular PoC is, considering that all PoC are deemed to share more similarities than differences.

The third and final criterion behind group identification is *centrality*—the key concept behind chapter 4's PoC ID scale. This concept captures the degree to which a given social category, or group, is critical to a person's sense of self. It is an individual difference, in which the more central a category is to a person, the more important it is to them as a key feature of how they view and define themselves in relation to others in particular moments and contexts (Ellemers, Spears, and Doosje 1997, 2002; Leach et al. 2010; Oakes, Haslam, and Turner 1994; Turner et al. 1987). For example, when a member of a distinct minority group claims to identify as a PoC, they are essentially confirming that the PoC category is crucial to their self-image. In other words, it is an important aspect of how they see themselves and navigate their social and political worlds at a given moment or time. It bears emphasizing here that "group consciousness is not group identity" (McClain et al. 2009: 476). Centrality is the extent to which a category is an important reflection of one's self-image—it is identity, unvarnished (Ellemers, Spears, and Doosje 1997; Leach et al. 2008). In contrast, group consciousness is identity "*politicized* by a set of ideological beliefs about one's group's social standing, as well as a view that collective action is the best means by which the group can improve its status and realize its interests" (McClain et al. 2009: 476, emphasis in original). If centrality is the cognitive "hardware" that informs a person about how important a category is to their sense of self, then consciousness is the cognitive "software" of beliefs, strategies, and outlooks that puts identity into political action—a process that depends on the opportunity structure of a setting (e.g., Doosje, Spears, and Ellemers 2002; Jardina 2019; Pérez 2015a, b).

As an individual difference (cf. Leach et al. 2010), the key distinction in identity centrality is the nuance between low- and high-identifiers (Ellemers, Spears, and Doosje 1997, 2002; Pérez 2015a, b). Low-identifiers are individuals for whom a given category is a generally weaker reflection of themselves. High-identifiers are people for whom a group is essential to how they see themselves. These shades of category importance have major repercussions for how individuals respond to in-group and intergroup stimuli (Huddy 2001). Specifically, higher levels of centrality sensitize individuals to in-group threats. In a classic study, for example, Sellers and Shelton (2003) found that Black Americans who viewed the category Black as more central to their self-image were more likely to detect threats of discrimination by Whites.

These and other studies (Doosje, Ellemers, and Spears 1995; Leach et al. 2010; Pérez et al. 2019; Spears, Doosje, and Ellemers 1997) suggest we should expect a healthy degree of centrality when it comes to PoC. More specifically, we should observe relatively high levels of this attachment's importance to individual minorities, with wide dispersion among this robust average, which should neatly distill into that difference between low- and high-identifiers. Critically, however, these centrality levels should vary negligibly by the actual composition of PoC. That is, insofar as being a PoC is central to oneself, this sense of importance should be minimally affected by whether other PoC are from one's racial in-group or another racial minority.

## Ships in Thick Fog

The three psychological processes explained in the preceding section are foundational to my claim that PoC ID is socially and politically meaningful.

But in the real world of intergroup politics, a thick fog hangs over this trio of vessels, making it exceedingly difficult to pinpoint and corroborate their presence and operation among minorities. The source of this heavy mist is what researchers formally recognize as social desirability bias.

The idea is this: to gauge the degree to which minorities view PoC as a single group, scholars need to ask these individuals their views about it. But in asking minorities to self-report their perspectives about PoC, analysts run the risk of eliciting, not individuals' pure, honest opinions, but their personal opinions adjusted for what they believe others feel they should think. This nebulous mix of genuine opinion and social pressure makes it quite challenging to fully isolate what individual minorities truly believe about PoC.

Two solutions to this challenge are in order, both drawing on prior knowledge about human nature (Schwarz 2007; Tourangeau, Rips, and Rasinski 2000). The first is a clear-eyed recognition of how social desirability bias operates, with a key emphasis on the word *social*. This type of response bias gums up the expression of opinions because individuals detect a palpable sense of social pressure to respond in a certain way (Crowne and Marlowe 1960; see also Duff et al. 2007; Hanmer, Banks, and White 2013). Maybe it is *what* a survey question asks that increases this pressure. Or perhaps it is *when* a survey question is asked. Or—most relevant to our purposes—*how* a survey question is asked. There is no getting around the fact that in gauging minority views of PoC, researchers must ask about a social entity that is widely recognized, which opens the door to social desirability bias. But even if that door is opened, scholars can quickly shut it closed by short-circuiting the pressure minorities might feel when answering questions about PoC. One strategy is to consider limiting people's ability to control their responses to these types of queries. That is, instead of allowing individuals to complete questions about PoC at their own pace—which allows them the luxury of time to modify their answers in light of social pressure—we might instead direct them to complete questions quickly, under time constraints—which saps one's ability to respond to this tension (cf. Fazio and Towles-Schwen 1999). By encouraging people to answer swiftly, researchers can tap into what is known as automatic thinking: quick, low-effort, and impulsive thoughts that reflect a person's own views and are less contaminated by social desirability (Pérez 2016; Ranganath, Smith, and Nosek 2008).

The second way to dissipate this fog around minority opinions about PoC is to observe their automatic thoughts about the miscellaneous groups nested under PoC. Especially critical here is the ability to observe people's reactions to their own racial in-group in comparison with other racial/ethnic groups. To the extent that we see minority individuals responding to all PoC in ways that are more similar than dissimilar, we can be more confident about just how coherently they view this larger entity encompassing so many unique groups.

But there is a wrinkle here, too. Researchers cannot credibly ask people to react serially to various groups because that is enough to trigger the response bias we seek to avoid here (cf. Sniderman and Carmines 1997; Sniderman and Piazza 1993). That is, asking people to react to one racial group after another is likely to tip them off that a researcher wishes to see how unbiased they are—and so they respond unbiasedly. What should we do here? The way out I offer is to ask different individuals about distinct groups without the former ever knowing that this is, in fact, what is taking place.

## The "I Feel Your Pain" Experiments

The solutions I just proposed—rapid and randomized responses to survey questions—are the cornerstones of a trio of online survey experiments I designed to uncover evidence of *self-stereotyping, in-group homogeneity,* and *identity centrality* among minority individuals. I call these the "I Feel Your Pain" experiments.

The thrust behind these experiments and their name is this. When minority individuals witness a racial affront, do they react in the same way—with alacrity, resolve, and affirmation—if the aggrieved party is from a community of color that is *not* immediately their own? If the psychological principles I have been banging about are worth their salt, the answer has to be yes. Insofar as PoC recognize themselves as such, their sense of being a clear, coherent, and personally meaningful collective should vary inappreciably by whether in-group members are Black, Latino, Asian, or some other minority. A consistency in reaction is key to this hypothesis.

If, however, Blacks respond differentially to Blacks, Latinos respond differentially to Latinos, and Asians respond differentially to Asians, then we have here little more than in-group favoritism based on more narrowly defined and unique racial groups: a PoC without their explicit recognition as such (Branscombe, Schmitt, and Harvey 1999; Branscombe and Wann 1994; Huddy and Virtanen 1995). In fact, classic social identity theory leads us to expect that when one's immediate racial or ethnic in-group is threatened, say, by racially insensitive comments, one is more likely to respond with *greater* in-group favoritism—a behavioral bias toward one's narrower in-group—rather than a more generalized bias toward groups in positions comparable to one's own (Branscombe and Wann 1994; Craig and Richeson 2012; Pérez 2015a).

Table 5.1 underlines the pull of this behavioral tendency with results from a separate experiment I helped implement in nationally representative

TABLE 5.1. Perceived discrimination triggers in-group favoritism among minorities

|  | Latino adults | | Asian adults | |
| --- | --- | --- | --- | --- |
|  | Latinos over Blacks | Latinos over Whites | Asians over Blacks | Asians over Whites |
| Perceived Discrimination | 3.29** (1.59) | 3.52** (1.65) | 2.68** (1.35) | 1.63* (1.19) |
| Control article (constant) | 13.13** (1.15) | 10.47** (1.19) | 13.52** (.97) | 8.93** (.85) |
| N | 807 | 807 | 942 | 947 |

Note: Data are from parallel surveys of Latino and Asian American adults conducted via GfK's platform (Hopkins et al. 2020). **$p < .05$, *$p < .10$; one-tailed tests are used given prior accumulated evidence on this behavioral response (see text for details).

samples of Latino and Asian American adults.[1] This study manipulated perceptions of racial discrimination by randomly assigning Latino and Asian adults to read an article highlighting the prevalence of racial bias against one's immediate in-group in US society or a control article discussing "lonesome George," a tortoise on the Galapagos Islands that is the last of its species.[2] After reading their assigned article, all respondents evaluated their own racial in-group, African Americans, and Whites on an individual and random basis by using a 0 to 100 scale, with higher values indicating greater favorability toward a group. Using these items, I take ratings of one's in-group (e.g., Latinos) and subtract from it ratings of a specific out-group (e.g., Blacks), thus constructing battle-tested measures of in-group favoritism (cf. Kinder and Kam 2009). Table 5.1 shows that heightening perceived discrimination against Latinos and Asian Americans leads group members to express more favoritism toward their in-group. Consider Latinos in the control, who rate co-ethnics about 13 points more positively than Blacks and about 10 points more positively than Whites, on average. In light of sharper perceptions of discrimination, Latinos rate their in-group an additional 3.29 points more positively than Blacks and 3.52 points more positively than Whites, with comparable increases emerging among Asian American adults. Thus, heightening minorities' sense of discrimination toward their unique in-group can trigger, not a broad embrace of other racial minorities or a backlash against Whites, but a more parochial bias toward others who are like them. From this angle, then, unearthing evidence of favorable

1. These studies are based on joint work with Dan Hopkins (Political Science, University of Pennsylvania) and Cheryl Kaiser (Psychology, University of Washington) that examines the roots of partisanship among Latinos and Asian Americans. I thank Dan and Cheryl for allowing me to use these data for this purpose.

2. Full wording of treatment for Latino adults is provided in the appendix to this chapter. The same wording was adapted to Asian adults (see Hopkins et al. 2020).

reactions toward minority groups nested under PoC demands a more nuanced approach. In particular, it requires observing what occurs when distinct minority groups experience similar discriminatory sentiments and actions.

## Research Design

I conducted the "I Feel Your Pain" experiments during 2018 and 2019. Because all three studies share some core features, I describe their design in detail here. In each experiment, African American, Latino, and Asian American adults were invited to participate in brief online surveys about current affairs. Accordingly, participants were asked for their feedback about whether a developing news story was, in their opinion, worthy of further media coverage. All participants read the same news story, which described an altercation at a high-end restaurant in Los Angeles owned by a celebrity chef. The crux of the incident, participants were informed, was caught on audio by another customer at a nearby table and disseminated to news reporters. It was now participants' job to evaluate the transcript of this recording for newsworthiness.

Figure 5.1 displays a screenshot of the treatment. It starts with a minority couple bringing to the attention of a White waiter that their food order was incorrectly filled, with the race/ethnicity of the couple—Black, Latino, or Asian—varying at random. In the middle of trying to explain themselves, the couple is then brusquely interrupted by the White waiter, who explains that he heard them order something else, noting:

> Besides, it doesn't help that I couldn't understand your English very well when I took your order. I mean, no offense, but sometimes it's really, really hard to understand people like you when you talk. I asked you several times and I heard steak, not salad. Maybe next time you can practice saying your order in your head before opening your mouth.

Notice that the waiter does not actively discriminate against the couple. Yet his words rebuke them for their impertinence. It is precisely the kind of microaggression that routinely reminds non-Whites about their secondary status in US society (Kuo, Malhotra, and Mo 2017; Sue 2010). From debates about the use of African American vernacular English, to the heavily accented use of English by some Latino and Asian Americans, language is often used as a litmus test for minorities' full inclusion in the US (Baugh 2000; Garcia Bedolla 2005). To question a PoC's handling of English is to underscore their continued marginalization as minorities (Zou and Cheryan 2017).

After reading the report, participants completed some manipulation checks that gauged whether the news story registered with respondents in the intended

The incident in question revolves around a recent altercation at a high-end restaurant in Los Angeles, California that is managed by a celebrity chef. The confrontation, which involved [a Black/an Asian/a Latino] couple and a White waiter, was caught on audio by an unidentified customer at a nearby table, who then shared the clip with reporters earlier this week.

Here is an excerpt from that recording:

[Asian/Black/Latino] male customer: "Excuse me, but my wife didn't order this sirloin steak. She actually doesn't eat meat and asked for the cobb salad without bacon."

[Asian/Black/Latino] female customer: "Yeah, when you asked me for my order, I told you, twice, that I don't eat meat. It upsets my stomach and…"

White male waiter: "Look, lady, let me stop you right there. In case you can't tell, we're pretty busy here tonight with lots of other customers. Besides, it doesn't help that I couldn't understand your English very well when I took your order. I mean, no offense, but sometimes it's really, really hard to understand people like you when you talk. I asked you several times and I heard steak, not salad. Maybe next time you can practice saying your order in your head before opening your mouth."

…[inaudible commotion] …

…[audio ends]…

FIGURE 5.1. Visual and wording of experimental treatment

way: that is, as an instance of racial hostility. These items vary across studies, and I describe them further in my discussion of the results from each experiment. However, immediately following these manipulation checks, participants in all three studies answered three items tapping levels of *self-stereotyping* as PoC, *perceived homogeneity* of PoC, and *PoC ID*. Using a seven-point scale, participants indicated their degree of agreement that "I am similar to the average person of color" (self-stereotyping), "People of color have a lot in common with each other" (in-group homogeneity), and "Being a person of color is an important part of how I see myself" (identity centrality). The key detail here is that participants in each experiment were given no more than 15 seconds to complete each statement as it sequentially and randomly appeared on their screen, thus engaging a more automatic and deeply affective mode of thinking (cf. Ranganath, Smith, and Nosek 2008). What do we learn from a collection of studies with this basic design? Let's begin answering this question by taking a closer look at its first installment.

## "I Feel Your Pain"—Study 1

In this experiment, I partnered with Survey Sampling International (SSI) to recruit African American ($N = 804$), Latino ($N = 800$), and Asian American ($N = 802$) adults to participate in my study.[3] Adults from each minority group were randomly assigned to read the news transcript I previously described or to a control group that offered no information whatsoever. For all participants, the minority couple in the news transcript was matched to their specific racial/ethnic in-group. My basic expectation is that minority respondents will react to the microaggression in the news article in a substantively similar way. That is, although the news story should register as a negative encounter between a minority couple and a White waiter, one's affinity for PoC should not shift dramatically just because one's own racial/ethnic in-group is involved. Statistically, this means we should observe negligible treatment effects. That is, minorities' answers to the last three items in my interview schedule should be minimally impacted by the race/ethnicity of the aggrieved couple.

But how minimally? To better guide the interpretation of my results, I establish a benchmark, a priori, for what I mean by *negligible* effects (Rainey 2014). In published experiments, a shift of one-fifth of a standard deviation—a Cohen's $d$ of .20—is considered the lower bound of a meaningful effect: a change in an outcome that is worth caring about and exploring further (Cohen 1992). Anything lower is generally deemed statistical debris. How did participants in this study perform by this metric?

Figure 5.2 displays the average responses to the statement concerning one's self-stereotyping as a PoC. These replies are displayed for participants from each racial/ethnic group and by experimental condition. Recall that the control group received no information. Our treatment effects, then, can be understood as deviations from this control condition, which is depicted by the darker bars. Seen this way, it is clear that while the responses of participants from racial/ethnic group bounce around a tiny bit here and there, the general pattern is one of consistency in response.

Consider the reactions of African Americans. Blacks in the control group report a self-stereotyping level as PoC that is $M = .538$ on a 0–1 range. This value then increases mildly, but reliably, to $M = .594$ ($p < .05$, two-tailed). Lest we get too excited about the statistical significance of this result, however, this shift is, alas, substantively small ($d = .187$). Similar shifts characterize Latinos'

---

[3]. In this chapter's appendix, I report basic demographic characteristics and balance checks for all three sets of "I Feel Your Pain" Experiments.

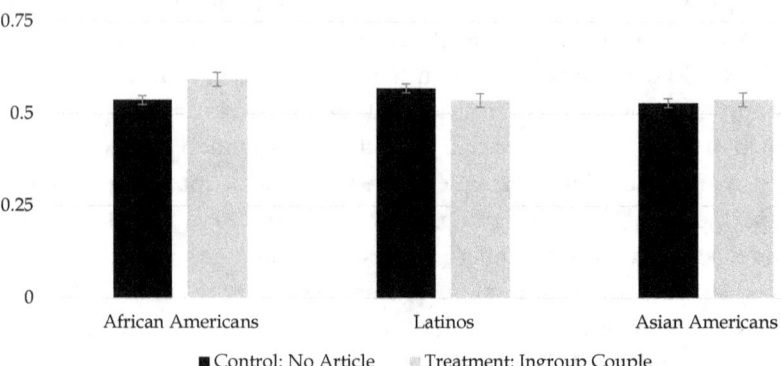

FIGURE 5.2. Self-stereotyping as PoC by racial group: "I Feel Your Pain"—Study 1

and Asians' degree of self-stereotyping as PoC. Latinos in the control report a self-stereotyping level of M = .570, yet among Latinos who read about an affront toward their co-ethnics, this level changes negligibly (M = .537, $p <$ .085, two-tailed, $d$ = .120). In turn, Asian Americans in the control report a degree of self-stereotyping coming in at M = .530. This level then shifts, insignificantly, by a tiny amount when Asians read about an Asian couple that is berated by the White waiter, thus yielding yet another trivial effect (M = .539, $p <$ .578, two-tailed, $d$ = .039).

Comparable patterns emerge for minorities' replies to the statement "People of color have a lot in common with each other" (in-group homogeneity). Figure 5.3 shows African Americans in the control perceive PoC to be fairly homogeneous (M = .585). This value then shifts by a modest amount when Blacks read about a Black couple reprimanded by the White waiter (M = .565, $p <$ .316, two-tailed, $d$ = .072). Latinos manifest a negligible effect on this outcome, too. In the control, they report perceiving PoC as fairly homogeneous (M = .588). This perception hardly changes when they read about a co-ethnic couple that is upbraided by the White waiter (M = .561, $p <$ .145, two-tailed, $d$ = .103). Not to be outdone, Asian Americans in the control also perceive PoC as quite homogeneous (M = .550): a value that negligibly changes if they read about an Asian couple being rebuked by the White server (M = .541, $p <$ .612, two-tailed, $d$ = .071).

This general affinity toward PoC that Blacks, Latinos, and Asians seem to feel hardly shifts when we examine PoC ID levels as well. Figure 5.4 displays

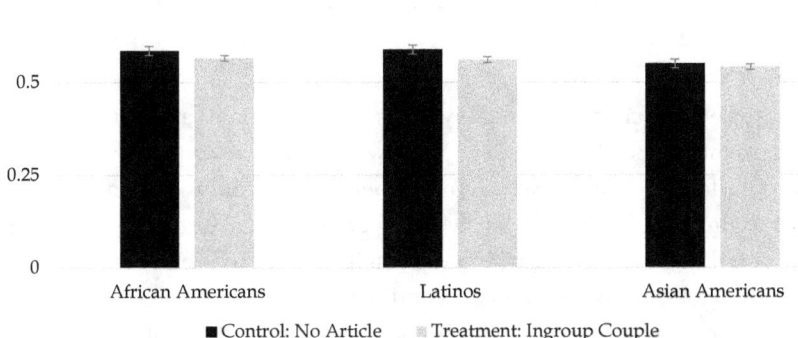

FIGURE 5.3. Perceived homogeneity of PoC by racial group: "I Feel Your Pain"—Study 1

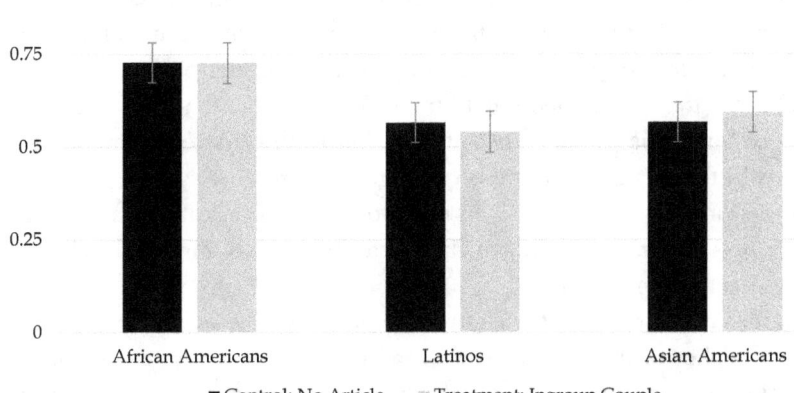

FIGURE 5.4. Centrality of PoC ID by racial group: "I Feel Your Pain"—Study 1

replies to the statement "Being a person of color is an important part of how I see myself" (identity centrality). Blacks in the control express a very high degree of PoC ID (M = .728), and this level changes negligibly when they read about the altercation involving a Black couple and the White waiter (M = .726, $p < .928$, two-tailed, $d = .007$). In turn, while Latinos in the control report a milder PoC ID level than Blacks (M = .566), this robust value barely shifts in the treatment condition (M = .541, $p < .232$, two-tailed, $d = .084$). Asian Americans exhibit a parallel pattern, too: in the control, they report a PoC ID level

TABLE 5.2. Average ratings of news story as negative: Study 1

|  | African Americans | Latinos | Asian Americans |
|---|---|---|---|
| Mean rating [95% CI] | .784 [.756, .812] | .794 [.770, .818] | .784 [.759, .811] |

of M = .567, which changes negligibly when they read about an Asian couple's mistreatment by the White waiter (M = .593, $p < .150$, two-tailed, $d = .102$). A more uniform set of answers across experimental conditions and groups is hard to imagine. In fact, the unswerving nature of these responses is even more remarkable when we recall that participants offered their responses to each of these questions under a 15-second limit.

As further evidence of this consistency in response across PoC, a meta-analysis that pools these three studies ($N = 2,406$) reveals an average treatment effect across the three main outcomes (scaled together) that is both substantively tiny and statistically indistinguishable from zero at the conventional 5% level (mean $d = .077, p < .061$, two-tailed) (Goh, Hall, and Rosenthal 2016).

But perhaps the patterns we observe here emerge, not because of minorities' steadfast commitment to PoC, but because the microaggression they read about is too underwhelming to influence their reaction. I have more to say about this across the next two studies, but in this first experiment, participants in the treatment condition reported how negatively they perceived the news story they read about. This rating occurred on a scale from 1 = "very positive" to 5 = "very negative," which I rescale here to a 0–1 interval. Table 5.2 displays the relevant results.

Because participants in the control did not read a news story, we cannot compare replies to this item *between* conditions; however, we can compare perceptions of the story *across* racial/ethnic groups in the treatment condition. From this angle, Blacks, Latinos, and Asians all construed the article they read as very negative, with a mean rating that is about three-fourths of the scale and statistically insignificant gaps in ratings between groups (as evidenced by overlapping 95% confidence intervals). This pattern is inconsistent with the claim that Study 1's treatments did not work as designed.

## "I Feel Your Pain"—Study 2

The results from Study 1 suggest the affinity for PoC that racial/ethnic minorities sense is both relatively steadfast and automatic. That is to say, it does not vary substantially by whether one's racial in-group is involved in the altercation with a member of a dominant out-group (i.e., White waiter). But what

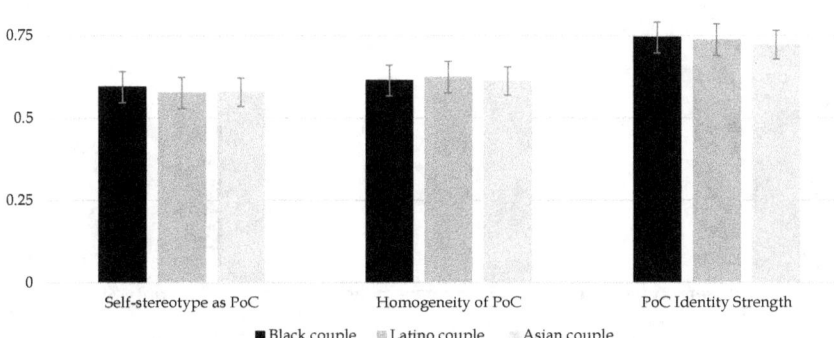

FIGURE 5.5. Black affinity for PoC by race of couple: "I Feel Your Pain"—Study 2

if the minority couple that is berated by the waiter is not from their racial in-group—does their affinity for PoC shift drastically then? If it does, it would imply that minorities' sense of being a PoC is only as strong as the bond they feel toward their own racial group. But if it does not, it would indicate that minorities' kinship with other PoC is as broad as the diversity of this group itself. Deciding between these alternatives was the goal of the second "I Feel Your Pain" experiment, which I administered with fresh SSI samples of Black ($N$ = 1,763), Latino ($N$ = 1,764), and Asian American ($N$ = 1,794) adults.

All details in this second study are the same as in the previous one, except two. First, this second experiment replaces the "pure" control group with an article focusing on a couple from one's racial in-group. This condition is the baseline in all subsequent analyses, which lets me gauge minorities' reaction to the altercation with the White waiter when one's own racial in-group is involved versus when a racial out-group is involved. Second, instead of one treatment, there are now two, with each one focused on a specific minority out-group. Thus, for example, Black adults in the baseline condition read an article about a Black couple that is berated by the White waiter, and other Black participants read the same article focused on a Latino or Asian American couple. The same protocol was followed for Latino and Asian participants.

What does Study 2 reveal? The same pattern of steadfast commitment to PoC as in Study 1—except, this time, the pattern emerges irrespective of whether the offended minority group is from one's racial in-group or a minority out-group. As figure 5.5 shows, Blacks' affinity toward PoC is consistent regardless of whether they read about a Black, Latino, or Asian couple. For instance, going from left to right, Blacks who read about a Black couple that

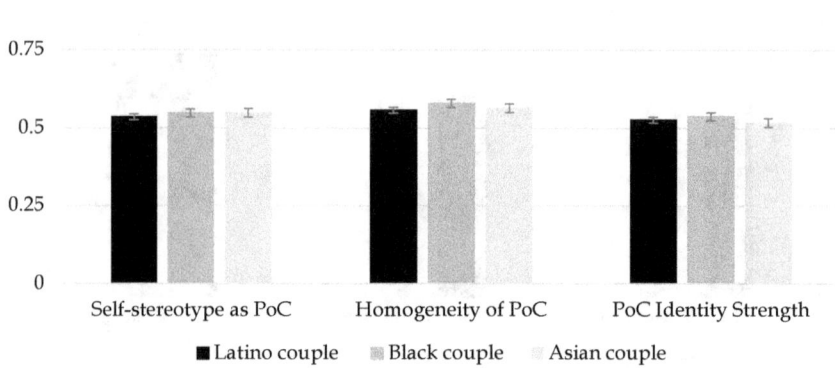

FIGURE 5.6. Latino Affinity for PoC by race of couple: "I Feel Your Pain"—Study 2

is reprimanded by the White waiter self-stereotype themselves as PoC at M = .594. This value changes negligibly if Blacks read about a Latino couple (M = .576, $p < .246$, two-tailed, $d = .070$) or Asian couple (M = .580, $p < .354$, two-tailed, $d = .055$) receiving the brunt of the waiter's tirade.

Parallel patterns arise in Blacks' perceived homogeneity of PoC and their PoC ID strength. African Americans who read about a Black couple provoking the White waiter's ire believe PoC to be quite homogeneous (M = .614). This value shifts, negligibly, if Blacks read about a Latino (M = .624, $p < .496$, two-tailed, $d = .038$) or Asian couple (M = .612, $p < .900$, two-tailed, $d = .008$). In turn, Blacks who read about a Black couple that is berated by the waiter express a very high PoC ID level (M = .744). But again, among Blacks who read about a Latino (M = .737, $p < .648$, two-tailed, $d = .026$) or Asian couple (M = .722, $p < .169$, two-tailed, $d = .080$), this reported PoC ID level hardly shifts.

The results for Latinos and Asian Americans closely replicate these patterns. Figure 5.6 shows that Latinos who read about a Latino couple report a solid level of self-stereotyping as PoC (M = .535), yet this value barely moves when they read about a Black (M = .547, $p < .413$, two-tailed, $d = .046$) or Asian (.548, $p < .381$, two-tailed, $d = .049$) couple. In turn, Latinos who read about a Latino couple berated by the White server perceive PoC as quite homogeneous (M = .557). But again, this value shifts trivially if they read about a Black (M = .578, $p < .142$, two-tailed, $d = .084$) or Asian (M = .565, $p < .615$, two-tailed $d = .028$) couple. And, in terms of PoC ID, Latinos in the control report a level of M = .526, which changes inappreciably when Latinos read about the waiter rebuking a Latino (M = .537, $p < .527$, two-tailed, $d = .037$) or Asian (M = .518, $p < .645$, two-tailed, $d = .027$) couple.

Asian Americans' performance on these measures of affinity for PoC are displayed in figure 5.7. Similar to Blacks and Latinos, Asian Americans also self-stereotype themselves as PoC at a relatively high level if they read about the White waiter deriding an Asian couple (M = .520). But this value shifts, modestly, if Asians read about a Black (M = .530, $p < .430$, two-tailed $d = .045$) or Latino (M = .547, $p < .037$, two-tailed, $d = .119$) couple. Further, in what is now a very familiar pattern, Asians who read about an Asian couple bearing the waiter's comments perceive PoC as fairly homogeneous (M = .546)—a view that barely shifts if they read about a Black (M = .557, $p < .381$, two-tailed, $d = .049$) or Latino (M = .560, $p < .270$, two-tailed, $d = .058$) couple. Finally, even Asians' sense of PoC ID remains steadfast. Asian participants who read about an Asian couple that is rebuked by the White waiter express a vigorous PoC ID level (M = .562). This level, though, remains statistically identical if they read about a Black (M = .573, $p < .473$, two-tailed, $d = .042$) or Latino (M = .574, $p < .425$, two-tailed $d = .045$) couple.

Study 2's results are also comparable to those in Study 1 in one other respect. Following the experiment, all participants reported how negatively they viewed the news story they read. This means they judged the story when it portrayed a couple from their racial/ethnic group, as well as a story that portrayed a couple from the two remaining racial/ethnic out-groups. Table 5.3 delivers the punch lines of these ratings.

Looking across the rows, individuals from each racial/ethnic group consistently rated the story as *very* negative regardless of the couple's racial/ethnic identity. Indeed, these ratings generally cross 75% of this scale's range, with most differences between them being substantively small and statistically insignificant. This further supports my inference that the lack of appreciably

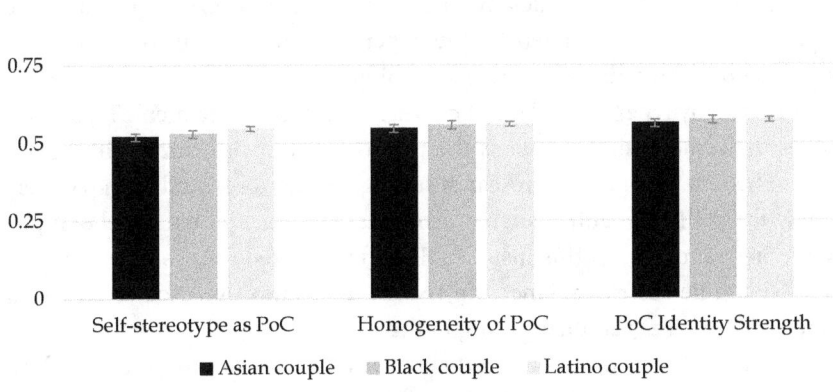

FIGURE 5.7. Asian affinity for PoC by race of couple: "I Feel Your Pain"—Study 2

TABLE 5.3. Average ratings of news story as negative (0–1 range): Study 2

|  | Black couple | Latino couple | Asian couple |
|---|---|---|---|
| Blacks' rating [95% CI] | .757 [.734, .780] | .741 [.719, .763] | .738 [.716, .7611] |
| Latinos' rating [95% CI] | .766 [.745, .787] | .770 [.749, .790] | .769 [.749, .789] |
| Asians' rating [95% CI] | .772 [.752, .792] | .766 [.746, .786] | .786 [.767, .806] |

large shifts in minorities' affinity for PoC is unlikely driven by an underwhelming and unengaging news story.

## "I Feel Your Pain"—Study 3

Up to this point, we have before us a collection of experiments revealing a major finding. In the heat of in-group versus out-group relations, the affinity that racial/ethnic minorities feel toward PoC does not vary dramatically by who a PoC is. Indeed, in both studies so far, the presence of a combative out-group member—the White waiter—is sufficient to construct a solid wall of support for PoC, irrespective of the racial/ethnic origins of the minority couple taking the waiter's verbal abuse. This unerring affirmation of PoC by PoC is all the more remarkable because it replicates across two independent studies, with very large samples, and with a focus on individuals' more automatic opinions toward PoC.

Nevertheless, there is an important alternate explanation I have yet to rule out: it is quite plausible that the unswerving reactions of PoC emerge across my studies, not because PoC stand firmly behind a couple that has been *racially* offended, but because, more simply, the waiter's behavior is deemed unprofessional and rude. From this angle, minorities' unflinching reactions across both studies arise because PoC construe the waiter's behavior as boorish and uncouth, but not racially insensitive. Hence, PoC's response to the plight of other PoC is muted by the experience of poor customer service, which is both workaday and underwhelming.

Is this really true? To find out, I conducted a third experiment. This study shares the same basic features as the previous ones, with three minor revisions. The first change is the research setting. I undertook Study 3 in partnership with Prolific, an online survey firm that manages a global panel of high-quality respondents. In this instance, Prolific gathered for me large samples of self-identified African American ($N = 554$), Latino ($N = 504$), and Asian American ($N = 622$) adults residing in the US.

The second revision to this study involves the control group. To test for a "rudeness" explanation, the control condition in this study directs participants to read the same story as before, except the waiter now derides the language use of a southern White couple. By design, this couple is White, just like the waiter, which holds race constant. But by describing this couple as being from the American south, they, too, serve as a lightning rod for the waiter's criticisms, since southerners are known to speak distinctly with a regional drawl (Kinzler and DeJesus 2013; Lippi-Green 2012). In this way, participants who read about this southern White couple's encounter with the waiter are compared to those participants who read about the same encounter when a member of their racial/ethnic in-group is involved.

The third revision I made was to slightly expand the type of manipulation checks asked immediately after the experiment itself. Specifically, all participants used a scale ranging from 1 = "strongly disagree" to 7 = "strongly agree" to complete three statements: (1) "The waiter behaved rudely toward the couple," (2) "The waiter's response to the couple was unprofessional," and (3) "The waiter's comments were racially insensitive." Whereas the "rudeness" explanation would lead us to expect minor differences in response between experimental conditions for the first two items, my working assumption that PoC are reacting to a *racial* incident should produce clear and resounding differences on the third item. That is, Blacks, Latinos, and Asians should all construe the White waiter's comments as racially insensitive.

## Similar Patterns, New Insights

So, what does this last experiment teach us? A lot we did not learn from the first two studies, actually. Let's begin with minorities' affinity toward PoC. Figure 5.8 displays the results for African Americans, across all three main outcomes of interest, when they read about the southern White couple's or the Black couple's encounter with the waiter. All responses here are recoded to range from 0 to 1, with higher values indicating stronger agreement with a statement about the waiter's behavior. Simply eyeballing this graph should reaffirm the main pattern we have seen before. That is, changes in Blacks' sense of self-stereotyping as PoC ($d = .012$, $p < .882$, two-tailed), their perceived homogeneity of PoC ($d = .109$, $p < .187$, two-tailed), and their strength of PoC ID are all substantively negligible ($d = .054$, $p < .517$, two-tailed).

Not to be outdone, Latinos and Asian Americans in this study replicate this same general pattern, as seen in figures 5.9 and 5.10, respectively. Whether Latinos read about a southern White couple or a Latino couple that is berated by the White waiter, their expressed levels of self-stereotyping ($d = .072$, $p < .419$), perceived homogeneity ($d = .081$, $p < .362$), and PoC ID ($d = .060$, $p < .499$) also hardly shift at all. In turn, Asian Americans' sense of self-stereotyping ($d = .109$,

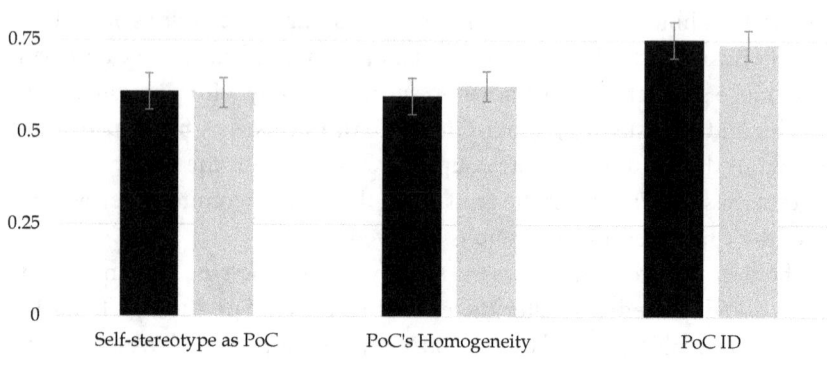

FIGURE 5.8. Black affinity toward PoC: "I Feel Your Pain"—Study 3

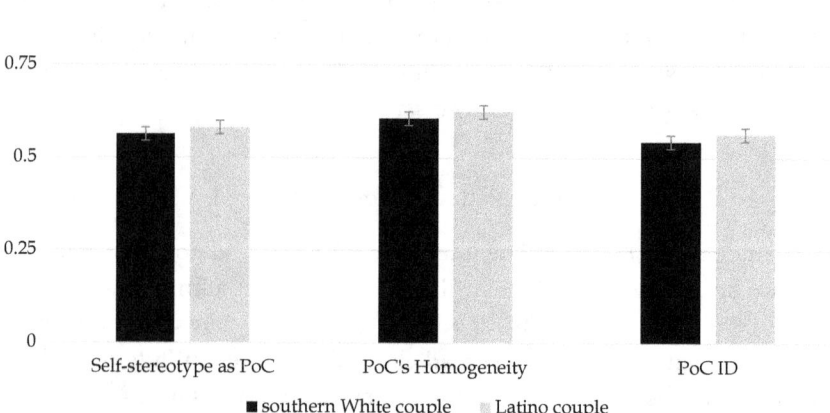

FIGURE 5.9. Latino affinity toward PoC: "I Feel Your Pain"—Study 3

$p < .175$, two-tailed), perceived homogeneity ($d = .022$, $p < .786$, two-tailed), and PoC ID ($d = .032$, $p < .694$, two-tailed) all negligibly change as well between experimental conditions. Combined, these additional experiments suggest, in line with the previous ones, that racial minorities' affinity toward PoC is generally invariant with respect to the specific group of color. Indeed, consistent with this inference, a meta-analysis pooling these three studies ($N = 1,711$) reveals the average treatment effect across my three main outcomes (scaled together) is substantively and statistically insignificant (mean $d = .045$, $p < .321$, two-tailed) (Goh, Hall, and Rosenthal 2016).

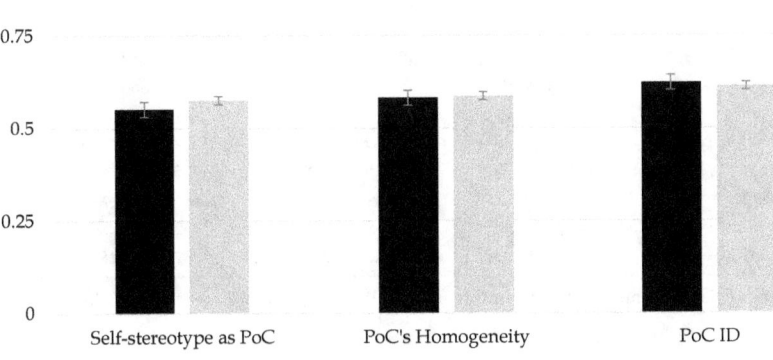

FIGURE 5.10. Asian affinity toward PoC: "I Feel Your Pain"—Study 3

Of course, one way to interpret these results is to suggest that, hand-in-glove, they fit with the "rudeness" explanation I laid out earlier. Since the White waiter's behavior is primarily construed as rude and unprofessional by racial/ethnic minorities, they react the same way even when a southern White couple is upbraided by the waiter. After all, rudeness and lack of professionalism have no racial boundaries.

Or do they? Recall that one of this study's innovations is the suite of items asking participants to report their perceptions of the waiter they read about: specifically, their assessment of the waiter as rude, unprofessional, and—most crucially—racially insensitive. These replies are displayed in table 5.4 as mean differences on a 0–1 range, with higher values reflecting greater agreement with a statement about the waiter.

Embedded in this table are some new and illuminating results pertaining to PoC. Let's begin with African Americans' sense of the White waiter's rudeness. Compared with Blacks who read about a southern White couple (M = .912), those African Americans who read about a Black couple that is berated by the White waiter report a marginally stronger sense that the server is rude (M = .937, $p < .089$, two-tailed; $d = .141$). A comparable trend is observed for Blacks' perceptions of the White waiter's lack of professionalism. Relative to Blacks in the control (M = .950), African Americans who read about the Black couple's altercation with the server perceive the waiter to be just as unprofessional (M = .954, $p < .697$; $d = .032$). However, when Blacks' assessment of the waiter's comments as racially insensitive is taken into account, we see an eye-popping difference. Specifically, African Americans who read about the southern White

TABLE 5.4. Ratings of waiter by racial group and experimental condition: Study 3

|  | Rude waiter | Unprofessional waiter | Racially insensitive waiter |
|---|---|---|---|
| *African Americans* | | | |
| Southern White couple | .912 [.892, .934] | .950 [.936, .965] | .425 [.382, .466] |
| Black couple | .937 [.918, .955] | .954 [.939, .970] | .882 [.860, .904] |
| *Latinos* | | | |
| Southern White couple | .911 [.891, .932] | .942 [.926, 957] | .520 [.477, .563] |
| Latino couple | .932 [.915, .951] | .952 [.936, .968] | .853 [.826, .880] |
| *Asian Americans* | | | |
| Southern White couple | .911 [.894, .927] | .930 [.914, .946] | .526 [.490, .562] |
| Asian American couple | .935 [.921, .950] | .951 [.938, .964] | .876 [.856, .896] |

Note: Entries reflect agreement with statements (0–1 interval), with 95% confidence intervals in brackets.

couple's experience with the waiter slightly disagree that his comments are racially insensitive (M = .425). But when African Americans read about a Black couple's encounter with the same waiter, their construal of the server's comments as racially crass jump, massively, by 46 percentage points (M = .882, d = 1.243, p < .01, two-tailed), thus placing Blacks firmly in the camp of interpreting the waiter's words as unmistakably hostile in a racial sense.

Latinos' responses parallel those of their African American peers. Consider Latino perceptions of the waiter's behavior as rude, which remain consistent across the conditions with the southern White (M = .911) and Latino (M = .932, p < .117, d = .140) couples. Consider, also, Latinos' construal of the waiter's behavior as unprofessional, which is also invariant across the southern White (M = .942) and Latino (M = .952, p < .370, d = .080) couple conditions. Notice, however, that just like African Americans, Latino evaluations of the waiter's comments as racially insensitive change dramatically across experimental conditions. Latinos in the control, who read about a southern couple, report neither agreement nor disagreement that the server's comments were racially insensitive (M = .520). But when Latinos read about a Latino couple, this assessment significantly rises by several points (M = .853, p < .01, d = 1.001), which also places Latinos firmly in the camp of interpreting the waiter's words as racially motivated.

Asian Americans reveal a similar set of results to members of the other two minority groups. In the control, for example, when Asian Americans read about a southern couple, their perceptions of the waiter as rude and unprofessional register at M = .911 and M = .930, respectively. In turn, when Asian Americans read about their co-ethnics being reprimanded by the same waiter, these perceptions hardly shift in a substantive sense (M = .935, d = .176, p < .029, two-tailed; and M = .951, d = .159, p < .047, two-tailed, respectively). What does change dramatically is Asians' sense of the waiter's racial insensitivity.

Whereas in the control, Asian perceptions of the waiter's comments as racially tinged are at M = .526, these perceptions sharpen dramatically among Asians who read about their co-ethnics being rebuked by the same waiter (M = .876, $d$ = 1.128, $p$ < .01, two-tailed). What all three minority groups share, then, is the perception of the White waiter's behavior as baldly hostile in a racial sense.

## Implications and Next Steps

This chapter began with a simple question: given the wide-ranging diversity of distinct racial and ethnic groups, do minorities perceive themselves as a unified and coherent PoC? Having now reached the conclusion of this chapter, we have in hand harder evidence to reply with a more resounding yes. This singular finding dispels many uncertainties about this pan-racial category, while pointing to new questions about it. Let's begin with what the evidence actually clarifies.

The rich diversity of PoC is a double-edged sword. At times, the heterogeneity of these communities is a source of strength and a badge of honor: a quintessential feature used by PoC to define themselves, particularly with respect to Whites (Skrentny 2002; Vidal-Ortiz 2008). Yet at other times, the unique histories, aspirations, and political goals of these communities can be, and have been, a root of discord, disunity, acrimony, and even hostility between these very same groups (cf. Benjamin 2017; Bobo and Hutchings 1996; McClain and Johnson Carew 2017; McClain and Karnig 1990; Vaca 2004). How can both of these be true?

The answer, my evidence suggests, has to do with *how* minorities view themselves in specific moments. Insofar as they see themselves as members of unique racial and ethnic groups, their perspective will be, perforce, narrower, more circumspect, and strictly focused on their immediate co-ethnics. But if and when minorities cast their gaze toward PoC in general, these same minority individuals reorient their perspective toward this larger group, under which sundry minority communities are nested. This shift in vantage point leads members of specific minority groups to offer the benefits of in-group favoritism to all assorted minorities nested under the banner of PoC.

This is precisely what the "I Feel Your Pain" experiments underscored over and over. Insofar as PoC is a socially meaningful category, members will view it as a coherent and distinct entity that is, to important degrees, critical to how minority individuals see themselves individually. The cognitive and affective significance of this category therefore induces minority individuals to see themselves as part of a much broader collective. It is not that they forget that they are African American, Latino, Asian American, or members of other minority groups. Rather, it is that they project these smaller groups onto this larger assemblage, where each component community is interchangeable and worthy of the compassion, affirmation, and support that any bona fide member should receive (cf. Wenzel, Mummendey, and Waldzus 2007).

There are limits to this generosity of spirit, of course—limits set down by prior work. The findings in this chapter establish only that PoC is a distinct entity that exceeds the tighter confines of one's proximate racial or ethnic in-group. The evidence, however, does not address, and cannot directly speak to, the operation of this category in settings characterized by conflict over expressive or material interests (e.g., Benjamin 2017; Carter 2019; Cutaia Wilkinson 2015; McClain et al. 2005). But having established the meaningfulness of PoC, my theoretical framework does anticipate what could happen in such contexts. In particular, my framework suggests paying special attention to the frame of reference for PoC (cf. Turner et al. 1987, 1994). If the intergroup context is driven by relations between Whites and non-Whites, PoC ID's salience and influence on minorities' individual judgments and choices should increase, since Whites would serve as the frame of reference. But if the intergroup context is driven by relations between different minority groups, then it should be more difficult to sustain PoC ID and easier to amplify the influence of racial ID on individual judgment and choice, *especially when scarce resources are at stake* (Zou and Cheryan 2017). In this sense, my theoretical framework points to some conditions when PoC ID matters for politics, as well as some conditions when its political effects wane—conditions that we examine in detail in subsequent chapters (see especially chapter 7).

The evidence in this chapter, moreover, does not address, and cannot directly speak to, variation in the composition of PoC, an expansion or shrinking of its boundaries, and the strengthening or weakening of its behavior as a whole. We already detected hints that these aspects are not firmly set in stone, at least for some PoC. For example, we observed that even on the three questions asked about this group, there was a neat ordering of responses, with African Americans expressing greater overall affinity for PoC, followed by Latinos, and then followed by Asian Americans. This pattern raises the tantalizing possibility that, in general, some individuals might feel more invested in this shared category than other people. It also nods at the prospect that some minority groups might be deemed clearer representations of PoC. An understanding of these latter dynamics has implications for how we understand intra- and intergroup relations for and by PoC. Clarifying what makes these processes tick, and how they are shaped by politics, are the goals of the chapter we turn to next.

## APPENDIX

## Auxiliary Results

TABLE 5.A1. Subjects' demographic characteristics: "I Feel Your Pain"—Study 1

|  | African Americans | Latinos | Asian Americans |
|---|---|---|---|
| US-born | 95% | 82% | 51% |
| Age (years) | 44 | 40 | 46 |
| College-educated | 53% | 43% | 76% |
| Female | 52% | 50% | 53% |
| Democrat | 87% | 69% | 61% |
| Mexican [Chinese] | — | 44% | 44% |
| Puerto Rican [Filipino] | — | 22% | 14% |
| Cuban [Indian] | — | 4% | 5% |

TABLE 5.A2. Subjects' demographic characteristics: "I Feel Your Pain"—Study 2

|  | African Americans | Latinos | Asian Americans |
|---|---|---|---|
| US-born | 95% | 84% | 57% |
| Age (years) | 44 | 41 | 46 |
| College-educated | 42% | 44% | 69% |
| Female | 59% | 54% | 57% |
| Democrat | 86% | 68% | 62% |
| Mexican [Chinese] | — | 45% | 33% |
| Puerto Rican [Filipino] | — | 19% | 15% |
| Cuban [Indian] | — | 7% | 5% |

TABLE 5.A3. Subjects' demographic characteristics: "I Feel Your Pain"—Study 3

|  | African Americans | Latinos | Asian Americans |
|---|---|---|---|
| US-born | 95% | 84% | 57% |
| Age (years) | 44 | 41 | 46 |
| College-educated | 42% | 44% | 69% |
| Democrat | 86% | 68% | 62% |
| Mexican [Chinese] | — | 45% | 33% |
| Puerto Rican [Filipino] | — | 19% | 15% |
| Cuban [Indian] | — | 7% | 5% |

TABLE 5.A4. Randomization Check: "I Feel Your Pain"—Study 1

|  | Treatment assignment | | |
|---|---|---|---|
|  | Blacks | Latinos | Asians |
| US-born | .012 (.079) | .032 (.048) | −.024 (.036) |
| Age | −.001 (.001) | .001 (.001) | .001 (.001) |
| College-educated | .019 (.037) | .028 (.037) | .065 (.042) |
| Female | −.047 (.037) | .023 (.037) | −.056 (.036) |
| Democrat | .039 (.053) | −.076* (.038) | .075* (.036) |
| N | 804 | 800 | 802 |
| Block test: null; all covariates = 0 | $p < .472$ | $p < .232$ | $p < .057$ |

Note: *$p < .05$, two-tailed.


TABLE 5.A5. Randomization check: "I Feel Your Pain"—Study 2

|  | Treatment Assignment | | | | | |
|---|---|---|---|---|---|---|
|  | Blacks | | Latinos | | Asians | |
| US-born | −.224 (.243) | .036 (.258) | .153 (.153) | .109 (.154) | −.195 (.115) | −.044 (.115) |
| Age | .003 (.003) | −.002 (.003) | −.001 (.004) | −.005 (.004) | .001 (.004) | .000 (.003) |
| College educated | .231* (.115) | .287* (.115) | −.045 (.115) | −.023 (.116) | .011 (.122) | −.061 (.121) |
| Female | .053 (.114) | .111 (.115) | −.226* (.113) | −.035 (.114) | .075 (.115) | .237 (.115) |
| Democrat | .072 (.161) | .194 (.165) | .154 (.120) | .093 (.120) | −.217 (.117) | −.117 (.117) |
| N | 1,900 | | 1,900 | | 1,900 | |
| Block test: null; all covariates = 0 | $p < .239$ | | $p < .495$ | | $p < .230$ | |

Note: *$p < .05$, two-tailed.


TABLE 5.A6. Randomization check: "I Feel Your Pain"—Study 3

|  | Treatment assignment | | |
|---|---|---|---|
|  | Blacks | Latinos | Asians |
| US-born | —[a] | −.155 (.206) | .043 (.129) |
| Age | .003 (.006) | −.002 (.007) | −.001 (.008) |
| College-educated | −.143 (.113) | −.039 (.118) | .012 (.114) |
| Democrat | .173 (.161) | .063 (.114) | .009 (.103) |
| N | 554 | 496 | 621 |
| Block test: null; all covariates = 0 | $p < .239$ | $p < .495$ | $p < .996$ |

Note: *$p < .05$, two-tailed.
a All African Americans in this study were US-born.

TABLE 5.A7. Balance tests: "I Feel Your Pain"—Study 1

|  | Control | Treatment | Test statistic |
|---|---|---|---|
| *Blacks* | | | |
| US-born | 95% | 95% | $\chi^2 (1) = .005, p < .942$ |
| Age | 45 years | 43 years | $\chi^2 (63) = 49.97, p < .883$ |
| College-educated | 52% | 55% | $\chi^2 (1) = .891, p < .345$ |
| Female | 55% | 50% | $\chi^2 (1) = 2.152, p < .142$ |
| Democrat | 86% | 87% | $\chi^2 (1) = .238, p < .626$ |
| Mexican [Chinese] | — | — | — |
| Puerto Rican [Filipino] | — | — | — |
| Cuban [Indian] | — | — | — |
| *Latinos* | | | |
| US-born | 82% | 83% | $\chi^2 (1) = .055, p < .814$ |
| Age | 39 years | 41 years | $\chi^2 (66) = 60.81, p < .658$ |
| College-educated | 41% | 44% | $\chi^2 (1) = .737, p < .393$ |
| Female | 44% | 49% | $\chi^2 (1) = .004, p < .948$ |
| Democrat | 72% | 65% | $\chi^2 (1) = 3.453, p < .063$ |
| Mexican [Chinese] | 45% | 42% | $\chi^2 (1) = .238, p < .626$ |
| Puerto Rican [Filipino] | 21% | 23% | $\chi^2 (1) = .238, p < .626$ |
| Cuban [Indian] | 4% | 5% | $\chi^2 (1) = .238, p < .626$ |
| *Asians* | | | |
| US-born | 52% | 51% | $\chi^2 (1) = .055, p < .814$ |
| Age (years) | 46 | 47 | $\chi^2 (1) = .271, p < .603$ |
| College-educated | 73% | 79% | $\chi^2 (1) = 3.549, p < .060$ |
| Female | 56% | 50% | $\chi^2 (1) = 3.296, p < .069$ |
| Democrat | 58% | 64% | $X^2 (1) = 3.646, p < .056$ |
| Mexican [Chinese] | 40% | 48% | $\chi^2 (1) = 5.676, p < .017$ |
| Puerto Rican [Filipino] | 15% | 13% | $\chi^2 (1) = .298, p < .585$ |
| Cuban [Indian] | 5% | 5% | $\chi^2 (1) = .002, p < .964$ |

TABLE 5.A8. Balance tests: "I Feel Your Pain"—Study 2

|  | Control | Latino couple | Asian couple | Test statistic |
|---|---|---|---|---|
| *Blacks* | | | | |
| Mexican [Chinese] | — | — | — | — |
| Puerto Rican [Filipino] | — | — | — | — |
| Cuban [Indian] | — | — | — | — |
| US-born | 95% | 95% | 94% | $\chi^2 (2) = 1.37, p < .51$ |
| Age | 44 yrs. | 44 yrs. | 45 yrs. | $\chi^2 (138) = 31.57, p < .64$ |
| College-educated | 44% | 37% | 43% | $\chi^2 (2) = 7.22, p < .03$ |
| Females | 60% | 57% | 59% | $\chi^2 (2) = 1.04, p < .59$ |
| Democrats | 87% | 85% | 86% | $\chi^2 (2) = 1.58, p < .45$ |
| *Latinos* | | | | |
| Mexican [Chinese] | 47% | 42% | 45% | $\chi^2 (2) = 3.76, p < .153$ |
| Puerto Rican [Filipino] | 19% | 21% | 19% | $\chi^2 (2) = 1.038, p < .60$ |
| Cuban [Indian] | 6% | 7% | 6% | $\chi^2 (2) = .68, p < .71$ |

TABLE 5.A8. (Continued)

|  | Control | Latino couple | Asian couple | Test statistic |
|---|---|---|---|---|
| US-born | 84% | 84% | 82% | $\chi^2 (2) = 1.48, p < .48$ |
| Age | 41 yrs. | 40 yrs. | 42 yrs. | $\chi^2 (130) = 150.50, p < .11$ |
| College-educated | 44% | 44% | 45% | $\chi^2 (2) = 0.23, p < .89$ |
| Females | 51% | 55% | 56% | $\chi^2 (2) = 4.21, p < .12$ |
| Democrats | 69% | 68% | 66% | $\chi^2 (2) = 1.34, p < .51$ |
| Asians |  |  |  |  |
| Mexican [Chinese] | 34% | 31% | 33% | $\chi^2 (2) = 1.34, p < .51$ |
| Puerto Rican [Filipino] | 14% | 16% | 16% | $\chi^2 (2) = 1.28, p < .53$ |
| Cuban [Indian] | 4% | 6% | 5% | $\chi^2 (2) = 1.89, p < .39$ |
| US-born | 60% | 58% | 54% | $\chi^2 (2) = 4.05, p < .13$ |
| Age | 46 yrs. | 46 yrs. | 46 yrs. | $\chi^2 (2) = 138.66, p < .61$ |
| College-Educated | 69% | 68% | 69% | $\chi^2 (2) = 0.61, p < .74$ |
| Females | 54% | 60% | 56% | $\chi^2 (2) = 4.65, p < .10$ |
| Democrats | 65% | 62% | 59% | $\chi^2 (2) = 4.15, p < .13$ |

TABLE 5.A9. Balance Tests: "I Feel Your Pain" Experiment—Study 2

|  | Southern White couple | [Black/Latino/ Asian] couple | Test statistic |
|---|---|---|---|
| Blacks |  |  |  |
| Mexican [Chinese] | — | — | — |
| Puerto Rican [Filipino] | — | — | — |
| Cuban [Indian] | — | — | — |
| US-born | — | — | — |
| Age | 30 yrs. | 30 yrs. | $\chi^2 (35) = 131.57, p < .245$ |
| College-educated | 40% | 36% | $\chi^2 (2) = 7.22, p < .03$ |
| Democrats | 86% | 89% | $\chi^2 (1) = 1.022, p < .312$ |
| Latinos |  |  |  |
| Mexican [Chinese] | 53% | 54% | $\chi^2 (1) = .110, p < .740$ |
| Puerto Rican [Filipino] | 15% | 10% | $\chi^2 (1) = 3.101, p < .078$ |
| Cuban [Indian] | 6% | 9% | $\chi^2 (1) = 1.558, p < .212$ |
| US-born | 92% | 90% | $\chi^2 (2) = .700, p < .403$ |
| Age (years) | 28 | 28 | $\chi^2 (39) = 25.94, p < .946$ |
| College-educated | 44% | 45% | $\chi^2 (1) = .052, p < .820$ |
| Democrats | 53% | 55% | $\chi^2 (1) = .176, p < .675$ |
| Asians |  |  |  |
| Mexican [Chinese] | 34% | 31% | $\chi^2 (1) = .276, p < .599$ |
| Puerto Rican [Filipino] | 14% | 16% | $\chi^2 (2) = 1.598, p < .206$ |
| Cuban [Indian] | 4% | 6% | $\chi^2 (2) = 1.344, p < .246$ |
| US-born | 60% | 58% | $\chi^2 (1) = .130, p < .719$ |
| Age (years) | 46. | 46. | $\chi^2 (36) = 34.92, p < .520$ |
| College-educated | 69% | 68% | $\chi^2 (1) = .001, p < .975$ |
| Democrats | 65% | 62% | $\chi^2 (1) = .035, p < .851$ |

# BIAS AGAINST LATINOS IS ALIVE

BY: J.L. HALEY

## ASSOCIATED PRESS

LOS ANGELES – On a recent Sunday afternoon, several residents of this heavily Latino neighborhood gathered to plan an upcoming block party. But before the talk could turn to party planning, the neighbors wanted to discuss something far less entertaining: the prevalence of anti-Latino bias in their lives. Person after person reported experiences with discrimination, from having been called slurs like "wetback" to having been stereotyped as illegals or subjected to racist jokes.

Those stories match up with data collected by the University of California's Survey Research Center. The Center's new survey shows that Latinos face widespread discrimination. The study, which surveyed 5,000 Latinos and 5,000 Whites from throughout the U.S., revealed that Latinos routinely face discrimination and inequality in politics, employment, education, and in everyday interpersonal interactions.

## RACISM STILL PERVASIVE

The data showed that stereotypes and negative attitudes about Latinos have remained pervasive. The study revealed that between 70% and 75% of the surveyed White respondents held prejudiced attitudes against Latinos. White respondents generally rated Latinos as more untrustworthy, unintelligent, and less competent than Whites.

## PERPETUAL FOREIGNERS

Emerging from these data, the view of Latinos as not quite "real" Americans is one of the most common stereotypes. The overwhelming majority of Latinos surveyed reported being frequently asked "Where are you really from?" and being praised for their "good" English.

## LATINOS SHUT OUT POLITICALLY

The survey uncovered widespread prejudice, and so helps explain a major challenge facing Latinos in the U.S.: a political system that does not represent them well, and at times, targets them. Latinos now account for over 17% of the American population, and yet less than 9% of Members of Congress are Latino.

FIGURE 5.A1. Sample treatment in Hopkins et al. (2020)

# 6

# Galvanizing People of Color

When Professor Manning Marable trained the American public's attention on the rapid rise of people of color (PoC) in the early 1990s, he saw hidden in those demographics the glimmer of a political eventuality. The idea, lying in plain sight to him, was that demographic growth would ultimately be attended by political power, with PoC regularly acting in unison to achieve shared political, economic, and social goals. One of these objectives, for Marable at least, was attaining greater economic empowerment for minority communities. As he saw it:

> Civil rights organizations should become more aware of . . . patterns of African-American and Latino consumer spending. They should consider targeting White corporations which have heavy shares of minority consumer markets but which have done little or nothing to promote minority hiring or joint ventures. A reasonable share of such profits must be ploughed back into Hispanic and Black communities, and the managerial ranks of such firms must reflect ethnic and gender diversity. If such companies refuse to negotiate, the economic clout of minorities should be used to reward our genuine friends and to punish our enemies.

Marable's fiery words lay out a tactical blueprint for political action by PoC that, in theory, would seem to generalize across several issue domains. But this roadmap presumes that PoC already recognize who their genuine friends are and who are the enemies they must punish. While this may be true in some cases, it is unlikely in the realm of politics, where the demarcation between friend and foe is usually at the center of public battles. Indeed, when it comes to PoC, these political clashes typically entail racial and ethnic minorities determining who really counts as PoC and what PoC must reach for collectively. Hence, what Marable foresaw as ineluctable—the political galvanization of PoC—might be better viewed as highly variable and in need of theoretical clarification.

This is the principal business of the chapter at hand: to illuminate some of the conditions under which PoC ID becomes politically activated and consequential. To this end, I again reach back into social identity theory (SIT) to retrieve a concept that can illuminate the political galvanization of PoC: the notion of in-group threat. SIT suggests that individual group members vary incrementally, appreciably, and reliably in terms of how central a category is to their self-image, something clearly captured by the PoC ID measure I validated back in chapter 4. Along this continuum, individuals for whom a given category is highly central to their self-definition tend to be acutely sensitive to group-centered stimuli, especially of a negative or critical variety.

This basic insight suggests that high-identifying PoC should be especially responsive to threats directed at their shared in-group. But threats issued from whom and with what effects? This is a question of the threat's source. Given how heterogeneous PoC are, does it matter that a threat is communicated by one of their own—an in-group member—rather than by someone beyond the ranks of their group—for instance, an out-group member? The objective here is to ascertain whether political galvanization on the basis of threat is more effective when it is led internally by PoC, rather than externally by an out-group force.

In terms of the consequences of threat against PoC, SIT also suggests that the observed political pattern among PoC should be one of unity and uniformity. In the wake of threat to PoC, in-group members should express feelings, beliefs, and outlooks that broadly enhance the well-being of racial and ethnic minorities. In other words, irrespective of whether one is African American, Asian American, Latino, or a member of another racial or ethnic minority group, PoC will respond to in-group threat by making political decisions that promote the welfare of all PoC, regardless of whether the immediate beneficiaries of those choices are from one's own racial or ethnic in-group. Thus, in the heat of a threat issued to PoC, Asian Americans and Latinos will, for example, vigorously support the #BlackLivesMatter movement, while African Americans and Asian Americans will stand behind Latinos when opining about undocumented immigration. To paraphrase Marable, PoC will, in times of crisis, stand by their genuine friends.

This chapter presents the results of three large online experiments that test this anticipated interaction between in-group threat and PoC ID. Each of these studies—collectively dubbed the "Political Galvanization" experiments—randomly assigned 1,200 Black, 1,200 Asian, and 1,200 Latino adults to a control group with no information or one of two treatments issuing a threat to PoC. In one treatment, a minority spokesperson communicates a threat to minorities (i.e., "PoC are targets of racial intimidation, vandalism, and violence"). In the other treatment, a White supremacist issues a threat to minorities (i.e., "Whites are the target of racial intimidation, vandalism, and violence by PoC"). Since the study formally appraises individual differences in the strength of PoC ID among all participants, this general design puts me in a position to analyze when and which PoC react to these pronounced dangers to their shared in-group.

Consistent with Marable's intuition and SIT's insights, I find that stronger PoC ID levels shape minority support for policies that combat hate crimes, curb police brutality, and bolster voting rights—all domains that widely impact PoC. I also uncover that higher PoC ID levels heighten support for initiatives and policies that are more narrowly associated with specific minority groups, such as #BlackLivesMatter.

Thus, whether a policy proposal broadly affects all PoC or only some of them, high-identifying PoC firmly stand behind their peers. But I also uncover an unanticipated effect. Whether a threat to PoC is expressed by another minority or issued by a White nationalist—or whether a threat is issued at all—this difference between high- and low-identifiers emerges across experimental conditions. This pattern suggests it takes very little to politicize this motley group of racial and ethnic minorities that I call PoC, because this attachment is already highly accessible to racial and ethnic minorities in the US. Hence, although not as inevitable as Marable assumed, these results imply that the political galvanization of PoC might be easier and smoother than what their diverse ranks imply.

### The Interplay between Identity and Threat

To more fully appreciate the hypothesized dynamic between PoC ID and in-group threat at the core of this chapter, it is useful to rehearse here some of what SIT and its offshoots teach us about this general relationship (Tajfel and Turner 1979; Turner et al. 1987). The theory maintains that all people—not just those of color—are motivated to uphold a positive self-image, which they achieve, in part, by ensuring that their in-group(s) compares favorably with sundry out-group(s) (Tajfel and Turner 1986). But this positive differentiation is not an innate group trait. Alas, "social context . . . determines the evaluative flavor of any . . . group" (Ellemers, Spears, and Doosje 2002: 165).

In the racial and ethnic landscape of the US, the evaluative flavor of PoC is conditioned by its lower position in America's racial hierarchy—a hierarchy where non-Hispanic Whites are still the larger and predominant racial group

(Jardina 2019; see also Knowles and Lowery 2011; Lowery, Knowles, and Unzueta 2007; Unzueta and Lowery 2008). Nevertheless, although PoC share a lower station in America's racial order, this does not necessarily mean they internalize or endorse the devalued status implied by their lower rank—quite the contrary. As chapter 4's in-depth interviews demonstrate, racial and ethnic minorities see in PoC a source of pride, a badge of honor, and a point of celebration—all stemming from the fact that they are racially and ethnically different and outside the (White) mainstream (Brewer 1991).

This process, known as *social creativity*, in which individuals rearrange the terms of comparison between their in-group and an out-group, enables PoC to draw that sense of self-worth *despite the objectively lower rank of racial and ethnic minorities*. Indeed, by converting into strengths the reputed negative attributes of minorities, PoC are generally able to draw that sense of self-worth that SIT says is so important.

This is the positive distinctiveness that is at stake when PoC encounter a threat—that is, any potential dragging-down of the otherwise positive worth that individual racial and ethnic minorities attach to this broadly shared category. Here, SIT also provides some guidance in terms of what we should expect when the positive worth of an in-group is undermined. In particular, SIT explains *when* and among *whom* we should expect a reaction to in-group threat. If an identity enhances self-regard, then a stimulus undermining this process will jeopardize the positive worth group members attach to an identity. In light of in-group threat, SIT predicts that high-identifying members will bolster the imperiled group (Ellemers, Spears, and Doosje 2002), which social and political research firmly establishes (cf. Ellemers 2001; Ellemers, Spears, and Doosje 1997; Leach et al. 2008, 2010; Pérez 2015a, b). This means individual differences in PoC ID are crucial to its political impact, with higher levels yielding evaluations that potentially improve PoC's well-being. It also means that in the wake of threat, high-identifying PoC will judge politics in a way that bolsters racial minorities' general welfare.

Figure 6.1 depicts the intuition behind this hypothesis. On the y-axis, we have a hypothetical outcome: expressed solidarity with PoC. As Leach and his associates explain it, solidarity is an "investment of the self in coordinated activity with those to whom one feels committed" (2010: 147). As a situational feature of intergroup life, solidarity is highly variable and likely to spike when an in-group (e.g., PoC) is under threat—that is, precisely when an in-group is in distress and needs individual members to invest in its rescue. Thus, we should expect expressions of solidarity to surge in light of threat.

This is where the x-axis come in. Each of the quantities in figure 6.1 depicts the effect of PoC ID on expressed solidarity with PoC in the absence of

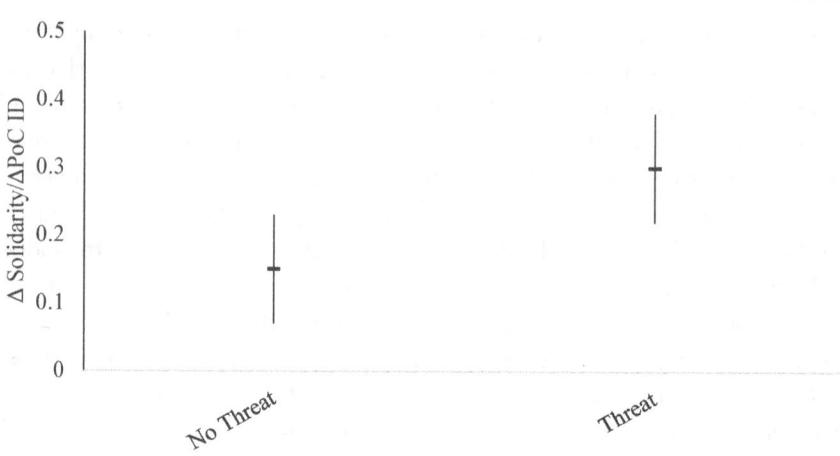

FIGURE 6.1. PoC ID heightens solidarity with PoC under threat

threat or in the presence of threat to PoC, with 95% confidence bands around each estimate. The clear break between both point estimates captures the essential point of my two-part hypothesis: in both conditions, higher PoC ID levels boost expressed solidarity with PoC. However, in light of threat to PoC, that positive association should grow in strength: an indication that a sense of threat to PoC propels PoC to manifest more solidarity with their peers. Let us turn to the actual test of this expectation.

## The "Political Galvanization" Experiments

To assess my two-pronged hypothesis, I administered three concurrent survey experiments on African American, Asian American, and Latino adults—what I dub the "Political Galvanization" experiments. These experiments were embedded in the "People of Color" surveys I analyzed back in chapter 4. Recall that after consenting to participate, respondents briefly reported some demographic data, followed by batteries of three to four items appraising one's racial identity, national identity, and—most important for our purposes here—one's identification as a PoC. Each of these identities was assessed with statements on Likert scales from 1 = "strongly disagree" to 7 = "strongly agree." Specifically, respondents expressed degree of agreement with assertions like "Being a person of color is a major part of how I see myself," "In general, identifying as [Black/Asian/Latino] is central to who I am as an individual," and "Identifying as American is crucial to my self-image" (cf. Leach et al. 2008). For all item wordings, please see the appendix to this chapter.

## DISTRACTER TASK AND MANIPULATION

After these statements were completed, all respondents participated in a distracter task right before the actual experiment. This activity directed respondents to count the number of dots appearing on their screens, with participants completing four such exercises. After this personally involving task, respondents were randomly assigned to one of three conditions: (1) a control group with no information, (2) a condition in which a minority spokesperson (matched to one's race) communicated a threat to PoC, or (3) a condition in which a White nationalist communicated a threat against PoC. Table 6.1 details the two treatments.

A perusal of these treatments reveals that both aim to heighten a sense of threat against PoC by connecting specific racial minorities (i.e., Asians, Blacks, and Latinos) to this category. Moreover, each treatment, in its own way, places the general well-being of PoC in danger. The main difference between these conditions boils down to the source of the threat, and by extension, the nature of the reaction it implies among racial and ethnic minorities who more strongly identify as PoC. In particular, the in-group treatment depicts a PoC communicating a threat against fellow PoC. This individual, matched to one's own racial/ethnic group, highlights a variety of challenges that minorities face as a result of systemic racism against PoC. In this message, the source also prescribes a way to buoy PoC in light of this threat: namely, that PoC should come together, proactively, to politically push back against these racist currents.

In contrast, participants in the out-group condition are exposed to a threat communicated, externally, by a White supremacist—a resoundingly clear

TABLE 6.1. Wording for PoC treatments

| *In-group treatment* | *Out-group treatment* |
|---|---|
| **A large group of Black, Asian American, and Latino leaders** met in Washington, D.C. a few days ago to discuss common challenges facing their communities. **James Washington, a Black leader in attendance and spokesperson for the assembled group**, explained to reporters: "People of color must recognize that racism is still alive in the United States. I'm talking about Blacks, Asians, Latinos—*all* people of color. Our communities are increasingly the target of racial intimidation, vandalism, and even violence. It's 2018. This cannot stand any longer! We must come together to end this hate toward us." | **A large group of white nationalists** met in Washington, D.C. a few days ago to discuss common challenges facing their communities. **James Miller, one of the attendees and spokesperson for the assembled group**, explained to reporters: "Whites must recognize the dangers of too much diversity in the United States. I'm talking about Blacks, Asians, Latinos—*all* people of color. White communities are increasingly the target of racial intimidation, vandalism, and even violence by people of color. It's 2018. This cannot stand any longer! Whites must come together to end this hate toward us." |

out-group member. This source, too, places the well-being of PoC in danger, but by contending that PoC are the source of some of his group's trials and tribulations. Hence, the prescribed response for PoC in this condition is for them to be reactive, rather than proactive—that is, to scramble together to prop their pan-racial group against the mobilization of White supremacists. This sharp contrast between treatments should enable me to judge the degree to which threat to PoC ID depends on the source communicating it.

### BOLSTERING POC

The prediction following from SIT is that in light of threat to PoC, members of distinct racial and ethnic minorities—particularly those who more strongly identify as such—should rally behind their shared pan-racial group. To appraise the extent to which this wall of support is erected by PoC, I had participants report two varieties of opinions following their assignment to experimental condition. These are the same outcomes I described and analyzed in chapter 4, so I simply refer to them here by name. The first class of outcomes gauges the extent to which individual PoC feel a strong sense of affinity and bond with fellow PoC and their presumed allies, as manifested in their expressed *solidarity with* PoC, *favorability toward* PoC *(relative to Whites)*, and *favorability toward Democrats (relative to Republicans)*. The anticipated bond with and rallying behind PoC should also manifest in support for policies that broadly impact and benefit members of this shared pan-racial group. To this end, I evaluate my experiments' effects on *policies broadly impacting minorities*, which includes support for stronger *voting rights*, limiting *police brutality*, and combating *hate crimes*. These are issue areas in which members of most or all minority groups stand to make gains or see their general well-being improve. For example, reinforcing voting rights advances the general welfare of most racial and ethnic minorities. Similarly, curbing police brutality improves the general safety and security of many racial and ethnic minority communities. All minority groups, moreover, stand to reap the rewards of combating hate crimes against non-White communities. Finally, I also appraise my experiments' impact on *support for policies narrowly impacting minorities*–issue domains that are more narrowly associated with a specific minority group. For example, regardless of one's personal take about the #BlackLivesMatter, this movement is explicitly linked to African Americans. In a similar vein, I reason, the issue of undocumented immigration is more narrowly associated with Latinos, while the realm of legal immigration is more strongly linked to Asian Americans. Hence, I expect that an activated sense of PoC ID will lead racial and ethnic minorities to increase their support for #BlackLivesMatter, boost their endorsement of Deferred Action for Childhood Arrivals (DACA), and strengthen backing for visas for legal immigrants.

## The Galvanization of PoC

Under what circumstances does identifying as a PoC become politically relevant? My theoretical framework anticipates that direct threats to PoC should activate PoC ID, thus leading it to have political effects on minority individuals.

Recall that to test this activation prediction, I designed an experiment where minority individuals were randomly assigned to a control group with no information or one of two conditions emitting a threat to PoC. The main difference between these latter two treatments boils down to whether this threat is communicated by a member of the in-group (i.e., a Black, Asian, or Latino leader) or a member of an out-group (a White nationalist leader). Per my activation hypothesis, I expect that relative to the control group, PoC ID should have a larger impact in each of the treatment conditions. This pattern would imply that each form of threat can activate this identity and make it more influential among various minority groups.

This set of expectations can be directly tested via interactive analyses, in which each treatment is multiplied by respondent's level of PoC ID, while holding constant individual differences in racial identity, American identity, and ideology. This empirical strategy has two advantages, as outlined by Kam and Trussler (2016). The first is that, since PoC ID is not randomly assigned, its moderating influence on the treatments can be better isolated with respect to other key predispositions that are related to PoC ID and the outcomes in focus. The second benefit is that any variation in our outcomes that is explained by PoC ID and its interactions with each treatment is purged of the influence that these other key predispositions might have in shaping each outcome. In order to facilitate interpretation of these interactive analyses, figure 6.2 displays the marginal of effect of PoC ID for each experimental condition by outcome and racial group (The appendix explains and reports these interactive results in detail).

## PoC ID, Threat, and Minority Politics

Careful perusal of figure 6.2's patterns reveals two dominant patterns. First, for Blacks, Asians, and Latinos, the effect of PoC ID in the control condition is generally substantial, positive, and reliable. That is, in the absence of any

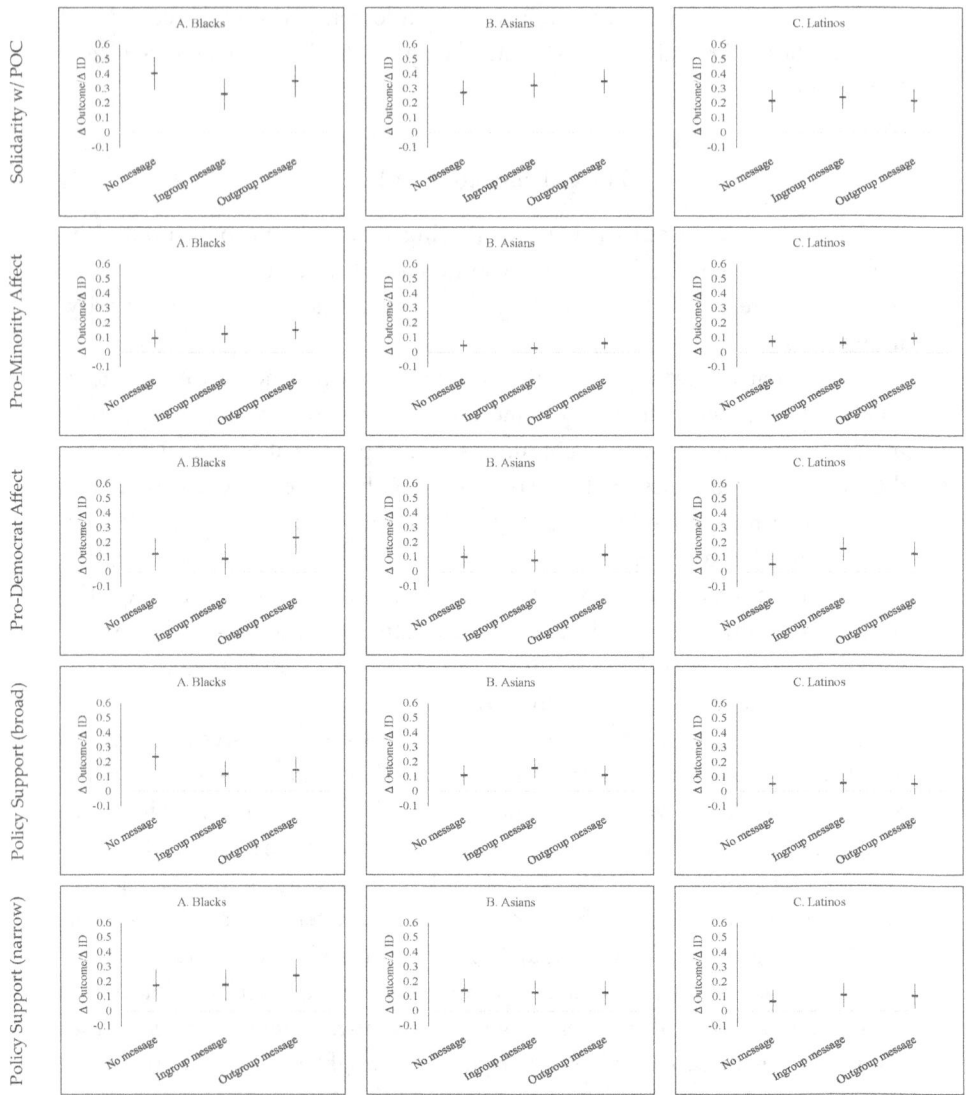

FIGURE 6.2. Activation of PoC ID and its effects on social and political opinions
Note: OLS estimates. Panels display marginal effects of PoC ID across experimental condition by racial group (with 95% confidence intervals). For each panel, $N = 1,200$. Models include racial identity, American identity, and liberal ideology as covariates.

prompting, higher levels of PoC ID reliably and substantially impact each of the outcomes under question—and among each of the racial and ethnic minority groups under investigation. More specifically, higher levels of PoC ID in the control group heighten solidarity with PoC, pro-minority sentiment, pro-Democrat feelings, support for policies broadly affecting minorities, and even support for policies narrowly impacting some minorities, with most of these effects ranging between 10 and 20 percentage points—a nontrivial amount. What is more, this general pattern is manifested by all PoC under examination. Irrespective of whether one is Black, Asian, or Latino, the more central the category PoC is to a person's self-definition, the more they display this general trend of bolstering this pan-racial group.

Given that this hearty pattern is displayed in the absence of any prompting and independently of other key forms of attachment, these results suggest that PoC ID is already a fairly accessible form of identity for members of all three minority groups under analysis. Indeed, consistent with this claim, the effects of PoC ID hardly budge when Blacks, Asians, and Latinos are exposed to messages that threaten this attachment; and if they do budge, they fail to do so in a statistically reliable way, as evidenced by the general overlap in the confidence intervals attending these estimates in each panel. There are two ways to interpret this lack of interaction between PoC ID and treatments. The first is that these treatments, in particular, fail to further heighten the association between PoC ID and each of the outcomes under investigation. This is a fair criticism, but only up to a point. Remember, the treatments here are unabashedly clear about the stakes involved for PoC: "we" face a collection of threats, tied to systemic racism, that "we" can beat back only by coming together as a unified force.

The fact that PoC ID levels don't have a stronger impact on the political views of PoC in light of such strong and direct threats suggests a different question: why are PoC ID levels already so mentally accessible for racial and ethnic minorities? In the next section, I provide further answers about this unanticipated pattern. But first, let me speak further about the other empirical pattern I hypothesized about.

Recall that part of my reasoning about PoC ID implied that, regardless of experimental condition, the impact of this attachment is such that it produces a homogeneous pattern of opinions among disparate racial and ethnic minority groups. This is indeed what the various panels in figure 6.2 seem to indicate. That is, insofar as PoC ID is a highly accessible attachment among racial and ethnic minorities, this pattern is more similar than dissimilar for all three PoC groups under analysis. This matters because one of the central claims of this book is that when PoC ID is mentally activated among PoC, it should produce judgments and evaluations that generally enhance the well-being of racial and ethnic minorities.

The visual evidence in figure 6.2 is highly consistent with this claim. Looking across the panels, it is difficult to detect a consistent pattern of disjointedness or meaningful differences of opinion between African Americans, Asian Americans, and Latinos. Indeed, the general pattern is one of uniformity of feelings, opinions, and beliefs on the basis of one's PoC ID. Most impressive here, perhaps, is the fact that such homogeneity of opinion emerges across domains where all racial and ethnic minorities are implicated (e.g., strengthening voting rights) as well as domains in which only a specific minority group is the focus (e.g., support for #BlackLivesMatter). Taken together, then, these layers of evidence bolster the inference that PoC ID serves to narrow differences of opinion among diverse racial groups in the United States.

## But Why Is PoC ID So Accessible? Obama, Trump, and a Resurgent Racial Politics

Although unanticipated, the highly accessible nature of PoC ID among racial and ethnic minorities demands further explanation. While I cannot rule out definitively that the absence of an interaction between PoC ID levels and the treatments in this study arise from these particular manipulations being relatively ineffective, I will suggest here that a more comprehensive answer might have to do with the "nature of the times" as it concerns US racial politics.

The astute reader will recall that the "Political Galvanization" experiments were administered online during February 2018, a little over one year after Donald Trump had been inaugurated President of the United States. Candidate Trump was iconoclastic when it came to norms of public discussions surrounding race and ethnicity. Throughout his campaign, he publicly and vociferously derided, derogated, or outright devalued a variety of racial and ethnic minority groups, including Latinos, African Americans, and Muslim Americans. Indeed, he launched his campaign with a vitriolic attack on Mexicans as "drug dealers" and "rapists" (e.g., Farris and Silber Mohammed 2018; Silber Mohammed and Farris 2019). Candidate Trump continued this type of discourse as he transitioned to his role as President Trump, except his rhetoric was matched by exclusionary policies and initiatives, including an attempted ban on Muslim immigrants and intensified efforts to arrest and deport undocumented (mostly Latino) immigrants (e.g., Collingwood, Lajevardi, and Oskooii 2018). The virulence of Trump's anti-minority rhetoric and policy proposals suggests that perhaps, just perhaps, levels of PoC ID have increased and become generally accessible for racial and ethnic minorities as a result. That is, Trump's regular focus on racial and ethnic minorities has encouraged them to more regularly think of themselves broadly as PoC, thus boosting their baseline levels of this form of identity.

But Trump is not the only visible politician who in recent memory has made racial politics salient. Immediately preceding him was President Barack Obama: America's first African American president (Tesler 2016; Tesler and Sears 2010). One of Obama's foci, too, was racial and ethnic minorities. Yet his emphasis and logic were different. If it can be said that Donald Trump has used racial and ethnic minorities—and their alleged shortcomings—to politically mobilize some White Americans, then Barack Obama relied on racial and ethnic minorities in a more affirmative sense as a way to build a broader electoral coalition that cut across various racial and ethnic minority groups. His public statements lamenting the fatal shootings of Black youth by police officers (Lee 2016), his efforts at incorporating undocumented immigrant youth through policy revisions (Shear 2014), his assemblage of a presidential cabinet that reflected the racial and ethnic diversity of the United States (Moseley 2017)—these and other signature moves underscore the very real possibility that, when it comes to racial and ethnic minorities, President Obama also helped increase the general accessibility of PoC ID among them, making it harder to heighten it further in the short run.

Insofar as this reasoning about Obama, Trump, and racial rhetoric is correct, it implies that the mental accessibility of the category, PoC, has grown in consequence. As a result, even in the control condition of my experiment, where PoC ID is not prompted, this pan-racial attachment should already have a reliable and meaningful association with outcomes of interest, just as we observed in figure 6.2.

Hence, any treatment to activate PoC ID further—that is, to make it more accessible—is more likely than not to fail due to this "pretreatment" of charged racial rhetoric. As Jamie Druckman and Thomas Leeper (2012: 875) explain it, when an "experiment explores a communication that regularly occurs in 'reality,' then reactions in the experiment might be contaminated by those 'regular' occurrences prior to the experiment." In the case of PoC ID, the regular flow of rhetoric around racial and ethnic minorities could have made this identity more accessible to non-White individuals *prior to* my experiment, which means that another single exposure to this general class of discourse—no matter how strong—is unlikely to activate PoC ID even further.

This sounds plausible, I think, but how can we assess, rather than merely speculate, that this reasoning is correct? The fundamental challenge here is that PoC ID—the very construct in whose trajectory over time we are interested in—has only been measured since 2018, when I first validated my PoC ID

TABLE 6.2. Number of PoC cases in ANES samples by year and race/ethnicity

|  | 1992 | 2000 | 2002 | 2004 | 2008 | 2012 | 2016 |
|---|---|---|---|---|---|---|---|
| Blacks | 253 | 139 | 106 | 146 | 470 | 951 | 333 |
| Latinos | 171 | 99 | 75 | 90 | 437 | 913 | 351 |
| Asians | — | — | — | — | — | 81 | 113 |

Note: Entries represent minimum number of available cases for analysis of feeling thermometer ratings of African Americans, Asian Americans, and Latinos.

scale (see chapter 5). Thus, we have a firm sense of what PoC ID looks like after Obama, and in the wake of Trump, but no sense of how it may have evolved before then. Without a measure that allows us an look over time at PoC ID, we are left unable to further address the idea of pretreatment and its implications for the "Political Galvanization" experiments.

Perhaps. But there are, even in social science, various ways to skin a cat, so to speak. While there is simply no way to go back in time to administer my PoC ID measure, there is a way to proxy for this attachment in order to track its longitudinal course, even if crudely. What we need for this task is a measure that, while not PoC ID itself, is substantially correlated with it. To this end, I draw on the cumulative file of the American National Election Studies (ANES), focusing on its African American, Latino, and Asian American respondents and their feeling thermometer ratings of African Americans, Asian Americans, and Latinos. These thermometer ratings invite ANES respondents to use a 0 to 101 scale to rate how "warm" or "favorable" they feel toward a social or political group, in this case, a specific racial or ethnic minority in the US.

The virtue of these ratings is that, when scaled together, they form a valid gauge of the positive affect toward PoC that non-White individuals feel, which chapter 5 taught us is robustly correlated with PoC ID. Seizing on this insight, I utilize data for African American, Asian American, and Latino respondents in the ANES for all years when the three relevant feeling thermometer ratings were administered (1992–2016). Of course, the main challenge with ANES data, as scholars of racial and ethnic politics are well aware, is that the number of Black, Asian, and Latino respondents in any one yearly cross-section of the ANES pales in comparison to non-Hispanic Whites, who predominate these samples. I therefore restrict the following analysis to all yearly samples in which the number of each non-White group hovers around 100. This yields analyzable samples for multiple years, as displayed in table 6.2.

The first step in this exercise involves verifying that a scale of favorability toward PoC correlates positively, substantially, and reliably with my PoC ID scale. To this end, I reach back into my "People of Color" surveys (conducted in 2018) to create two valid and reliable scales. The first of these indices is comprised of three indicators: favorability toward Blacks, Asian Americans, and Latinos. The second of these is my scale of PoC ID. Pooling across surveys and minority respondents, I factor analyze these items, anticipating the emergence of two substantive variables: favorability toward PoC and identification as a PoC. The virtue of factor analyzing these data is that we obtain an estimate of the correlation between these two constructs that is free of random and systematic measurement error.

The appendix contains the relevant results. The main takeaway is that this analysis yields a correlation of $r = .41$, $p < .01$, two-tailed, between our scale of favorability toward PoC and our scale of identity as a PoC. This is a substantial association between two distinct concepts. Indeed, in the absence of any conceptual knowledge, we might even be tempted to conclude that both types of items are capturing something in common. Alas, we do have that conceptual knowledge, which informs us that robust correlation notwithstanding, feelings toward PoC are not conceptually identical to identifying as a PoC (cf. Wong 2010). There are at least two reasons for this distinction. First, group identification involves recognition of one's membership in a group, as well as the emotional significance one attaches to this membership—it is the thoughts and feelings that one appends to group membership (Tajfel 1981). In contrast, favorability toward a group involves, more strictly, feelings toward a group.

This affect is less tethered to one's membership in a group. Indeed, one can have positive feelings toward a group without identifying with a group. For example, some Whites can feel sympathy toward African Americans (Chudy 2019), yet we do not conclude from these feelings that Whites *identify* with and as Blacks. Second, empirically speaking, although feelings toward PoC are more variable and liable to change, identification as a PoC is relatively more stable and more resistant to dramatic changes (Leach et al. 2008). Thus, I take this correlation between both concepts as evidence that feelings toward PoC is a reasonable and conservative proxy for PoC ID, which permits a look back in time at its evolution.

Figure 6.3 provides us this temporal peek. There we see displayed the average correlation between feelings of Blacks, Asians, and Latinos for each of the racial/ethnic minority groups under investigation. The idea behind this operationalization is as follows. Over time, insofar as PoC see themselves as a pan-racial category, as PoC ID implies, their positive feelings toward each other should increase and become more tightly interwoven. According to this logic, two major patterns should stand out from figure 6.3. The

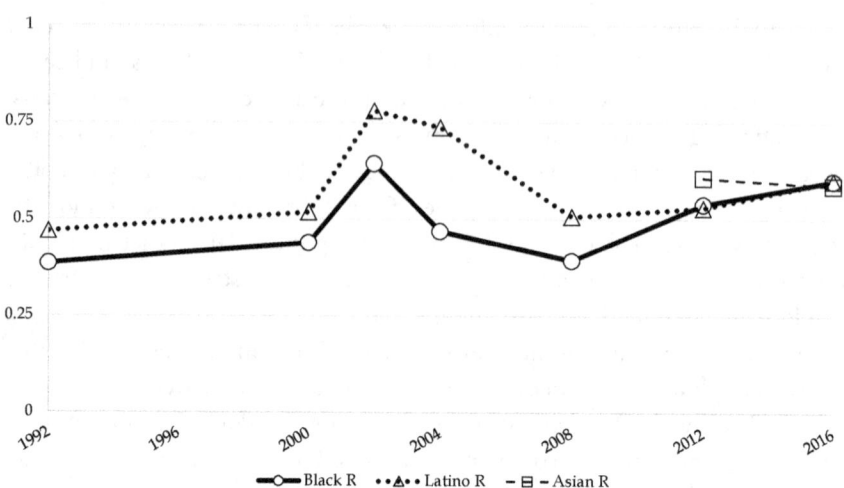

FIGURE 6.3. Average interitem correlation between thermometer ratings of Asians, Blacks, and Latinos by year and respondent race (R)

first involves the steep ascent in association between interminority feelings for most of the racial/ethnic groups under analysis. Consider the trend line for African Americans. Whereas the average association between their feelings toward their group and other minorities comes in at a respectable $r = .39$ in 1992, this association increases to .60 by 2016. This growing interlacing of feelings toward PoC among African Americans is consistent with my stylized description of racial politics in the wake of Obama's and Trump's presidencies, implying that levels of PoC ID are probably already heightened and thus chronically accessible. But there is also another descriptive lesson here: this tightening affective bond between PoC predates both Obama and Trump, suggesting that they perhaps have cemented it rather than caused it.

Further inspection of the figure reveals that African Americans are not unique in their warming feelings toward PoC. The trend line for Latinos displays a pattern that is similar in thrust and scope to the one revealed by African Americans. Whereas the average correlation between positive feelings toward Blacks, Latinos, and Asians among Latinos starts at $r = .47$, this association climbs to around $r = .55$ by 2016. Given the relatively smaller samples of Latinos, I have less confidence in the numerical estimate of interitem correlation over time, but I am confident in the direction and change over time in these quantities, which suggest a general increase in the interlacing of one's feelings toward PoC, broadly.

And what about Asian Americans? Although their numbers are too paltry to permit a credible analysis extending back to 1992 (see table 6.2), their raw numbers in 2012 and 2016 allow some provisional insights. In particular, figure 6.3 shows that in these two years, the average correlation between Asian Americans' feelings toward Blacks, Latinos, and Asians approximate those of Latinos. Thus, while we cannot observe well the trajectory of this intertwining, we can say that within the sample at hand, the available trends for Asian Americans are not entirely discrepant relative to the other racial and ethnic minorities under analysis.

The bottom line, then, when considering this analysis as well as my earlier experimental results, is twofold. First, high-identifying PoC appear inclined to support policy proposals and initiatives that enhance the general well-being of their peers, irrespective of whether these efforts broadly affect all PoC or just some of its constituent groups. This support manifests itself in a robust and uniform way across various PoC groups. Second, at least in contemporary times, racial minorities' sense of identification as a PoC is a chronically accessible form of identity, easily called to mind to influence the type of political judgments and decisions that have repercussions for racial and ethnic minorities writ large.

## Lessons Learned and Next Steps

The United States is poised to soon become a majority-minority nation. Indeed, in states like California and Hawaii, this demographic trend is already reality (US Census Bureau 2018). There are many implications for racial and ethnic minorities who are awash in this sea of diversity. But the one I have highlighted here is that they now face a stronger incentive to identify as PoC—that is, to forge a new identity under the banner of being non-White. Identifying as PoC, I contend, enables members of disparate racial minorities to unify and collectively mobilize to enhance their general welfare by focusing on shared grievances. Across a trio of survey experiments, I uncovered evidence establishing that PoC ID is a highly accessible attachment that leads to robust and uniform support for political efforts that broadly benefit distinct racial and ethnic minority groups.

Several implications flow from these results, but perhaps one of the more important ones concerns the mechanisms sustaining the collective action of diverse racial groups. The literature on racial and ethnic coalition building in the US stiffly challenges the assumption that minorities have interests and aspirations that "naturally" align with each other, as Marable's opening epigraph implies (cf. McClain and Johnson Carew 2017). Instead, this literature demonstrates that it takes much active effort, strategizing, and persuasion to unify and politically mobilize these motley individuals (cf. Benjamin 2017; Jones-Correa, Wallace, and Zepeda-Millán 2016; McClain and Karnig 1990). My results here continue in this longer and distinguished tradition by further backing out of this seeming unity of minority groups and demonstrating that a greater sense of commonality among them is sometimes underpinned by a shared sense of *identity* that can be called to mind by politics. My findings therefore suggest that greater political unison among Blacks, Asians, Latinos, and other minorities arises—not because each distinct group sacrifices its own ambitions for the sake of a greater whole—but because members of highly heterogeneous groups sometimes see themselves as belonging to the same collective, replete with its own set of overlapping grievances and hopes. In this way, my work throws new light on just how complex racial minorities are in terms of the identities they choose at different moments in politics.

But perhaps the larger implication of my analyses in these chapters is the degree to which one's identification as a PoC is a mentally accessible and politically powerful attachment. My experimental results suggest that PoC ID's activation requires minimal sparking because this attachment is already highly accessible. While this pattern was unanticipated on my part, it is not completely unexplained. As my analyses over time of ANES data suggest, the generally accessible nature of PoC ID among racial and ethnic minorities is a pattern that appears to have been affirmed by the more race-centered politics of the Obama and Trump presidencies. Thus, while both presidents did not cause or even necessarily ride a wave of PoC ID fervor into office, their race-rich discourse has served to forge a stronger and more consistent connection between identifying as a PoC and expressing political views and outlooks that broadly benefit all racial and ethnic minorities.

At this point, it might be tempting to infer from these results that PoC ID matters all the time in politics. But such a conclusion would be both premature and misaligned with the theoretical framework guiding this chapter, which expects PoC ID to rise (and fall) in its political influence. Having found that PoC ID is already quite accessible in the minds of racial and ethnic minorities, it might instead make more sense to consider what kinds of political conditions can break down this activation. That is, if PoC ID is highly salient among racial and ethnic minorities, what type of conditions might *reduce* its impact in politics? To be sure, some scholars might consider this approach normatively undesirable; yet clarifying the conditions under which PoC ID becomes less politically relevant for minorities would deepen our knowledge about the limits of this new identity, while allowing us to more fully appreciate the diversity of racial minorities in American society. That is the express goal of the next, and last, empirical chapter in this book.

## APPENDIX

### Question Wordings

You will now be asked your opinions about some social groups you may identify with. These are people who may be like you in their ideas and interests and feelings about things. Please respond to each statement by indicating how much you agree or disagree with it.

#### RACIAL IDENTITY

Overall, being [Black/Asian/Latino] is important to my sense of what kind of person I am.
In general, identifying as [Black/Asian/Latino] is central to who I am as an individual.
I feel good about being [Black/Asian/Latino].

1. Strongly disagree
2. Disagree
3. Somewhat disagree
4. Neither agree or disagree
5. Somewhat agree
6. Agree
7. Strongly agree

#### PERSON OF COLOR IDENTITY

The fact that I am a person of color is an important part of my identity.
Being a person of color is a major part of how I see myself.
I often think about the fact that I am a person of color.
I am glad to be a person of color.

1. Strongly disagree
2. Disagree
3. Somewhat disagree
4. Neither agree or disagree
5. Somewhat agree
6. Agree
7. Strongly agree

## AMERICAN IDENTITY

Generally, being American is important to who I am as an individual.
Identifying as American is crucial to my self-image.
Being American gives me a good feeling.

1. Strongly disagree
2. Disagree
3. Somewhat disagree
4. Neither agree or disagree
5. Somewhat agree
6. Agree
7. Strongly agree

## OUTCOMES

In the next section, you will read statements about some ideas that Congress is working on. Using the response options provided, please indicate how much you oppose or support each idea.

Combat Hate Crimes

- Providing harsher penalties for hate crimes.
- Improving hate crime reporting and data collection.

Strengthen Voting Rights

- Strengthening federal laws to protect voting rights.
- Requiring all states to automatically register eligible adults to vote.

Curb Police Brutality

- Setting stricter criteria for the use of deadly force by police officers.
- Limiting police officers' ability to engage in racial profiling.

1. Strongly oppose
2. Oppose
3. Somewhat oppose
4. Neither oppose, nor support
5. Somewhat support
6. Support
7. Strongly support

Support #BlackLivesMatter

- Limiting the protest activities of #BlackLivesMatter and other movements like it.

Support DACA

- Renewing temporary relief from deportation for undocumented immigrants brought to the US as children.

Support Legal Immigration

- Increasing the number of visas available to legal immigrants.

1. Strongly oppose
2. Oppose
3. Somewhat oppose
4. Neither oppose, nor support
5. Somewhat support
6. Support
7. Strongly support

### FEELING THERMOMETER RATINGS

Next, please use the scale provided to indicate how favorable or unfavorable you feel toward the following groups or individuals.

Asians
Blacks
Latinos
Whites
Democrats
Republicans

1. Very unfavorable
2. Unfavorable
3. Somewhat favorable
4. Neither unfavorable nor favorable
5. Somewhat favorable
6. Favorable
7. Very favorable

## SOLIDARITY WITH PEOPLE OF COLOR

You are nearing the end of the survey. Please reply to the statements below using the response options provided.

I feel solidarity with people of color.
People of color have a lot in common with each other.

1. Strongly disagree
2. Disagree
3. Somewhat disagree
4. Neither agree or disagree
5. Somewhat agree
6. Agree
7. Strongly agree

### Explanation and Reporting of Interactive Results from Experimental Analyses by Racial Group

These analyses are the basis of the results depicted in figure 6.4, in which I examine the extent to which threats to PoC ID activate this attachment among Blacks, Asians, and Latinos. To this end, I interact each of my two experimental conditions with levels of PoC ID (with the control group as the baseline condition). Since PoC ID is observed, rather than manipulated, I follow the advice of Kam and Trussler (2016) by including levels of racial identity, American identity, and liberal ideology as covariates.

The results in the following tables generally suggest that significant interactions between treatment(s) and levels of PoC ID are sparse. Indeed, a series of block $F$-tests further confirm this by suggesting that it is generally difficult to reject the null hypotheses that the interactions in each regression are indistinguishable from zero. This general absence of substantively and statistically significant interactions indicates a lack of activation relative to the control groups. In fact, for most outcomes under analysis, the impact of PoC ID is both meaningful and reliable at conventional levels, further suggesting that PoC ID is already a highly accessible attachment.

TABLE 6.A1. PoC ID generally predicts support for minority-oriented policy regardless of message: Black respondents

| | Solidarity w/ PoC | Pro-minority affect | Pro-Democrat affect | Strengthen voting rights | Curb police brutality | Combat hate crimes |
|---|---|---|---|---|---|---|
| PoC ID | .406** (.056) | .098** (.030) | .122** (.055) | .254** (.064) | .163** (.064) | .293** (.066) |
| PoC ID × in-group | −.024** (.011) | .028 (.037) | −.033 (.067) | −.025* (.013) | −.012 (.013) | −.021 (.014) |
| PoC ID × out-group | −.001 (.069) | .055 (.037) | .110 (.068) | −.017 (.074) | .004 (.014) | −.031* (.015) |
| In-group message | .152** (.065) | −.023 (.035) | .055 (.064) | .154** (.078) | .086 (.079) | .141 (.087) |
| Out-group message | .065 (.067) | −.056 (.036) | −.088 (.066) | .108 (.083) | −.017 (.086) | .156* (.086) |
| Racial ID | .207** (.036) | .057** (.020) | .092** (.036) | .086** (.040) | .129** (.040) | .048 (.039) |
| American ID | .029 (.024) | −.135** (.013) | .030 (.023) | .170** (.029) | −.057* (.024) | .066** (.027) |
| Liberal | .073** (.020) | .028** (.011) | .213** (.020) | .125** (.023) | .158** (.022) | .172** (.024) |
| Constant | .156** (.042) | .496** (.023) | .372** (.042) | .332** (.052) | .573** (.050) | .413** (.054) |
| $R^2$ | .257 | .150 | .169 | .144 | .123 | .130 |
| Interactions = 0? | $F(2, 1,911) = 2.33$, Prob > F = .098 | $F(2, 1,191) = 1.07$, Prob > F = .342 | $F(2, 1,191) = 2.50$, Prob > F = .083 | $F(2, 1,191) = 1.85$, Prob > F = .158 | $F(2, 1,191) = .67$, Prob > F = .509 | $F(2, 1,191) = 2.38$, Prob > F = .093 |

TABLE 6.A2. PoC ID generally predicts support for minority-oriented policy regardless of message: Black respondents

| | Support #BlackLivesMatter | Increase visas | Support DACA | Omnibus scale, broad | Omnibus scale, narrow |
|---|---|---|---|---|---|
| PoC ID | .236** (.092) | .106 (.083) | .186** (.082) | .237** (.045) | .176** (.056) |
| PoC ID × in-group | −.011 (.018) | .101 (.100) | −.027 (.099) | −.019* (.009) | .001 (.011) |
| PoC ID × out-group | .000 (.019) | .208** (.102) | −.011 (.101) | −.015 (.009) | .011 (.012) |
| In-group message | .069 (.107) | −.060 (.097) | .055 (.095) | .127** (.053) | .021 (.065) |
| Out-group message | −.002 (.109) | −.178* (.099) | .006 (.097) | .083 (.054) | −.058 (.067) |
| Racial ID | .151** (.059) | .083 (.054) | .088* (.053) | .088** (.029) | .107** (.036) |
| American ID | −.156** (.039) | −.142** (.035) | .011 (.035) | .060 (.191) | −.096** (.024) |
| Liberal | .219** (.033) | .132** (.030) | .157** (.030) | .152** (.016) | .169** (.020) |
| Constant | .389** (.069) | .522** (.063) | .414** (.062) | .439** (.034) | .442** (.042) |
| $R^2$ | .097 | .072 | .067 | .190 | .157 |
| Interactions = 0? | $F(2, 1,911) = .24$, Prob > F = .790 | $F(2, 1,191) = 2.06$, Prob > F = .128 | $F(2, 1,191) = .04$, Prob > F = .963 | $F(2, 1,191) = 2.43$, Prob > F = .089 | $F(2, 1,191) = .59$, Prob > F = .552 |

TABLE 6.A3. PoC ID generally predicts support for minority-oriented policy regardless of message: Asian respondents

|  | Solidarity with PoC | Pro-minority affect | Pro-Democrat affect | Strengthen voting rights | Curb police brutality | Combat hate crimes |
|---|---|---|---|---|---|---|
| PoC ID | .273** (.043) | .048** (.019) | .100** (.039) | .140** (.048) | .157** (.049) | .040 (.041) |
| PoC ID × in-group | .008 (.009) | -.003 (.004) | -.004 (.008) | .011 (.010) | .006 (.011) | .001 (.009) |
| PoC ID × out-group | .013 (.009) | .003 (.004) | .002 (.009) | -.004 (.010) | .003 (.011) | .002 (.009) |
| In-group message | .019 (.045) | .020 (.020) | .025 (.033) | -.031 (.050) | -.020 (.051) | -.023 (.043) |
| Out-group message | -.058 (.044) | -.013 (.020) | -.017 (.032) | .020 (.049) | -.029 (.051) | -.010 (.043) |
| Racial ID | .147** (.032) | .056** (.014) | .007 (.030) | .074** (.036) | .065* (.037) | .115** (.031) |
| American ID | -.024 (.026) | -.051** (.011) | -.050** (.023) | .016 (.028) | -.003 (.029) | .163** (.025) |
| Liberal | .166* (.022) | .053** (.010) | .417** (.020) | .182** (.024) | .246** (.025) | .162** (.021) |
| Constant | .248** (.034) | .421** (.015) | .321** (.031) | .468** (.037) | .443** (.039) | .474** (.033) |
| $R^2$ | .246 | .087 | .305 | .102 | .135 | .129 |
| Interactions = 0? | $F(2, 1,911) = .97$, Prob > $F$ = .378 | $F(2, 1,191) = .91$, Prob > $F$ = .404 | $F(2, 1,191) = .30$, Prob > $F$ = .742 | $F(2, 1,191) = 1.00$, Prob > $F$ = .369 | $F(2, 1,191) = .19$, Prob > $F$ = .830 | $F(2, 1,191) = .45$, Prob > $F$ = .636 |

TABLE 6.A4. PoC ID generally predicts support for minority-oriented policy regardless of message: Asian respondents

|  | Support #BlackLivesMatter | Increase visas | Support DACA | Omnibus scale, broad | Omnibus scale, narrow |
|---|---|---|---|---|---|
| PoC ID | .224** (.064) | .014 (.057) | .186** (.082) | .112** (.035) | .142** (.042) |
| PoC ID × in-group | -.135 (.083) | .016 (.012) | -.004 (.016) | .008 (.007) | -.003 (.009) |
| PoC ID × out-group | -.153* (.083) | .016 (.012) | -.002 (.016) | .000 (.008) | -.003 (.009) |
| In-group message | .108** (.054) | -.069 (.060) | .055 (.095) | -.025 (.036) | .022 (.044) |
| Out-group message | .120** (.053) | -.107* (.059) | .006 (.096) | -.006 (.036) | .003 (.044) |
| Racial ID | -.081* (.048) | .170** (.043) | .088* (.053) | .084** (.026) | .050 (.032) |
| American ID | -.111** (.038) | -.113** (.034) | .011 (.035) | .059** (.021) | -.075** (.025) |
| Liberal | .438** (.032) | .280** (.029) | .157** (.030) | .196** (.018) | .365** (.021) |
| Constant | .270** (.050) | .476** (.045) | .414** (.062) | .461** (.027) | .354** (.033) |
| $R^2$ | .165 | .120 | .067 | .185 | .249 |
| Interactions = 0? | $F(2, 1,911) = 2.02$, Prob > $F$ = .134 | $F(2, 1,191) = 1.14$, Prob > $F$ = .321 | $F(2, 1,191) = .01$, Prob > $F$ = .963 | $F(2, 1,191) = .79$, Prob > $F$ = .453 | $F(2, 1,191) = .06$, Prob > $F$ = .945 |

TABLE 6.A5. PoC ID generally predicts support for minority-oriented policy regardless of message: Latino respondents

| | Solidarity w/ PoC | Pro-minority affect | Pro-Democrat affect | Strengthen voting rights | Curb police brutality | Combat hate crimes |
|---|---|---|---|---|---|---|
| PoC ID | .217** (.038) | .077** (.020) | .052 (.039) | .024 (.041) | .108** (.045) | .020 (.039) |
| PoC ID × in-group | .004 (.009) | -.002 (.005) | .017* (.009) | .009 (.009) | -.003 (.010) | -.003 (.009) |
| PoC ID × out-group | -.000 (.009) | .003 (.005) | .012 (.009) | -.003 (.009) | .003 (.010) | .000 (.009) |
| In-group message | -.002 (.040) | .018 (.021) | -.078* (.042) | -.019 (.044) | .014 (.048) | .037 (.042) |
| Out-group message | -.028 (.041) | -.010 (.021) | -.063 (.042) | .019 (.044) | -.021 (.048) | -.007 (.042) |
| Racial ID | .222** (.030) | .076** (.016) | .171** (.031) | .197** (.033) | .205** (.036) | .212** (.031) |
| American ID | .021 (.027) | -.087** (.014) | -.064** (.027) | .063** (.029) | -.093** (.032) | .134** (.028) |
| Liberal | .122** (.022) | .041** (.012) | .371** (.023) | .131** (.024) | .265** (.026) | .139** (.023) |
| Constant | .274** (.033) | .441** (.017) | .306** (.034) | .452** (.035) | .465** (.039) | .431** (.034) |
| $R^2$ | .226 | .127 | .274 | .094 | .169 | .122 |
| Interactions = 0? | $F(2, 1,911) = .11$, Prob > $F$ = .899 | $F(2, 1,191) = .63$, Prob > $F$ = .533 | $F(2, 1,191) = 1.97$, Prob > $F$ = .140 | $F(2, 1,191) = .82$, Prob > $F$ = .439 | $F(2, 1,191) = .16$, Prob > $F$ = .853 | $F(2, 1,191) = .09$, Prob > $F$ = .911 |

TABLE 6.A6. PoC ID generally predicts support for minority-oriented policy regardless of message: Latino respondents

| | Support #BlackLivesMatter | Increase visas | Support DACA | Omnibus scale, broad | Omnibus scale, narrow |
|---|---|---|---|---|---|
| PoC ID | .008 (.061) | .070 (.051) | .127** (.052) | .051 (.032) | .068* (.039) |
| PoC ID × in-group | .015 (.014) | .003 (.012) | .003 (.012) | .001 (.007) | .007 (.009) |
| PoC ID × out-group | .013 (.014) | -.001 (.012) | .007 (.012) | -.000 (.007) | .006 (.009) |
| In-group message | -.094 (.066) | .010 (.055) | .016 (.056) | .010 (.034) | -.024 (.041) |
| Out-group message | -.068 (.066) | .016 (.055) | -.003 (.056) | -.003 (.034) | -.018 (.042) |
| Racial ID | .085* (.049) | .335** (.041) | .284** (.042) | .205** (.026) | .235** (.031) |
| American ID | -.141** (.043) | -.151** (.036) | -.113** (.037) | .035 (.022) | -.135** (.027) |
| Liberal | .374** (.036) | .234** (.030) | .323** (.030) | .178** (.019) | .311** (.0230) |
| Constant | .403** (.053) | .381** (.044) | .333** (.045) | .449** (.028) | .373** (.034) |
| $R^2$ | .116 | .162 | .201 | .184 | .258 |
| Interactions = 0? | $F(2, 1,911) = .66$, Prob > $F$ = .520 | $F(2, 1,191) = .06$, Prob > $F$ = .941 | $F(2, 1,191) = .16$, Prob > $F$ = .852 | $F(2, 1,191) = .01$, Prob > $F$ = .993 | $F(2, 1,191) = .35$, Prob > $F$ = .702 |

## Confirmatory Factor Analysis—Favorability toward PoC and PoC ID

TABLE 6.A7. Confirmatory factor analysis: favorability toward PoC and PoC ID

|  | Loading |
|---|---|
| *Method factor* | |
| Fact that I am PoC is important | .458* (.044) |
| Being PoC is a major part of me | 1.038* (.075) |
| I often think about being PoC | .458* (.044) |
| I am glad to be PoC | — |
| *PoC ID factor* | |
| Fact that I am PoC is important | 1.370* (.035) |
| Being PoC is a major part of me | 1.370* (.035) |
| I often think about being PoC | 1.133* (.023) |
| I am glad to be PoC | 1.133* (.023) |
| *Favorability toward PoC factor* | |
| Favorability rating – African Americans | 1.118* (.017) |
| Favorability rating – Latinos | 1.118* (.017) |
| Favorability rating – Asian Americans | .776* (.023) |
| *Inter-factor correlations* | |
| PoC ID factor with Favorability factor | .408* (.022) |
| Method factor with PoC ID factor | .085^ (.046) |
| Method factor with Favorability factor | −.092* (.035) |
| Confirmatory fit index/Tucker-Lewis index | .981/.963 |
| Root mean square error of approximation [90% CI] | .074 [.066, .083] |
| N | 3,600 |

Note: Entries are ML estimates with standard errors in parentheses. Pairs of similar loadings indicate they were fixed to equality to conserve degrees of freedom during estimation. A method factor for the PoC ID items was estimated to deal directly with residual variance between specific items. *$p < .05$, ^$p < .10$, two-tailed.

# 7

# Falling Apart

For most people of color (PoC), April 28, 2019, came and went like any other day. But on that early Sunday morning, a Black woman named Nadra Widatalla published a stinging editorial in the *Los Angeles Times* with the baldly unapologetic title: "The Term *People of Color* Erases Black People. Let's Retire It."

In her essay, Ms. Widatalla delivers an incisive rebuke of the category we have been studying across the previous chapters. The gist of her criticism is that PoC—a group that is supposed to be broadly inclusive of distinct racial and ethnic minorities—flattens the unique histories, experiences, and goals of these communities, particularly African Americans. As she puts it: "While every minority group faces its own challenges in America, a "one size fits all" mentality toward diversity erases the specific needs of the most vulnerable communities." Indeed, from where Ms. Widatalla sits—as a Black woman in largely White spaces—"the reality is that not all *people of color* suffer equally from the effects of institutional racism."

Ms. Widatalla's diatribe is relevant because it offers a clear glimpse into one of the most common challenges that any broadly inclusive group like PoC faces: how do *we* maintain a coherent group identity in light of the unique perspectives, needs, and objectives of *our* individual group members? This is the trouble with unity, the political scientist Cristina Beltrán (2010), reminds us. Insofar as a broadly inclusive group like PoC forges solidarity, it can do so at the expense of the special circumstances, challenges, and aspirations of individual group members. Thus, while African Americans, Asian Americans, Latinos, and other minority groups experience real and persistent inequalities with respect to Whites, it is also the case that, for example, the stain of slavery and its legacies might not be perceived as fully commensurate with the hardships and repercussions of immigrants' experiences.

Beyond sensitizing us to the inherent tensions below the surface of PoC, however, Ms. Widatalla's essay is enlightening for another reason: it sets into sharper relief the intuition behind *why* the unity of internally diverse groups is so difficult to maintain. Ms. Widatalla identifies as African American and as a PoC. Yet her own words reveal that her racial identity is more important than her PoC identity because she feels the distinctiveness of the former is drowned out in the cacophony of the latter. Yes, Ms. Widatalla is only one non-White individual expressing her own view about a sensed tension between her Black identity and her attachment to other PoC. But not unlike other minority individuals, she faces the challenge of navigating the straits between the Scylla of a unique racial identity and the Charybdis of sharing with others in being a racial or ethnic minority. When do PoC face this tension? How do they finesse it? And who, among them, best navigates this path? These are some of the central questions I tackle in this chapter.[1]

## From Many, One

The answers to these questions begin with acknowledgment that identification with any group entails creating, psychologically, an island of coherence amidst a sea of diverse group membership. This process is built around the basic psychological principles I introduced back in chapter 2. There, we learned about the important role that *distinctiveness* plays in mentally cementing a group among individuals. Recall that distinctiveness is what makes a particular in-group special or unique. It is the accumulation of the many things that make Blacks, Black; Latinos, Latino; or Asians, Asian. This can be an in-group's particular station in society (Sidanius and Pratto 1999; Carter and Pérez 2016), the specific experiences that an in-group has endured (Beltrán 2010; Carter 2019; Kim 2003), and/or some other unique aspect of the in-group and its current or past situation (Danbold and Huo 2015; Pérez et al. 2019). But whatever the source of an in-group's distinctiveness, this uniqueness is crucial because it defines an in-group while infusing it with cachet, thus enabling individuals to draw that sense of self-worth that follows from identifying with others. Like many aspects of all in-groups, however, this distinctiveness is intimately tied to the configuration of intergroup relations in a particular setting (Ellemers, Spears, and Doosje 2002).

---

1. As of this writing, Ms. Widatalla is a freelance writer and producer in Los Angeles. She maintains an active following on social media, including Twitter (@nadrawidatalla) and Instagram (@nadra.w).

With an in-group's distinctiveness intact, in-group members are infused with certainty and clarity about who, exactly, belongs in the in-group and, just as importantly, who does not. This line in the sand is the basis of one of the most fundamental triggers of identification with a group. By emphasizing an in-group's distinctiveness, members realize that its identity is of utmost relevance in the immediate context. "The primary concern here," Ellemers, Spears, and Doosje explain, "will be to express and affirm this identity (2002: 169)." Taken to the next level, this insight suggests an obverse pattern as well: insofar as the distinctiveness of an in-group is called into question, it's meaningfulness and relevance for a given situation is placed in doubt, making it *less* likely that it will influence intragroup behavior.

I review these tenets to underscore how the principles that govern whether an identity is relevant are the same principles regulating when that identity—in this case, PoC ID—might become less effective. Recall my theorized relationship between PoC ID and racial ID. In social identity theory's jargon, PoC ID is a superordinate attachment—a broad category encapsulating a person's unique racial identity. By this reasoning, one's racial identity is nested under one's *person of color* identity. When that nesting is complete, a *person of color* generally views members of one's specific racial group as interchangeable with members of other minority groups, thus extending the benefits of in-group favoritism to any and all individuals who fall under PoC ID's canopy (Gaertner et al. 1989; Tajfel and Turner 1986). This is precisely what we observed in chapter 5's "I Feel Your Pain" experiments, where members of distinct racial/ethnic groups stood by other PoC, regardless of whether a minority couple offended by a White waiter was from their own racial in-group or not.

However, when this nesting between PoC ID and racial ID is unsettled, the behavior of PoC is expected to change. In particular, one's panoramic and generous view of group membership should narrow to one's immediate racial or ethnic in-group. That is, one will become less likely to see other racial and ethnic minorities as interchangeable with members of one's own racial or ethnic in-group. How does this occur? I answer this below in more depth by braiding together the psychological insights I just discussed with some nitty-gritty realities of US intergroup relations.

### PoC—Parallel Stations?

When you converse with PoC, as I did in chapter 3, you learn that many of them emphasize the shared disadvantages they believe racial minorities endure with respect to Whites. As José García, a Latino person of color, stated during his interview: "A lot of the things that are going on today in the US, like racism, it's just by sight. And, if you see me walking next to someone that's Jewish or someone that's Italian, I am going to be the one who is going to be picked out as a person of color—as the other."

This sense of outsider status on the basis of not being White was further expressed by Lupe Ramírez, a Latina person of color. When asked why she thinks PoC are a coherent group despite socioeconomic nuances between them, she explained: "They've definitely had . . . similar experiences . . . of . . . discrimination or . . . instances . . . that they felt [discriminated against] . . . That's part of the othering that . . . comes from not being White . . . it comes from . . . not being a part of the dominant group."

These observations hint at a solid pecking order between racial groups, with Whites perched atop as the dominant and valorized group, and all PoC down below in a well of devaluation. This hierarchical view of intergroup relations is intuitive and firmly established in psychological research. As Jim Sidanius and his associates have repeatedly shown, a group's position in a racial order profoundly motivates the behavior of individual group members (cf. Carter and Pérez 2016; Sidanius et al.1997; Sidanius and Petrocik 2001; Staerkle et al. 2010). Dominant group members are generally driven to protect their privileged station. Subordinate group members are generally driven to improve their lowlier position.

This is a revealing insight, to be sure, but it is also a coarse one. Yes, PoC do stand at a collective disadvantage with respect to Whites. But look deeper, and you will find that racial and ethnic minorities also differ in terms of their social position with respect to Whites and other PoC (Carter 2019; Kim 2003; Kuo and Pérez n.d.; Masuoka and Junn 2013; Zou and Cheryan 2017). As Ebony Carter, an African American person of color I interviewed, shared with me: "I feel like people of color are oppressed, but I feel like Black people and Latin-Americans [are] oppressed the most." Indeed, as she further clarifies, "I wouldn't include . . . Asians or Asian Americans [in the category *PoC*] because I feel, like, here in the United States, people are targeted based on their skin color and . . . Asians typically don't have a darker skin color."

This sentiment is echoed by Linda Sánchez, another Latina PoC I spoke with. When asked about minority groups that are not widely considered PoC by her and her peers, she volunteered Asian Americans, saying, "I think they're usually left out . . . because, like, literally, people think people of color and it's like the color of your skin. And so, usually, when you see someone who's Asian, they have relatively the same [skin tone] as someone who is White." For this reason, Ms. Sánchez concludes, "Most . . . discrimination that continues is toward Mexicans and African Americans."

Karina Bello, another Latina PoC I interviewed, more finely underscored the differences in social position between various racial/ethnic minorities by describing Asian Americans as a "model minority," adding that many Blacks and Latinos do not consider Asians to be PoC because ". . . they get very much the rights that White folk do . . ." as a result of their model minority status.

The notion of Asian Americans as a model minority (Kim 2003; Zou and Cheryan 2017) acknowledges that they occupy a distinct station within America's racial hierarchy. Unlike other minorities, such as Blacks and Latinos, they are economically better off, on average, and relatively more socially valorized, on average. This is what Ms. Bello's comments point to. Yet just like other racial and ethnic minorities, Asian Americans are also excluded from the dominant group; which is to say, they still hold a subordinate position in America's racial order. Although this latter point is absent in the comments of Ms. Carter, Ms. Sánchez, and Ms. Bello, it is acknowledged by other PoC I interviewed. For example, Miriam Khoury, a PoC with Lebanese and Venezuelan roots, explained, although Blacks, Latinos, and Asians face distinct disadvantage in US society, "I wouldn't say a Black person is a person of color more than an Asian person is."

These insights from individual PoC drive home a key point: whether PoC share parallel positions in America's racial order is, fundamentally, a matter of perspective. Either *we*—meaning every PoC—are subordinated and devalued with respect to Whites. Or, alternatively, *they*—meaning some PoC, but not others—are stuck in an inferior and degraded position. These perspectives are deeply informed by *reality constraints*: the nuances in history, numbers, status, and power between in-groups and out-groups that structure intergroup relations in any one setting, such as the model minority narrative alluded to above (cf. Kim 2003; Waldzus et al. 2004; Zou and Cheryan 2017). The question before us, then, is whether perceptions about who counts as a *person of color* can also change according to shifts in the *reality constraints* that sometimes surround PoC? The answer, I will now try to persuade you, is yes.

## The "Distinct Stations" Experiment

To begin demonstrating how the sheer diversity of PoC can sometimes undermine its unity, I conducted the "Distinct Stations" experiment. This study's aim was to show how information about the varied positions of distinct minorities in a specific setting can shift views about who counts as a *person of color*.

The study took place on the campus of University of California, Los Angeles (UCLA), a setting that provides an unrivaled research opportunity. UCLA is an institution of higher learning where the historical trajectories of different

FIGURE 7.1. Control group: regional diversity
Note: Participants in this group read the following text: "Here is an important demographic fact about UCLA to consider: UCLA's undergraduates are some of the most regionally talented in the nation. Indeed, an estimated 74% of all UCLA students are from the state of California, with this segment of the undergraduate class already the largest and anticipated to continue growing. This increasing proportion of undergraduates includes individuals who are from northern California, central California, and southern California."

minority groups—e.g., African Americans, Asian Americans, and Latinos— rub against entrenched *reality constraints* produced locally by university life. Here is what I mean. In US society, Blacks, Asians, Latinos and other minorities are a rising share of the national population. At UCLA, however, non-Whites already comprise about three-fourths of the undergraduate population, which means, numerically, they are not minorities.[2] In US society, moreover, Latinos far outrank both Blacks and Asians in sheer population size. Yet at UCLA, Asian Americans swamp the numbers—and prestige—of Blacks and Latinos, with just over half of all PoC at UCLA being Asian

---

2. See *UCLA 2017–2018 Undergraduate Profile*, which estimates that 27% of undergraduates are White.

American. The question, then, is whether in a setting like this one, information about group positions can shift perceptions about who is a PoC?

To answer this, Asian and Latino undergraduates were invited to UCLA's Race, Ethnicity, Politics & Society (REPS) Lab, which I direct, to partake in a 10-minute survey about campus demographics. Data collection for this study occurred from March through May 2019. Efforts to recruit Black undergraduates, who are less than 5% of the student population, yielded insufficient numbers ($N < 50$) to properly analyze any data. Hence, I restrict my analysis below to Asian ($N = 141$) and Latino ($N = 250$) subjects.

Asian American and Latino subjects who consented to participate received a modicum of course extra credit in exchange. After completing a brief suite of demographic items, subjects were randomly assigned to one of three conditions providing information about the diversity of UCLA's campus. In the

FIGURE 7.2. Treatment: Asians predominate
Note: Participants in this group read the following text: "Here is an important demographic fact about UCLA to consider: UCLA's undergraduates are some of the most racially and ethnically diverse in the nation. Indeed, an estimated 74% of all UCLA students are people of color. Asian Americans form the largest segment of people of color on UCLA's campus at 54%. This substantial proportion of people of color includes individuals who are Chinese, Indian, Korean, Japanese, Vietnamese, Cambodian, among others."

FIGURE 7.3. Treatment: Latinos ascending
Note: Participants in this group read the following text: "Here is an important demographic fact about UCLA to consider: UCLA's undergraduates are some of the most racially and ethnically diverse in the nation. Indeed, an estimated 74% of all UCLA students are people of color, with Latinos as the fastest-growing segment of this group, having grown steadily by about 10% in less than a decade. This increasing proportion of people of color includes individuals who are Mexican, Puerto Rican, Cuban, Salvadoran, Dominican, and Guatemalan, among other groups."

control, subjects read a brief statement about the regional diversity of UCLA's undergraduates, which was accompanied by a word cloud underscoring this heterogeneity (figure 7.1). The two treatments delivered a similar message in a similar format. These treatments, however, highlighted the racial, rather than regional, diversity of UCLA's campus, as displayed in figures 7.2 ("Asians Predominate" Treatment) and 7.3 ("Latinos Ascending").

Post-treatment, subjects answered three items gauging the degree to which they viewed Blacks, Latinos, and Asians as prototypical PoC. Adapted from prior work on partisan perceptions (Heit and Nicholson 2010), subjects used a scale from 1 = "a very poor example" to 7 = "a very good example," to answer a simple question: "In your mind, how well do *Blacks* reflect the category *people of color*?" This item was then repeated by replacing *Blacks* with *Asians* and *Latinos*, with the order of items randomized across subjects. The replies here are the crux of my analysis below.

## Shifting PoC Prototypes

I wish to know whether information about the social position of racial/ethnic minorities can change their perceptions about who is a prototypical PoC. But before scouring for any shifts like these, it perhaps makes sense to explore these perceptions prior to subjects receiving any information. Table 7.1 reports the average perceptions that Latino and Asian American subjects have of PoC groups. These views are from the control group, which makes no reference to racial minority groups. What do we learn?

Several things, actually. First, we learn that even in a unique setting like UCLA, the perception of African Americans as *the* prototypical PoC has some staying power. As the first row in table 7.1 reveals, although Latino and Asian undergraduates far outnumber Black UCLA students, Latino and Asian subjects nonetheless rate Blacks as the most prototypical PoC, with ratings of 6.750 and 6.751, respectively. These values hover around the maximum of the response scale here and they align closely with the insights from the in-depth interviews in chapter 3, where many respondents singled out African Americans as the most reflective PoC example.

Second, notice that for both Asian American and Latino subjects, there is a clear hierarchy in these perceptions, with Asian and Latino participants rating African Americans as the most prototypical PoC, followed by Latinos as a close second, and then, several notches below, Asian Americans. This, again, comports with chapter 3's in-depth interviewees, many of whom explicitly identified Asian Americans as a minority group that loosely belongs in the category, PoC. It is also consistent with Asian Americans' placement in the racial order as a group that is marginalized with respect to Whites (just like other people of color), yet relatively valorized with respect to African Americans, Latinos, and other minorities (Kim 2003; Masuoka and Junn 2013; Zou and Cheryan 2017).

Third, although Asian and Latino subjects agree that Asian Americans are the least prototypical PoC, these subjects disagree about the extent to which this group is less reflective of PoC. In fact, Asian subjects view Asians as more prototypical PoC than Latino subjects do—by nearly a full point. Prior work construes these disagreements as indicative of a malleable sense of which groups

TABLE 7.1. Mean prototypicality ratings of PoC by race of participant (with 95% confidence intervals)

|  | Black prototypicality | Latino prototypicality | Asian prototypicality |
|---|---|---|---|
| Latino participants ($n = 70$) | 6.750 [6.570, 6.930] | 6.374 [6.179, 6.569] | 3.976 [3.531, 4.420] |
| Asian participants ($n = 51$) | 6.751 [6.611, 6.891] | 6.197 [6.001, 6.393] | 4.876 [4.473, 5.280] |

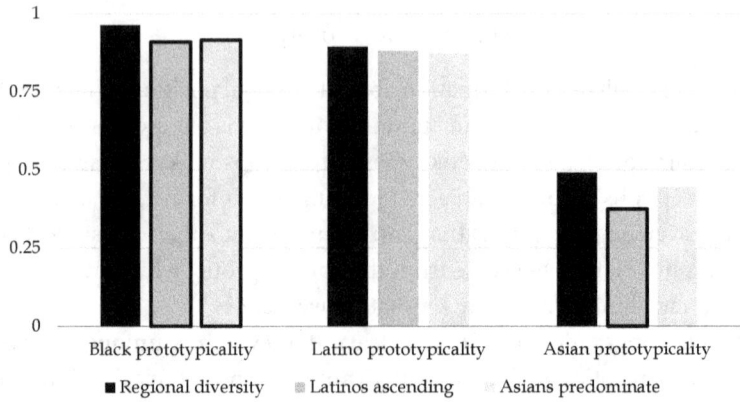

FIGURE 7.4. Prototypicality ratings by experimental condition: Latino subjects
Note: Outlined bars indicate a statistically significant difference at the 5% level (one-tailed) compared to the control condition.

are more worthy of membership in a shared category (Waldzus et al. 2004; Wenzel, Mummendey, and Waldzus 2007). This is an early sign that perhaps—just perhaps—the demographic information subjects received nudges their perceptions in expected directions. Does this actually occur?

The results for Latinos suggests it does. Figure 7.4 displays Latinos' prototypicality ratings (rescaled from 0 to 1) by racial/ethnic group and experimental condition, with full regression results reported in table 7.A1 in the appendix to this chapter. Given my strong directional predictions, which are based on accumulated work in this general area (cf. Brewer 1991; Gaertner et al. 1989, 1999; Tajfel et al. 1971; Tajfel and Turner 1986; Waldzus et al. 2004), I rely on one-tailed tests for my inferences. Figure 7.4 shows that compared to the control, where Latinos read about the regional diversity of UCLA's campus, Latinos who read about the demographic ascendance of their co-ethnics at UCLA view African Americans as less prototypical PoC ($-.053$, $p < .05$, one-tailed). This shift is reliably different from zero, as indicated by the bold line around the dark gray bar. A similar decrease occurs if Latinos read about the predominance of Asians at UCLA ($-.047$, $p < .05$, one-tailed). Both patterns imply that Latinos update their views of prototypical PoC based on the demographic information they receive.

These shifts in prototypicality ratings also arise in Latino views about Asian Americans. Again, relative to the control, Latinos who read about the ascendance of their co-ethnics at UCLA reliably downgrade their rating of Asians as prototypical PoC ($-.116$, $p < .05$, one-tailed). A negative trend also emerges if Latinos read about Asians' predominance at UCLA, although this shift is smaller and statistically insignificant ($-.044$, $p < .197$, one-tailed). These patterns suggest that insofar as Latino subjects already view Asian Americans as the least prototypical group within PoC, this information leads them to further sideline this group from this pan-racial category. In fact, the only instance where Latinos' prototypicality ratings fail to budge is when their own in-group is involved. Here, Latinos' sense of their in-group's prototypicality remains intact, suggesting that exposure to demographic information about PoC affects one's views of other groups as PoC, but not necessarily one's own.

What about Asian Americans—how do they react? Figure 7.5 suggests their responses generally mimic those of their Latino peers (with raw regression results in table 7.A2 in the appendix to this chapter). Specifically, when Blacks' prototypicality is concerned, Asian American subjects rate them as significantly less prototypical PoC if they are exposed to information about the predominance of Asians at UCLA ($-.0791, p < .01$, one-tailed), with a comparable decrease if they read about Latinos' ascendance on campus ($-.080, p < .01$, one-tailed). Similarly, Asians who either read about the majority status of Asian Americans as PoC at UCLA ($-.049, p < .079$, one-tailed) or the demographic climb of Latinos on campus ($-.061, p < .032$, one-tailed) rate Latinos as less prototypical PoC.

Finally, just like Latinos, Asian American views of their in-group as prototypical PoC remain consistent, even though their views of the other two minority groups shift.

The "Distinct Stations" experiment illuminates a specific circumstance under which the coherence and unity of the category, PoC, can start to unravel. This insight comes in two forms. First, the results reveal that, in the absence

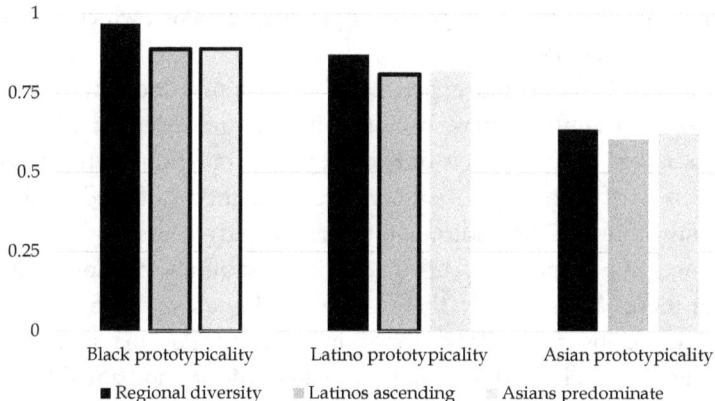

FIGURE 7.5. Prototypicality ratings by experimental condition: Asian subjects

Note: Outlined bars indicate a statistically significant difference at the 5% level (one-tailed) compared to the control condition.

of the treatments here, Asian and Latino participants see a clear hierarchy between racial and ethnic minority groups on campus, with African Americans far and away considered the most prototypical PoC, followed by Latinos, and then (and only then) by Asian Americans (Kim 2003; Masuoka and Junn 2013; Zou and Cheryan 2017). This implies that despite the *reality constraints* imposed by campus life at UCLA, Asian and Latino undergraduates identify themselves as PoC, yet still single out Blacks as the "best" example of this pan-racial category, and Asian Americans as the "weakest" instance of this broad group.

Second, this study teaches us that information about a group's position in a social setting can alter the perceptions one has about who, among PoC, is a prototypical example of this group. These shifts appear to be driven, in part, through an updating process, whereby minorities adapt their general understanding of PoC to the *reality constraints* of their immediate setting, which they are primed with. These constraints, however, also imply a clear pecking order between non-Whites at UCLA. Thus, as the higher-ranked group of non-Whites at UCLA, Asian Americans seem to update their views of PoC in a way that lets them preserve this more privileged rank, just as we would expect from prior work (e.g., Sidanius et al. 1997, Sidanius and Petrocik 2001). Consider, for example, Asians' reactions to Latinos. When Asian American subjects read about the numeric ascendance of Latinos at UCLA, they *downgrade* (rather than *upgrade*) their view of this group as prototypical PoC. Latinos, in turn, seem to update their view of PoC in a way that lets them improve their status within UCLA's order of non-White groups, again, just as prior work would lead us to expect (Carter and Pérez 2016). Specifically, when reading about the demographic predominance of Asian undergraduates, Latinos downgrade their view of Asian Americans as prototypical PoC, which is already relatively low to begin with.

Of course, this is only one experiment, and one that does not fully speak to whether these shifts in views of PoC influence individuals' political attitudes and beliefs. Indeed, this is one of the main limitations of this study: it is unable to clarify the range of outcomes that might be affected by shifting perceptions about PoC. In addition, the current study is less clear about how these changes in perceptions occur—that is, it does not fully pin down a mechanism for these effects. Finally, there is the usual bugbear of lab studies like this one: can we observe similar processes in samples of PoC that more broadly include adults beyond undergraduates (Sears 1986; McDermott 2011)? For these reasons, and others, I conducted a second study, what I call the "Distinct Experiences" experiment. Let us turn to this second effort next.

## PoC—Parallel Experiences?

The question about whether distinct groups of PoC share a similar station in America's racial order can also find expression in a related query: do sundry minority groups undergo similar experiences as PoC? Again, while there is no right or wrong answer here, there are at least two ways to answer this inquiry.

One way is to stress the similarities between the assorted groups that comprise PoC (Masuoka and Junn 2013; Zou and Cheryan 2017). Take the basic distinction of PoC as not being White, which many of the individuals I interviewed alluded to. Sara Reyes, a Filipina-American person of color I spoke with, expressed the following when I asked her to explain the category PoC to someone who might be unfamiliar with it:

> I'd explain it to them as people who aren't white, basically. For, for me, the definition of a person of color is someone who has a form of brownness, yellowness, or shade deeper than white in their skin . . . I'd say if you're a minority . . . in that your ethnicity or racial group . . . does not make up the majority, which is anything that isn't white, you are a person of color.

Clearly for Ms. Reyes, the distinctions between various PoC in terms of their skin tone are negligible. More important to her is the fact that all PoC are not White and excluded from the majority for this reason. For Ms. Reyes, all PoC share in this parallel experience.

These parallel experiences come in other forms, too, like the shared burden of racial disadvantage. Indeed, when I asked Ngoc Nguyen, a Vietnamese American PoC I interviewed, why the category PoC makes sense despite vast socioeconomic differences between racial and ethnic minority groups, she told me: "Even though someone can . . . be insulated from *some* race-based discrimination by having more money, I think there is an element of race-based discrimination that exists regardless of socioeconomic level." From Ms. Nguyen's perspective, then, America's tides of racial discrimination wash over all minority groups to a comparable degree.

For all of the parallel experiences that minorities might share, however, there are also shades of distinction—nuances that are flattened, elided, or outright ignored for the sake of the larger group's coherence (Kim 2003; Masuoka and Junn 2013; Zou and Cheryan 2017). This was precisely the point of Ms. Widatalla's editorial, which opened this chapter, and it is the second way to interpret the varied experiences of PoC in the US. From this angle, broad similarities shared by minority groups can become bones of contention. Take the notion of PoC being defined by some minorities as non-White (see chapter 3). While it might be true that PoC are generally darker than most Whites in the US, it is also true that some minority groups are noticeably darker than others on average (e.g., Hunter, Allen, and Telles 2001; Massey and Martin 2003).

Indeed, even within specific minority groups, skin tone varies widely, with some individuals displaying darker skin shades than others. Thus, not all PoC are exactly the same shade (e.g., Ortiz and Telles 2012; Ostfeld and Yadon n.d.).

But beyond such outward attributes, there are also degrees of distinction in terms of the experiences minorities go through or have undergone. Yes, PoC are disadvantaged socioeconomically and politically with respect to Whites, as some of my in-depth interviewees explained earlier. But this rip current of marginalization does not yank all minorities out to a sea of exclusion and despair in a strict one-to-one fashion (Kim 2003; Masuoka and Junn 2013; Zou and Cheryan 2017). Some minority groups simply take a heavier brunt of these waves. Consider Ebony Carter's insight here, one of the African American PoC I interviewed. When asked why Blacks come more easily to mind when she thinks about PoC, she explained:

> Well, I think . . . because of the history of African Americans, like them being slaves and them building the economy, but still not getting credit for it . . . I'm not saying that Asian American history isn't significant, but I feel like African American history is more significant because there's still racism today and, like, institutional racism—and I feel like African Americans . . . experience it more.

Of course, it is reasonable to think that only members of an in-group perceived as distinct think in this way. But the uniqueness of a group like African Americans seems to be recognized even by minority individuals who are outside of it. For example, Joanna Ocampo, a Filipina PoC I spoke with, explained:

> Growing up I only heard about the things that [Blacks] have gone through . . . You learn about slavery . . . So then it . . . trained me to think, like, not that everyone else didn't have problems, but it's, like, maybe the gravity of what happened to like African American or African people was so heavy that it's something that we . . . need to talk about.

Two lessons emerge from this brief discussion. The first one concerns the messiness of the world—especially the world of US racial and ethnic minorities—when it comes to facts on the ground. Given the range of diversity among PoC, defining and describing this group often entails a tradeoff between focusing on averages rather than variances. More simply put, a group like PoC exhibits clear tendencies like the ones we described above, but each of those averages is surrounded by nuances and exceptions that are sometimes tightly or widely dispersed around this groups' mean.

Consequently, the second lesson is about the meanings that are assigned to this range of diversity among PoC. In particular, when do PoC emphasize the average of their group to the detriment of these nuances—and, just as importantly, can these nuances undermine their group's coherence?

The answer, I will try to persuade you, is that much of it depends on which group is affirmed at any one time: PoC or one's racial/ethnic in-group. This simple mechanism, I will demonstrate, amplifies or diminishes PoC ID's influence across a swath of outcomes that include a sense of discrimination toward PoC, perceived competition with other minorities, and even preferences for policies affecting specific racial/ethnic minority groups. Let's turn to this experiment next.

### The "Distinct Experiences" Experiment

The "Distinct Experiences" study zeroes in on two key features of PoC: the range of diversity of group members and the varied ways in which this heterogeneity can be interpreted by them. To this end, $N = 290$ African American adults, $N = 295$ Latino adults, and $N = 308$ Asian American adults from Prolific's respondent panel completed a short online study described as an evaluation of US Census Bureau information.

In each sample, participants first reported demographic data that included their age, gender, and ideological orientation. This was followed by completion of two item batteries assessing degree of identification as a PoC and as Black, Latino, or Asian, with the order of these batteries randomized across respondents and separated by a distracter task involving the counting of triangles on a screen. The items gauging PoC ID used a scale from 1 = "strongly disagree" to 6 = "strongly agree" for participants to reply to two statements. I combine replies to these items into additive indexes, rescaled from 0 to 1, where higher values reflect stronger PoC ID levels (Black $\alpha = .638$; Latino $\alpha = .654$; Asian $\alpha = .697$). The two statements were as follows:

- The fact that I am a person of color is an important part of my identity.
- Being a person of color is unimportant to who I am as an individual.

In turn, Black, Latino, and Asian participants also used this same response scale to answer two statements concerning their degree of identification as Black, Latino, or Asian. Again, I folded replies to these items into additive indexes, rescaled from 0 to 1, where higher values indicate stronger levels of racial/ethnic identity (Black α = .692; Latino α = .675; Asian α = .600). The two statements were as follows:

- Overall, being [Black/Asian/Latino] is crucial to who I am as an individual.
- Identifying as [Black/Asian/Latino] is unimportant to my self-image.

After completing these identity items, participants reported other demographic data, including their education level and state of current residence. This was followed by another distracter task, which involved the counting of dots on a screen. It is after this last distracter task that the actual experiment took place.

The manipulation here consisted of information, attributed to the US Census Bureau, describing the growing percentage of Americans who are racial/ethnic minorities. In the baseline condition, these data were framed around the label PoC and the many similarities that members of this broad group reportedly share. After noting the numeric increase in PoC the bulletin explained:

> This increasing diversity rests on a common history shared by all people of color in the United States. For example, despite their differences, African Americans, Asian Americans, Latinos, Native Americans and other people of color still experience social and political exclusion. Indeed, the United States continues to marginalize people of color as outsiders and un-American, even though they were born here or have lived here for most of their adult lives. All people of color are treated in this peculiar way. In fact, the various forms of discrimination and prejudice that people of color now face is rooted in this unique legacy of hostility to all racial and ethnic minorities.

Notice what this PoC-Affirming treatment does. It makes salient a category, PoC, while at the same time stressing its uniqueness, maintaining that all PoC continue to experience social and political exclusion—a unique legacy of antipathy toward *all* racial and ethnic minorities. The message being driven home to Black, Latino, and Asian participants in this condition is that *we*—all PoC—are a single group uniquely tied together by our *shared* experiences with racial exclusion.

The second condition, in sharp contrast, treats participants with a different emphasis. Specifically, the "In-Group Distinctiveness" condition underscores the uniqueness of participants' own racial or ethnic in-group relative to PoC. Consider the wording in this distinctiveness condition as it pertains to African Americans:

> Nevertheless, this increasing diversity blurs the distinct histories each group has had in the United States. For example, it is very hard to compare African Americans' experience with slavery and its aftermath to the social and political exclusion faced by Asian Americans and Latinos. Indeed, the United States continues to marginalize many Blacks as second-class citizens, even though African Americans have been in this country since its founding. Other people of color are not treated in this peculiar way. In fact, the widespread discrimination and prejudice that Blacks now face is rooted in this unique legacy of slavery.

Notice that unlike the PoC-Affirming condition, this Black Distinctiveness condition highlights for Blacks how *they* are distinct from other PoC in light of their unique experiences and struggles as descendants of slaves. The message here is that Blacks are patently different from other PoC, with this notion of difference and nuance repeated for Latino and Asian American participants. Specifically, Latino participants in this condition read about the distinctiveness of their in-group:

> Nevertheless, this increasing diversity blurs the distinct histories each group has had in the United States. For example, it is very hard to compare Latinos' social and political exclusion to African Americans' experience with slavery and its aftermath. Indeed, the United States continues to marginalize many Latinos as foreigners, even though most of them were born in the U.S. or have lived here for most of their adult lives. Blacks are not treated in this peculiar way. In fact, the widespread discrimination and prejudice that many Latinos now face is rooted in this unique legacy of excluding individuals with Latino backgrounds.

In turn, Asian American participants read about their in-group's unique experiences:

> Nevertheless, this increasing diversity blurs the distinct histories each group has had in the United States. For example, it is very hard to compare Asian Americans' social and political exclusion to African Americans' experience with slavery and its aftermath. Indeed, the United States continues to marginalize many Asian Americans as foreigners, even though most of them were born in the U.S. or have lived here for most of their adult lives. Blacks are not treated in this peculiar way. In fact, the widespread discrimination and prejudice that many Asian Americans now face is rooted in this unique legacy of excluding individuals with Asian backgrounds.

By design, this second treatment underlines the special circumstances of one's particular racial/ethnic in-group, thus threatening the distinctiveness of the category, PoC. This is where those individual differences in group identity should become less relevant. If there are two conditions—one affirming the shared uniqueness of PoC, the other asserting the distinctiveness of one's racial/ethnic in-group—then we should expect PoC ID to structure one's political perceptions in the former condition, with this effect dissipating in the latter condition.

But what kinds of perceptions should these treatments affect? I expand here on the results of the "Distinct Stations" experiment by assessing multiple attitudes and outlooks. First, Blacks, Asians, and Latinos reported their perceived discrimination toward PoC. Using a scale from 1 = "very little discrimination" to 7 = "a lot of discrimination," participants answered "How much discrimination is there in the United States against [GROUP]?," with the group in focus (i.e., Blacks, Asians, Latinos, Native Americans, and Whites) randomized. I take mean perceived discrimination toward PoC and subtract perceived discrimination toward Whites, yielding *Perceived Discrimination toward PoC*, which reflects perceptions of discrimination toward PoC relative to Whites.

I also gauged Black, Latino, and Asian views of diversity among PoC, which I call *Minority Problems Too Different*. Using a seven-point scale from 1 = "strongly disagree" to 7 = "strongly agree," participants reported their agreement with the statement "The problems of Blacks, Latinos, and Asian Americans and other minorities are too different for them to be allies or partners." Higher values here reflect more agreement with this claim.

Using the same seven-point scale, participants also expressed their sense of zero-sum competition with racial minority out-groups. Specifically, Blacks indicated their degree of agreement with the statement "More political power for [GROUP] means less political power for Black Americans like me," with Asians and Latinos as the out-groups (in random order). I administered the same items to Asian and Latino participants, with the out-groups being Blacks and Latinos (for Asian participants) or Blacks and Asians (for Latino participants). I call this variable *Zero-Sum Perceptions*.

Participants also rated how favorably they feel toward a variety of groups, namely: Blacks, Asians, Latinos, Native Americans, Whites, all rated on an individual and random basis. These ratings occurred on scales ranging from 1 = "very unfavorable" to 7 = "very favorable." I take the average favorability rating of PoC groups and subtract from it one's favorability rating of Whites, resulting in *Pro-Minority Affect*, which indicates the degree to which one feels more positively toward PoC in relation to Whites.

Finally, participants reported their degree of support for policies focused on racial/ethnic minorities. Using a seven-point scale, they expressed agreement with: "Limiting the protest activities of #BlackLivesMatter and other movements like it," "Increasing the number of H1-B visas, which allow U.S. companies to hire people from foreign countries to work in highly skilled occupation, such as engineering, computer programming, and high-technology," and "Renewing temporary relief from deportation for undocumented immigrants brought to the U.S. as children." I dub these variables *Support for BLM*, *Support for H1-B Visas*, and *Support for DACA*, each of which more strongly implicates Blacks, Asian Americans, and Latinos, respectively (cf. Citrin and Sears 2014).

## Knocking the Wind Out of PoC ID

The idea behind the "Distinct Experiences" experiment is this. When racial/ethnic minorities are encouraged to think of themselves as PoC, their PoC ID should structure how they construe their social and political worlds. But if racial/ethnic minorities are encouraged to think more narrowly about their own in-group and how distinct it is in relation to PoC, the effect of PoC ID should weaken, if not vanish altogether. How far off the mark is this reasoning?

The results for Blacks suggest not by much.[3] Figure 7.6 depicts the marginal effect on an outcome that emerges when going from the lowest to highest PoC ID level among Blacks in each condition. Panel A shows that when PoC's uniqueness is affirmed, higher PoC ID levels reliably increase one's view that PoC endure more discrimination than Whites (1.630, $p < .004$, one-tailed). But when Blacks' distinctiveness is highlighted, this PoC ID's effect diminishes (.660, $p < .058$, one-tailed). Similarly, higher PoC ID levels decrease Blacks' agreement that the problems of minorities are too different for them to be allies (−1.339, $p < .064$, one-tailed). But if African Americans are reminded of Blacks' distinctiveness in relation to PoC, PoC ID's impact on this outcome is insignificant (.340, $p < .332$, one-tailed).

This general pattern emerges for *Zero-Sum Perceptions* and *Pro-Minority Sentiment*, too. Panel C shows that when Blacks construe themselves as PoC, higher PoC ID levels marginally decrease their perceived competition with Latinos (−.951, $p < .114$). Yet among Blacks who focus on African Americans' distinctiveness, PoC ID fails to impact this sensed competition (.313, $p < .362$, one-tailed). Blacks in the PoC-Affirming condition also see their PoC ID levels reduce perceptions of zero-sum competition with Asians (−1.194, $p < .067$,

---

3. The raw regression results for each racial group, as well as randomization tests and balance checks for each sample, are reported in tables A3–A10 in the appendix to this chapter.

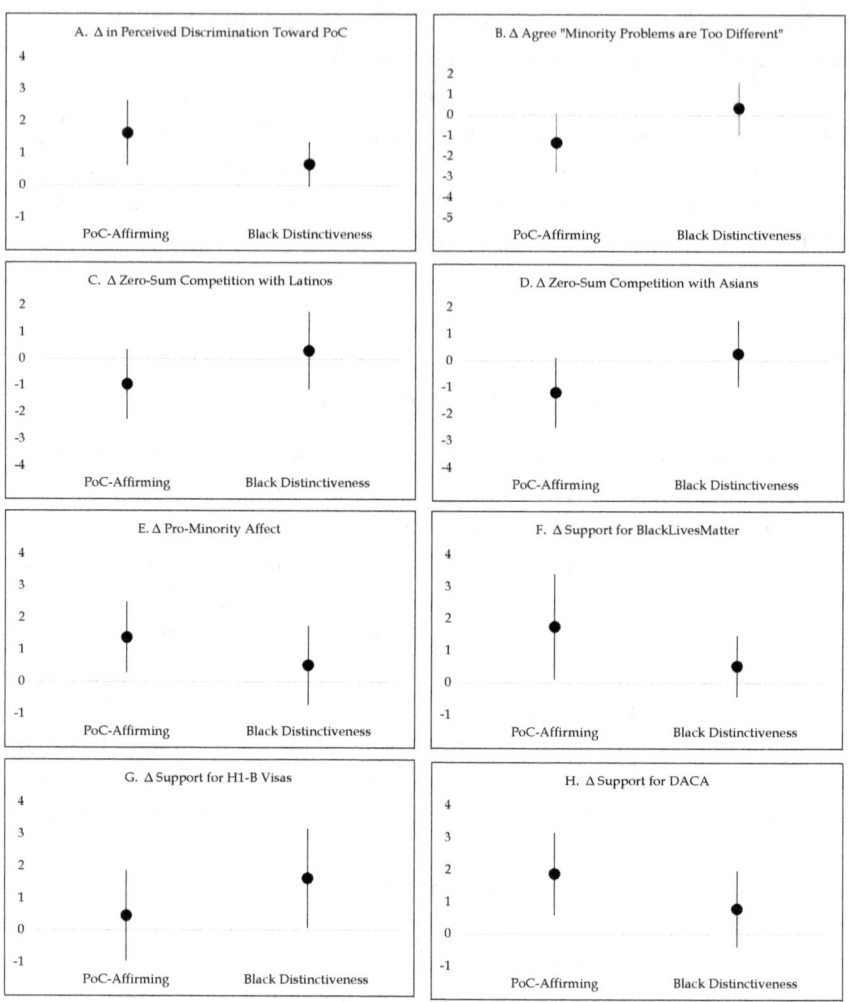

FIGURE 7.6. Effect of PoC ID: Black people

one-tailed). But in the Black Distinctiveness condition, Blacks' PoC ID levels insignificantly affect this perceived conflict (.279, $p < .356$, one-tailed). This dynamic spills onto Blacks' affect for PoC. As figure 7.6, panel E, shows, among Blacks in the PoC-Affirming condition, higher PoC ID levels heighten favorability toward PoC relative to Whites. But among African Americans in the Black Distinctiveness condition, this positive effect of PoC ID shrinks, statistically, to zero (.525, $p < .243$, one-tailed).

Finally, this general trend mostly receives support in the realm of policy opinions. Panel F shows that for Blacks in the PoC-Affirming condition, higher PoC ID levels boost support for #BlackLivesMatter (1.396, $p < .019$,

FALLING APART 167

one-tailed), yet in the Black Distinctiveness condition, PoC ID's effect weakens (.525, $p < .243$, one-tailed), with a comparable pattern for Black support of DACA. The one wrinkle here involves Black support for H1-B visas. As panel G shows, PoC ID levels have no impact on this policy in the PoC-Affirming condition (.468, $p < .292$, one-tailed). Curiously, though, this effect increases reliably in the Black Distinctiveness condition (1.637, $p < .041$, one-tailed).

So far, the evidence for Blacks suggests that reminding them about their racial in-group's distinct struggles and legacies is enough to undercut the influence of their PoC ID. Is this pattern unique to African Americans? The evidence for Latinos in this study suggests not. Figure 7.7 presents the same

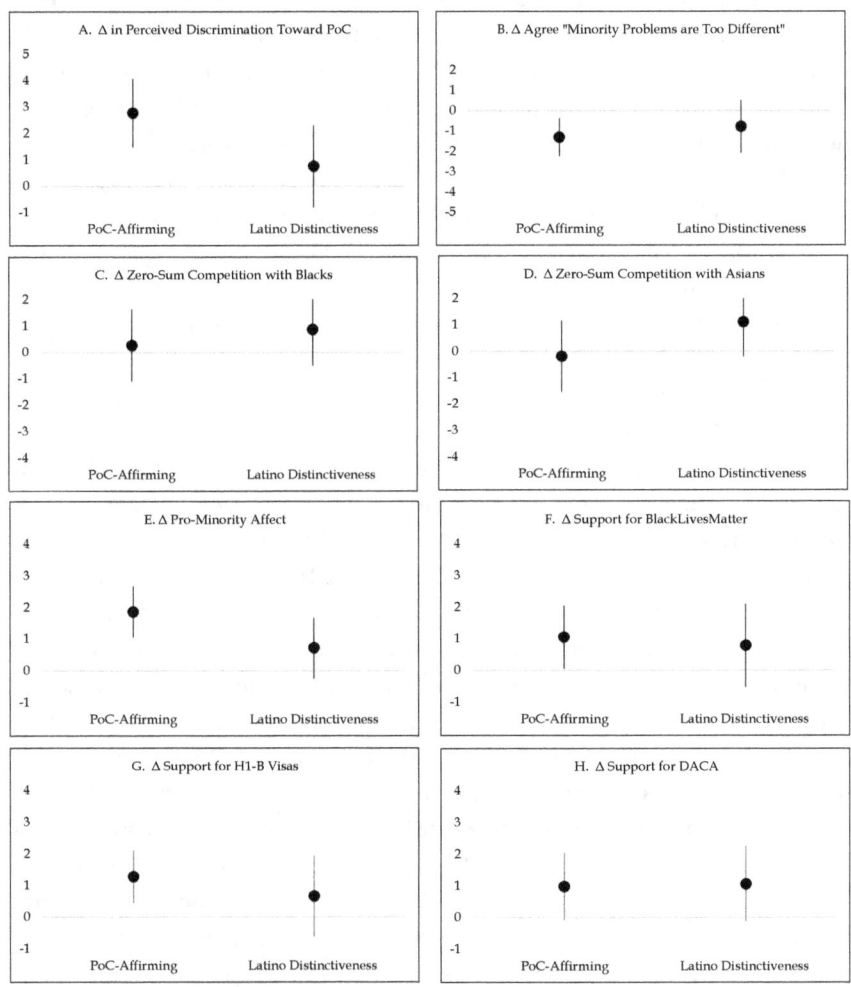

FIGURE 7.7. Effect of PoC ID: Latino people

type of graphs we viewed for African Americans, but this time, with a focus on Latinos. A quick scan of this figure reveals evidence that generally aligns with the results I uncovered for Black adults.

Consider panel A of figure 7.7. In the PoC-Affirming condition, higher PoC ID levels sharpen Latinos' sense of discrimination toward PoC (2.772, $p < .01$, one-tailed). Yet in the Latino Distinctiveness condition, this effect shrivels, statistically, to zero (.758, $p < .208$, one-tailed). Panel B further shows that when the distinctiveness of PoC is affirmed, higher PoC ID levels significantly reduce Latinos' view that the problems of minorities are too different for them to be allies (−1.306, $p < .011$, one-tailed): an effect that dissipates when Latino distinctiveness is underscored (−.785, $p < .159$, one-tailed).

Curiously, insofar as zero-sum competition with minorities is concerned, higher PoC ID levels *fail* to impact Latinos' perceived competition with Blacks (.271, $p < .372$, one-tailed) and Asians (−.189, $p < .409$, one-tailed) if the uniqueness of PoC is affirmed. But if Latinos' distinctiveness of Latinos is underscored, PoC ID levels trend toward boosting Latinos' sense of competition with Blacks .871, $p < .147$, one-tailed) and Asians (1.115, $p < .079$, one-tailed), although neither pattern is significant at conventional levels.

In contrast to these murkier findings, my predicted pattern emerges more clearly on Latinos' favorability toward PoC. Panel E shows that when the distinctiveness of PoC is underscored, higher PoC ID levels reliably increase Latinos' favorability toward racial/ethnic minorities in general (1.869, $p < .010$, one-tailed): an effect that weakens if Latinos' distinctiveness is highlighted (.721, $p < .108$, one-tailed).

Even crisper findings than these emerge on Latino support for policy initiatives. Consider Latinos' endorsement of #BlackLivesMatter. When the distinctiveness of PoC is stressed, higher PoC ID levels reliably boost Latino support for this movement (1.052, $p < .041$, one-tailed). But when the uniqueness of Latino is emphasized, this support shrinks dramatically (.785, $p < .162$, one-tailed). A comparable pattern arises for Latino support of H1-B visas. When the uniqueness of PoC is underlined, higher PoC ID levels heighten Latino support for these visas, which are strongly associated with Asian American immigration flows (Junn 2005; Zou and Cheryan 2017). But when Latinos' distinctiveness is pointed out, the effect of PoC ID shrivels substantially (.665, $p < .196$, one-tailed). The one small quirk here involves Latino support for DACA, which is strongly associated with their ethnic group. Panel H suggests that in the PoC-Affirming condition, higher PoC ID levels increase one's support for this policy measure (.989, $p < .064$): an effect that remains statistically identical in the Latino Distinctiveness condition (1.067, $p < .070$, one-tailed).

FALLING APART 169

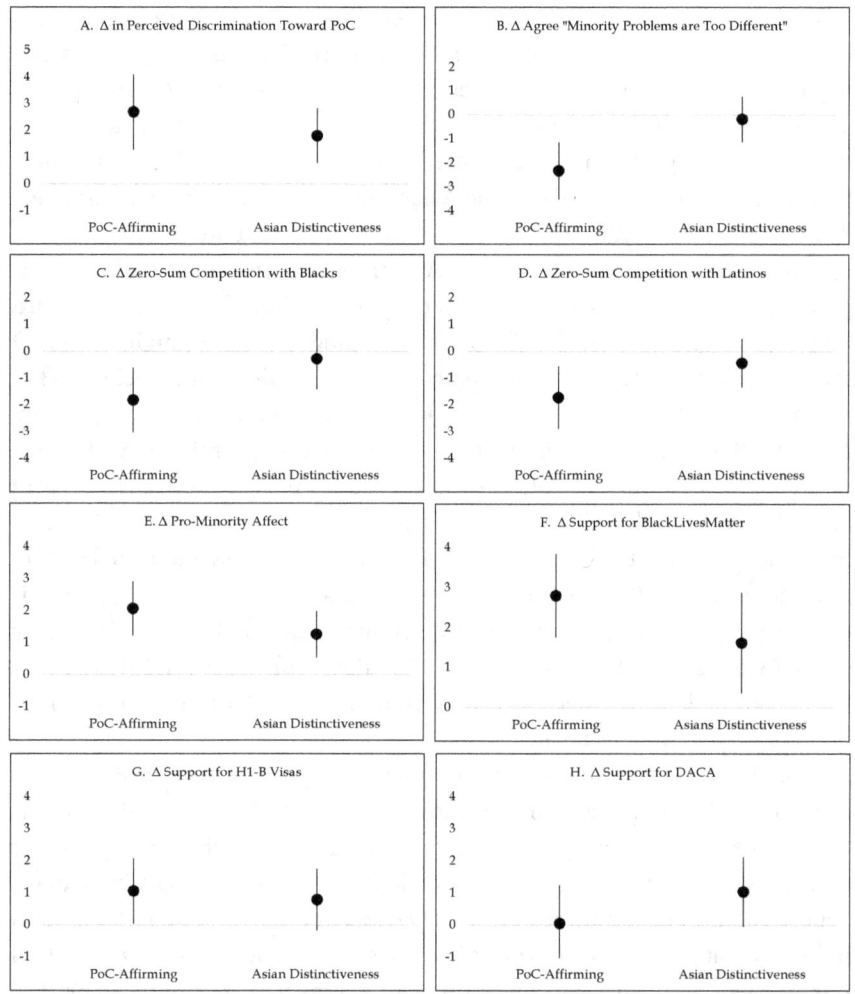

FIGURE 7.8. Effect of PoC ID: Asian people

Taken together, the findings for Latinos suggest that the switching "on" and "off" of PoC ID operates in the same general way as it does for Blacks, which extends the breadth of this mechanism. The remaining question is whether this dynamic also helps to explain PoC ID's operation among Asian Americans?

Figure 7.8 displays evidence suggesting that it does. Let's start with Asian Americans' sense of discrimination toward PoC. Panel A reveals that in the PoC-Affirming condition, higher PoC ID levels heighten Asian Americans' perceived discrimination toward PoC (2.692, $p < .01$, one-tailed). In the Asian

Distinctiveness condition, however, we see a reduction in these perceptions (1.805, $p < .01$, one-tailed). The anticipated pattern also arises in Asians' sense of partnership with other PoC. Panel B shows that in the PoC-Affirming condition, higher PoC ID levels reliably decrease Asian Americans' agreement that minorities' problems are too different from them to be allies or partners ($-2.326$, $p < .001$, one-tailed). In the Asian Distinctiveness, though, this effect drops both in size and significance ($-.183$, $p < .375$, one-tailed).

The distinctiveness of the Asian American experience also affects their perceived competition with other minority groups and their feelings toward them. Panel C shows that in the PoC-Affirming condition, higher PoC ID levels significantly reduce Asians' perceived competition with Blacks ($-1.823$, $p < .01$, one-tailed). This effect shrinks in size and significance ($-.279$, $p < .343$, one-tailed) when Asians' uniqueness is underscored. Similarly, if the outgroup is Latinos, higher PoC ID levels reduce Asian Americans' sense of competition with them if PoC's uniqueness is underlined ($-1.727$, $p < .010$, one-tailed): an effect that weakens if Asians' distinctiveness is affirmed ($-.430$, $p < .220$, one-tailed). This predicted pattern also manifests in Asian Americans' feelings toward PoC. As panel E reveals, higher PoC ID levels reliably boost Asian favorability toward PoC in the PoC-Affirming condition (2.069, $p < .01$, one-tailed). Yet this effect weakens in the Asian Distinctiveness condition (1.260, $p < .01$, one-tailed).

Finally, when we turn to Asian Americans' policy preferences, we observe a similar dynamic. Panel F shows that in the PoC-Affirming condition, higher PoC ID levels drastically increase Asian Americans' support for #BlackLivesMatter (2.795, $p < .01$, one-tailed), yet in the Asian Distinctiveness condition, this effect diminishes (1.618, $p < .05$, one-tailed). Similarly, panel G indicates that higher PoC ID levels boost Asian Americans' support for H1-B visas in the PoC-Affirming condition, with a weaker effect produced by PoC ID levels in the Asian Distinctiveness condition (.796, $p < .087$, one-tailed). The single blemish here involves Asian support for DACA. Panel H shows that in the PoC-Affirming condition, higher PoC ID levels *fail* to heighten Asian American support for DACA (.048, $p < .474$, one-tailed), but increase support for this measure in the Asian Distinctiveness condition (1.048, $p < .055$, one-tailed).

Looking across the results for African Americans, Latinos, and Asian Americans in the "Distinct Experiences" experiment, there is a basic underlying pattern in the data that is hard to miss. Higher PoC ID levels shape minorities' feelings, judgments, and policy preferences, *but only when the uniqueness of PoC is underscored*. This implies that in order for PoC ID to collectively shape the political opinions of racial/ethnic minorities, the category PoC must be made salient and its distinctiveness affirmed. This one-two punch appears to guide minorities' attitudes by directing them toward PoC as the relevant attachment to rely on in a setting, while reminding them about why they—and not others—share in its communion.

But there is another, perhaps less uplifting, side to this dynamic: insofar as one's attention is focused on one's narrower racial/ethnic group and its own particular experiences, the potency of PoC ID is vastly diminished. Simply affirming just how different one's immediate racial in-group is with respect to PoC is enough to zap the wider collective behavior this superordinate attachment engenders.

To further probe the robustness of this pattern, I performed a meta-analysis that pools across the three samples of Blacks, Latinos, and Asian Americans and focuses on the six outcomes that are strictly comparable between these groups (for results, see table 7.2) (Goh, Hall, and Rosenthal 2016).[4] A scan of the table from top to bottom for each outcome reveals that in the majority of outcomes under analysis—two out of three, to be exact—the influence of PoC ID is reliable and in the expected direction when this category is affirmed, yet significantly weaker when one's racial or ethnic distinctiveness is underlined. Even the two exceptions to this pattern (i.e., support for DACA and support for H1B visas) reveal an interesting twist: namely, PoC ID levels boost support for these policy measures when PoC are affirmed, and this effect continues even if the distinctiveness of one's racial or ethnic group is highlighted, which bolsters the case for a PoC ID that is politically meaningful and potent. Indeed, the steadfast influence of PoC ID on support for these immigration policies raises the possibility that in some issue domains, distinctiveness pressures might have a difficult time fully undermining the hold of PoC ID over members of some non-White groups, a possibility that future research should explore further. Ultimately, these additional results are all the more powerful because they align with what we see in the "real world" of minority politics. From Ms. Widatalla's call to erase the label *PoC* to the many nuanced experiences that, according to some PoC, different racial and ethnic groups undergo or have undergone (see chapter 3), the switch to a more comprehensive sense of being PoC seems to rest on the knife-edge construal of one's racial in-group as either patently similar to other minorities or vastly distinct from them.

---

4. The two outcomes excluded from this analysis are those focusing on individual perceptions of zero-sum competition with racial/ethnic minority out-groups, which vary across samples and, therefore, prevent me from undertaking analyses that are completely and fully comparable across samples.

TABLE 7.2. Mini meta-analysis of PoC ID under both experimental conditions

| | Perceived discrimination | Problems too different | Pro-PoC sentiment | BLM support | DACA support | H1-B support |
|---|---|---|---|---|---|---|
| PoC ID (affirming) | .254 [.166, .338] | −.187 [−.274, −.097] | .275 [.188, .357] | .216 [.126, .301] | .093 [.002, .184] | .135 [.044, .224] |
| PoC ID (distinctiveness) | .144 [.048, .238] | .049 [−.047, .143] | .134 [.039, .227] | .106 [.011, .199] | .114 [.019, .207] | .123 [.028, .216] |
| Null: Difference = 0? ($p <$ value, one-tailed) | No ($p < .040$) | No ($p < .050$) | No ($p < .001$) | No ($p < .040$) | Yes ($p < .370$) | Yes ($p < .425$) |

Note: Entries are average correlations ($r$) between PoC ID levels and each outcome under each experimental condition, controlling for levels of racial/ethnic ID and liberal ideology.

## Summary

This chapter began with an interest in explaining how the unity and coherence of PoC can unfurl. The collection of experiments I analyzed across the previous pages reveal several new insights on this front, all stemming from two considerations.

The first involves the interface between superordinate and subordinate identities that individuals often must manage. In the case at hand, the category *PoC* encapsulates a variety of unique racial/ethnic groups under a broader umbrella. This wide canopy envelops a suite of groups by giving them purpose, camaraderie, and the motivation to act on behalf of other PoC. The reasons for this are manifold, but they all boil down to a simple essence: can a credible case be made that PoC are a diverse but coherent group that belongs together? Insofar as the answer to this question is yes, the cognitive link between PoC ID and racial ID is bolstered, which facilitates the gathering of racial minorities under the banner PoC.

This coordinated action, though, is not a static feature of PoC; rather, it is, as social identity theorists have taught us (Ellemers, Spears, and Doosje 2002; Tajfel and Turner 1986), an attribute of the intergroup context. Moreover, this attribute can shift dramatically, the experiments here have taught us, simply on the basis of whether that interface between PoC ID and racial ID is weakened. In the collection of experiments reported here, the most revealing lesson is that this diminished connection between both attachments can occur for objective as well as subjective reasons. In the "Distinct Stations" experiment, for example, PoC shifted their perceptions of who counts as bona fide members of this group on the basis of factual information about its composite members in a particular setting. Thus, we learn that such facts can be construed in ways that galvanize or discourage PoC from acting in greater unison.

However, these experiments also suggest that the fortunes of PoC do not simply rest on objective matters of fact. Indeed, the plying and interpretation of subjective criteria seems to have comparable effects. As the "Distinct Experiences" experiments teach us, simply interpreting the experiences of racial and ethnic minorities as largely interchangeable or generally distinct is sufficient to amplify or undercut the influence of PoC ID levels on minorities' feelings, judgments, and policy preferences. When we consider that these experiments are the first of their kind among PoC, these implications are all the more deeply appreciated and informative.

## APPENDIX

TABLE 7.A1. Latino prototypicality ratings by experimental condition

|  | Blacks as prototype | Latinos as prototype | Asians as prototype |
|---|---|---|---|
| Latinos ascending | −.053* (.026) | −.013 (.027) | −.116* (.051) |
| Asians predominate | −.047* (.028) | −.200 (.028) | −.044 (.051) |
| Constant | .963* (.018) | .894* (.019) | .491* (.036) |
| N | 245 | 240 | 225 |

Note: *$p < .05$, one-tailed.

TABLE 7.A2. Asian prototypicality ratings by experimental condition

|  | Blacks as prototype | Latinos as prototype | Asians as prototype |
|---|---|---|---|
| Latinos ascending | −.080* (.032) | −.061* (.032) | .032 (.060) |
| Asians predominate | −.079* (.032) | −.049 (.035) | −.011 (.061) |
| Constant | .968* (.022) | .871* (.024) | .636* (.042) |
| N | 131 | 128 | 112 |

Note: *$p < .05$, one-tailed.

TABLE 7.A3. Influence of PoC ID on Black beliefs and opinions ("Distinct Experiences" experiment)

| | PoC discrimination | Too different | Zero-sum: Latinos | Zero-sum: Asians | Pro-PoC affect | BLM support | H1-B support | DACA support |
|---|---|---|---|---|---|---|---|---|
| PoC ID | 1.630* (.605) | −1.339^ (.875) | −.951 (.787) | −1.194^ (.793) | 1.396* (.667) | 1.753* (.994) | .468 (.852) | 1.302* (.666) |
| PoC ID × Black distinctiveness | −.969 (.740) | 1.678^ (1.163) | 1.263 (1.167) | 1.473^ (1.077) | −.871 (.981) | −1.227 (1.144) | 1.168 (1.250) | −.941 (.962) |
| Black distinctiveness | .266 (.437) | −.138 (.575) | .577 (.573) | .243 (.554) | .183 (.403) | −.220 (.636) | −.441 (.642) | −.024 (.538) |
| Black ID | .240 (.589) | 1.133^ (.860) | 1.713* (.717) | 2.070* (.739) | 1.240* (.592) | −.650 (.951) | .163 (.803) | −.120 (.653) |
| Black ID × Black distinctiveness | .786 (.724) | −1.839^ (1.142) | −2.385* (1.124) | −2.323* (1.041) | .382 (.855) | 2.167* (1.116) | −.517 (1.120) | 1.202 (.977) |
| Liberal | .222* (.047) | −.281* (.072) | −.209* (.063) | −.228* (.064) | .240* (.054) | .301* (.068) | .235* (.072) | .371* (.058) |
| Constant | 2.821* (.362) | 4.287* (.518) | 3.322* (.472) | 3.492* (.464) | −2.574* (.272) | 3.395* (.499) | 3.008* (.072) | 2.922* (.442) |
| N | 291 | 291 | 289 | 291 | 289 | 290 | 291 | 291 |

Note: *p < .05, one–tailed; ^p < .10, one–tailed.

TABLE 7.A4. Influence of PoC ID on Latino beliefs and opinions ("Distinct Experiences" experiment)

| | PoC discrimination | Too different | Zero-sum: Blacks | Zero-sum: Asians | Pro-PoC affect | BLM support | DACA support | H1-B support |
|---|---|---|---|---|---|---|---|---|
| PoC ID | 2.772* (.782) | −1.306* (.562) | .271 (.826) | −.188 (.820) | 1.869* (.486) | 1.052* (.600) | .989^ (.646) | 1.286* (.501) |
| PoC ID × Latino distinctiveness | −2.014* (1.228) | .521 (.969) | .600 (1.176) | 1.304 (1.141) | −1.147^ (.760) | −.267 (1.003) | .078 (.966) | −.621 (.930) |
| Latino distinctiveness | 1.627* (.564) | −.627^ (.462) | −1.142* (.586) | −.687 (.580) | .306 (.307) | .718^ (.525) | .245 (.518) | .172 (.442) |
| Latino ID | 1.001^ (.733) | .080 (.626) | −1.078 (.860) | −.380 (.865) | .639^ (.406) | 1.222* (.641) | .358 (.659) | .407 (.545) |
| Latino ID × Latino distinctiveness | −1.672^ (1.200) | .786 (.970) | .729 (1.222) | −.522 (1.203) | .031 (.696) | −1.420^ (1.024) | −.490 (.940) | −.306 (.948) |
| Liberal | −.003 (.091) | .038 (.061) | .143* (.074) | .102^ (.072) | −.038 (.048) | .024 (.073) | .076 (.071) | .083 (.072) |
| Constant | 1.000* (.599) | 2.896* (.404) | 3.846* (.492) | 3.781* (.495) | −.265 (.297) | 4.179* (.474) | 3.761* (.493) | 4.600 (.458) |
| N | 294 | 295 | 295 | 295 | 293 | 295 | 295 | 295 |

Note: *p < .05, one–tailed; ^p < .10, one–tailed.

TABLE 7.A5. Influence of PoC ID on Asian beliefs and opinions ("Distinct Experiences" Experiment)

| | PoC discrimination | Too different | Zero-sum: Blacks | Zero-sum: Latinos | Pro-PoC affect | BLM support | DACA support | H1-B support |
|---|---|---|---|---|---|---|---|---|
| PoC ID | 2.692* (.856) | −2.326* (.715) | −1.823* (.727) | −1.727* (.707) | 2.069* (.515) | 2.795* (.632) | .048 (.724) | 1.066* (.616) |
| PoC ID × Asian distinctiveness | −.887 (1.052) | 2.143* (.917) | 1.544^ (1.003) | 1.297^ (.899) | −.809 (.681) | −1.176 (.992) | .999 (.979) | −.270 (.849) |
| Asian distinctiveness | .477 (.662) | .023 (.605) | .336 (.604) | −.049 (.600) | −.457^ (.309) | .422 (.575) | −.681 (.642) | .634 (.501) |
| Asian ID | .411 (.862) | 1.302* (.755) | 1.696* (.770) | 1.342* (.778) | −.975* (.523) | −.338 (.619) | .011 (.821) | −.002 (.642) |
| Asian ID × Asian distinctiveness | .463 (1.127) | −2.086* (1.032) | −2.295* (1.122) | −1.608^ (1.037) | 1.757* (.724) | .426 (1.099) | .153 (1.110) | −.601 (.952) |
| Liberal | −.072 (.065) | .189* (.060) | .161* (.062) | .148* (.057) | 1.757* (.724) | −.148^ (.069) | −.020 (.062) | −.045 (.051) |
| Constant | 1.449* (.583) | 2.544* (.549) | 2.274* (.529) | 2.492* (.531) | .500^ (.321) | 4.649* (.501) | 4.919* (.572) | 5.099* (.051) |
| N | 308 | 309 | 309 | 309 | 309 | 309 | 309 | 309 |

Note: *p < .05, one-tailed; ^p < .10, one-tailed.

TABLE 7.A6. Randomization check: "Distinct Stations" experiment (Latinos)

|  | Asians predominate | Latinos ascending |
|---|---|---|
| US-born | −.433 (.474) | .456 (.477) |
| Mexican | −.606 (.489) | .457 (.421) |
| Democrat | .662 (.498) | −.078 (.437) |
| Female | −.449 (.555) | −.234 (.437) |
| N | 141 | |
| Null: covariates = 0? | $\chi^2 (8) = 9.74, p < .284$ | |

Note: Entries are coefficients from a multinomial logit, with the control group as the base category.
*$p < .05$, two-tailed.

TABLE 7.A7. Randomization check: "Distinct Stations" experiment (Asians)

|  | Asians predominate | Latinos ascending |
|---|---|---|
| US-born | .085 (.464) | .346 (.472) |
| Mexican | .310 (.432) | .317 (.422) |
| Democrat | .237 (.405) | .164 (.389) |
| Female | −.084 (.385) | −.245 (.367) |
| N | 244 | |
| Null: covariates = 0? | $\chi^2 (8) = 2.20, p < .974$ | |

Note: Entries are coefficients from a multinomial logit, with the control group as the base category.
*$p < .05$, two-tailed.

TABLE 7.A8. Balance check: "Distinct Stations" experiment (Latinos and Asians)

|  | Latinos | Asians |
|---|---|---|
| US-born | $\chi^2 (2) = .782, p < .676$ | $\chi^2 (2) = 1.546, p < .462$ |
| Mexican [Chinese] | $\chi^2 (2) = .787, p < .674$ | $\chi^2 (2) = 4.390, p < .111$ |
| Democrat | $\chi^2 (2) = .980, p < .861$ | $\chi^2 (2) = 2.665, p < .264$ |
| Female | $\chi^2 (2) = .392, p < .822$ | $\chi^2 (2) = 1.015, p < .602$ |

TABLE 7.A9. Randomization check: "Distinct Experiences" experiment (Blacks, Latinos, and Asians)

|  | Black distinctiveness | Latino distinctiveness | Asian distinctiveness |
|---|---|---|---|
| US-born | −.177 (.392) | .082 (.272) | −.210 (.177) |
| College-educated | −.127 (.151) | −.092 (.148) | .088 (.146) |
| Democrat | −.068 (.151) | .044 (.148) | −.057 (.147) |
| Female | .131 (.150) | −.169 (.150) | −.019 (.148) |
| Mexican [Chinese] | — | −.001 (.150) | −.022 (.156) |
| Null: covariates = 0? | $\chi^2 (4) = 2.05, p < .727$ | $\chi^2 (5) = 1.93, p < .859$ | $\chi^2 (5) = 2.06, p < .841$ |

TABLE 7.A10. Balance check: "Distinct Experiences" experiment (Blacks, Asians, and Latinos)

|  | Black distinctiveness | Latino distinctiveness | Asian distinctiveness |
|---|---|---|---|
| US-born | $\chi^2(1) = .219, p < .640$ | $\chi^2(1) = .096, p < .757$ | $\chi^2(1) = 1.542, p < .214$ |
| College-educated | $\chi^2(1) = .719, p < .396$ | $\chi^2(1) = .479, p < .489$ | $\chi^2(1) = .332, p < .565$ |
| Democrat | $\chi^2(1) = .453, p < .501$ | $\chi^2(1) = .097, p < .755$ | $\chi^2(1) = .212, p < .645$ |
| Female | $\chi^2(1) = .844, p < .358$ | $\chi^2(1) = 1.345, p < .246$ | $\chi^2(1) = .000, p < 1.00$ |
| Mexican [Chinese] | — | $\chi^2(1) = .039, p < .843$ | $\chi^2(1) = .061, p < .805$ |

CONCLUSION

# People of Color in a Diversifying World

Across the preceding seven empirical chapters, we have moved, piece by piece, toward a more complete portrait of people of color (PoC): who they are, what they think, what they believe, and how they express themselves—all within the realm of American politics. What does this portrait convey, and what does it portend for our understanding of racial and ethnic politics in a rapidly diversifying nation? Teasing out the political implications of PoC ID is the task ahead of us in this concluding chapter.

To this end, I explain how PoC ID deepens our understanding of identity formation in increasingly heterogeneous settings. I also discuss what PoC ID has to say about the ebb and flow of interminority conflict and cooperation in a world of neck-breaking racial and ethnic diversity. Lastly, I elaborate on what my findings indicate about the character of America's racial order and its consequences for mass politics. But before plunging into these much deeper conversations, let's start, first, with a quick review of what we have learned from the preceding chapters.

## Taking Stock

I started this book with a rough intuition: that in light of growing racial and ethnic diversity in the United States, non-White individuals face a variety of new motivations and opportunities to coalesce under a common banner of identity. I have used the foregoing chapters to bring that intuition to light, with the goal of distilling my reasoning into a handful of hypotheses that I have tested empirically. Here are my main conclusions, based on these efforts:

- The essence of PoC ID is its nesting capacity. Insofar as PoC ID affects the politics of a wide swath of US racial and ethnic minorities, it does so by cutting across and encapsulating the unique identities of these smaller groups. The power of PoC ID, then, resides in its ability to shape how assorted minority groups construe themselves, from uniquely Latino, African American, or Asian American, to distinctly as PoC. This panoramic outlook manifests itself, not only in the words and deeds of PoC, but also in the wall of support they build around their peers when they perceive the type of discrimination that all racial and ethnic minorities seem to endure at some point in their lives. Thus, while minority groups are not and cannot be identical, they can, under many circumstances, see themselves interchangeably as PoC.
- PoC ID is a unique attachment, independent of other identities held by PoC. It is also an individual difference: all minorities identify as PoC to a degree. These individual differences matter politically. The more strongly one identifies as a PoC, the more likely one is to express social and political opinions that enhance the well-being of racial and ethnic minorities. This includes support for policy proposals that broadly impact non-Whites, such as the strengthening of voting rights and measures against hate crimes, as well as support for "narrower" initiatives, like moral support for #BlackLivesMatter and more welcoming stances toward undocumented immigrants.
- PoC ID is a highly accessible form of group attachment. Put differently, it takes little effort to mentally activate this new identity. With minimal prompting from the political world, this form of attachment kicks into gear among racial and ethnic minorities, leading them to express attitudes and beliefs that put PoC in the best possible light or under more optimal political and social circumstances.
- PoC ID does not matter all the time. Just as it can be enlisted for political action, it can also be called back and defused. The key to this dynamic is distinctiveness; that is, the moment that members of any racial or ethnic minority group are reminded about their specific community's unique position, experiences, struggles, and aspirations, their ability to remain in solidarity with other PoC is challenged. In these circumstances, the group's panoramic generosity of PoC ID is replaced with narrower and more miserly views toward racial and ethnic minorities who are not in the same exact circumstances as them.

## Intergroup Conflict and Cooperation

What does this new knowledge imply for our collective understandings of diversity and politics? One major area my findings speak to is the interface between intergroup conflict and cooperation. In a mass democracy like the United States, conflict and cooperation are the lifeblood of politics. It is how elections are won and lost. It is how policy proposals become law or are discarded into oblivion. It is how institutions persist or crumble. But in traditional renditions of American democracy (Carey and McClellan 2001; Smith 1997), the masses operate as individuals. They are presumed to deliberate, arrive at, and vote their own *self*-interest. My findings, in contrast, underscore the group basis of American politics, demonstrating, yet again, that our political outcomes and practices are a strong function of how individuals coalesce into groups in order to press their political system, a point stressed repeatedly by Leonie Huddy and others (Huddy 2001, 2013; Marx 1998; Tajfel 1981).

My contribution here is nonetheless unique relative to these predecessors. When political scientists focus their attention on racial and ethnic minorities, their point of departure is typically one of two strong assumptions, often framed as mutually exclusive: either racial minorities are bound to cooperate because they all share a lowly status *or* they are bound to conflict because they are wildly different in terms of their social status and unique histories (Benjamin 2017; Cutaia Wilkinson 2015; McClain et al. 2005; McClain and Johnson Carew 2017). In contrast, I have treated these assumptions as end posts in a continuum of interminority politics, where conflict and cooperation between racial and ethnic minorities is neither inevitable nor avoidable, but instead driven by deep psychological motivations that find expression under certain conditions.

To this end, I begin with a clear-eyed look at reality. Racial and ethnic minorities are internally diverse, and very little unifies them, except perhaps their minority status and experiences with discrimination. Some scholars and political practitioners draw on these aspects of minority groups to argue or imply that minorities "naturally" belong together in a single group (e.g., Skrentny 2002; Vidal-Ortiz 2008; Yuen 1997). But as Natalie Masuoka, Jane Junn, and many others note, such commonalities rest on a knife's edge, given the varied placement of specific racial and ethnic minorities in America's racial order (e.g., Kim 2003; Masuoka and Junn 2013; Sidanius and Petrocik 2001; Zou and Cheryan 2017). These positions vary along innumerous dimensions, including how each group arrived to the United States, its treatment and persecution by US authorities, and the current inequities experienced by specific groups (Carter 2019; García 2012; Takaki 1989). Yet Zou and Cheryan (2017) also posit that the social position of all racial and ethnic minority groups vary, fundamentally, in terms of how inferior and foreign non-Whites are deemed to be. According to this parsimonious rendition, African Americans are, for example, held in lower esteem than other minority groups, such as Asians, but are considered more American than other groups, such as Latinos, who are deemed foreigners. In turn, Asian Americans are also widely considered foreign, but they are held in higher social esteem than are Blacks and Latinos (Kim 2003), who occupy the bottommost rungs of America's racial hierarchy. The point here is not to pinpoint which group "has it worse," but to underscore that all PoC occupy unique social positions that motivate their interpretation and reaction to the world around them, including the presence of other non-Whites (Perez and Kuo, forthcoming).

Indeed, these varying positions and experiences matter, especially if we aim to get a handle on when we might anticipate interminority conflict, rather than cooperation. Throughout the experiments described in this book, when we observed minorities acting in unison and solidarity with each other, the underlying basis of such action was a shared sense of identification—the broad notion that, as minorities, "we" are interchangeable members of the same group. For instance, in the "I Feel Your Pain" and "Political Galvanization" experiments, distinct racial and ethnic minority groups built a wall of support around PoC in reaction to circumstances that seemed shared by all PoC. The lesson here, then, is not that PoC must experience the exact same thing in order to engage in collective action, but rather that a deep sense of shared experience is sufficient for members of widely diverse groups to appreciate, and act upon, the common ground they hold as minorities (e.g., Sirin, Valentino, and Villalobos 2016a, b). This differs from previous findings. In social psychology, for example, Maureen Craig, Jennifer Richeson, and their colleagues have illuminated the psychology of coalition building among racial minorities, showing the major role that perceived similarity plays (e.g., Cortland et al. 2017; Craig and Richeson 2016). My work takes one more step further by showing that this perceived similarity actually coalesces into a broad sense of identity—that "you and I are one"—which can be activated quite easily by politics.

Just as importantly, the preceding chapters also establish that there is nothing ineluctable about this shared sense of PoC ID. Indeed, inasmuch as it can be called up by the realm of public affairs, it can also be deactivated by politics. This was demonstrated by the "Distinct Experiences" experiments, which highlighted the unique experiences, goals, and aspirations of each group—in other words, the variation in minority experiences that leads some groups to be more devalued or seen as more American by US society (Kim 2003; Zou and Cheryan 2017). By simply focusing on the distinctiveness of one's minority group, this trio of studies revealed that the wall of support that minorities build around each other can crumble under the stress of feeling that one's own unique trials and tribulations are underappreciated or overlooked.

Ultimately, then, the main lesson from all of these findings is that the future unfolding of interminority politics in the US will depend on firmly grasping this psychology, with political circumstances holding one important set of keys to propel racial and ethnic minority groups toward greater and lesser cooperation.

## Group Identity in Diverse Settings

Although I have primarily focused on intraminority politics in the United States herein, I believe the conceptual apparatus I have built to study this phenomenon is generic enough to travel to cases beyond the US or the specific groups I have studied. In particular, the interface between PoC ID and the many unique racial or ethnic IDs that US minorities possess offers an alternate way of understanding how new groups can, in a psychological sense, be created from preexisting configurations.

My results suggest that the existence and meaningfulness of a broad-based identity like PoC ID hinges, critically, on its ability to encapsulate and accommodate the variously unique racial and ethnic identities that minorities possess, as well as the distinct experiences they endure. This challenge is finessed when members of each racial and ethnic group cognitively nest their own subgroup identity under a broader attachment like PoC ID. This psychological process allows diverse individuals to redirect their attention away from their immediate subgroup to a much broader and widely shared megagroup. Just as importantly, this process also redirects the benefits of in-group favoritism by projecting them onto the new, broadly shared group (Gaertner et al. 1989, 1999; Levendusky 2018; Transue 2007; Wenzel, Mummendey, and Waldzus 2007).

None of this is particular to PoC ID. Indeed, this same framework can be adapted to throw light on how other US categories, often taken as given, achieve this status Consider, for example, a pan-ethnic category like Latino, or a pan-racial category like Asian American. Many political observers have questioned the meaningfulness of these broadly inclusive and internally heterogeneous megagroups (e.g., Beltrán 2010; de la Garza et al. 1992; Lien, Conway, and Wong 2004; McClain and Johnson Carew 2017; Wong et al. 2011). But this observation clashes with harder, empirical evidence establishing the impact of these categories on the individual political behavior of Latinos and Asian Americans (e.g., Barreto 2005; Kuo, Malhotra, and Mo 2017; Pérez 2015a, b). My findings bridge these perspectives by establishing that despite the heterogeneity between these subgroups, their ability to nest under a superordinate category depends on the ability of individuals to draw on some points of commonality and configure them into an entity that is cognitively and affectively shared (cf. Chandra and Boulet 2012; Cortland et al. 2017; Levendusky 2018; Posner 2005). Indeed, whether these groups are Mexicans, Puerto Ricans, and Cubans in the United States (Mora 2014); the Fon and Yoruba-Nagot in Benin (Ferree 2012); or the Chewas and Tumbukas in Zambia (Posner 2005), the ability of individuals to generate broader groups from preexisting categories is an empirical regularity with deeply psychological roots.

In this way, my book also speaks to smoldering debates about the constructivist versus primordialist nature of group identities: a debate that has raged mostly in comparative politics, but which has also sparked embers in American politics (e.g., Dawson 1994; García 2012). The primordialist view of ethnic identities construes them as deeply felt, historically rooted, and highly immutable (Barth 1969; Brass 1997; Kinder and Kam 2009). In contrast, the constructivist view of ethnic identities considers them to be dynamic and responsive to situational and institutional incentives (e.g., Chandra 2005; Posner 2005). The truth, as I and others see it, is likely somewhere in the middle of these extremes. While group identities can be created out of thin air in laboratory settings (Billig and Tajfel 1973; Tajfel et al. 1971; Tajfel and Turner 1986), in the real world of politics, they cannot just be conjured up out of nowhere (e.g., Ferree 2012).

More often than not, the creation of new identities rests on the reconfiguring of boundaries and rearrangement of attributes displayed by preexisting groups. Here, Kanchan Chandra's path-breaking conceptual work (2012) is instructive. Cutting through enormous detail of several groups, she teaches us that, at their psychological core, identities are nominal categories that are (re)combined with a specific set of attributes, usually through the efforts of political entrepreneurs. Against this backdrop, the findings from this book suggest that shifts in the social position of minorities in America's racial hierarchy have incentivized these marginalized communities to rearrange the narrower nominal categories they belong to and the attributes pinned to them into a new and broadly shared category—all in an effort to collectively press the political system and challenge their social position. In this way, my book's findings enhance the conceptual toolkit available to scholars aiming to better understand the development and consequences of group identity in diverse settings.

## Hierarchy and Intergroup Life

While this project has aimed to better understand the political psychology of PoC ID, one of my parallel objectives has been to demonstrate how this psychology is underpinned by changes in America's racial order. Since our country's inception, this hierarchy has been one in which Whites have predominated in terms of demographics, power, resources, and social status, with non-Whites arrayed below them (Kim 2003; Masuoka and Junn 2013; Sidanius and Pratto 1999). In traditional renditions, the non-White group that has received the most scholarly focus is Black Americans (Marx 1998; Omi and Winant 1986; Smith 1997), with less emphasis typically given to Asian Americans, Latinos, Muslim Americans, and Native Americans. The end result has been that scholars have generally treated this hierarchy in binary fashion, with Whites being demarcated sharply from Blacks (Kinder and Sanders 1996; Myrdal 1944). Besides ignoring the wide diversity of individuals pooling at the bottom of this racial well, this general approach has also presumed unerring stability in America's hierarchy. Yet two features of this order have gradually shifted in the past 50 years, encouraging scholars to reconsider how they construe the racial order between groups in the United States.

In terms of demographics, it is still the case that Whites occupy the top of this order. But in the past five decades, that foothold has started to loosen via an explosion in the raw numbers of non-Whites noted subsequently. In particular, the increased presence of Asian Americans and Latinos, combined with the presence of Blacks and other minority groups, has made the prospect of a majority-minority nation more within reach—a new development in our country's history. Indeed, this novelty is being captured in real time by growing research portraying a White population with many of its members hunkering down and lashing out—politically, socially, and economically—at anything that smacks of racial and ethnic diversity (Craig and Richeson 2014; Danbold and Huo 2015; Jardina 2019; Pérez et al. 2019).

Yet the changes in America's racial order have also meant strong rumblings down below, with a PoC ID providing clear evidence of the changing station of racial and ethnic minority groups. While these minority groups are still generally positioned below Whites in social, economic, and political terms, their exact position—especially with respect to each other—varies tremendously, making the emergence of PoC ID more of a puzzle than an obvious given. For example, as previously mentioned, although African Americans are generally viewed as a low status group in America's hierarchy, it is also the case that they are deemed more American than other minorities, such as Asians and Latinos. In turn, while Asians and Latinos are deemed less American than Blacks and Whites, Asians are considered higher status and, thus, closer to Whites than either Latinos or Blacks (Masuoka and Junn 2013; Zou and Cheryan 2017). How does PoC ID find fertile ground in a complicated setting like this one?

To understand why, one must focus on the psychology of group identity among racial and ethnic minorities. When hierarchies are stable and their prospects for change are limited, members of groups on the outs scramble for ways to bolster their group, even if it entails absolutely no change in their objective position in the hierarchy, what Henri Tajfel and his collaborators called *social creativity* (Tajfel 1981; Tajfel and Turner 1986). But when hierarchies are unstable and their prospects for change are palpable (Doosje, Ellemers, and Spears 1995), members of lower-ranked groups add to social creativity in a new way: they engage in *social competition* (Tajfel and Turner 1986). This is the notion that lower-ranked out-groups actively take the fight to a predominant group in order to change the actual position of their own group. My book suggests that PoC ID is one tool in minorities' arsenal of tactics and strategies to improve their position relative to White Americans.

## Bottom Line

Ultimately, my book's findings suggest that PoC ID is a new, unique, and real form of group attachment. This is important because it suggests that the political unity sometimes observed among racial and ethnic minorities is more than an alliance or partnership (Benjamin 2017; Cutaia Wilkinson 2015), more than solidarity or moral support (Cortland et al. 2017). and more than an ability to engage in perspective taking (Todd et al. 2011). It is, at its core, a shared form of identity in which members of distinct groups see one another interchangeably as a single, unified group.

This implies that as a new and unique form attachment, PoC ID has arrived and that scholars should further contend with its presence in US politics. That said, whether PoC ID is here to stay indefinitely remains more uncertain. If the birth of this new attachment is tied, in part, to the changing configuration of America's racial order, then some of its shelf life will also depend, in part, on where and how this hierarchy changes. This by no means implies that PoC ID is ephemeral. Alas, it has taken at least 50 years to get to a point where changing social, economic, and political conditions could nurture the emergence of a new form of identity. Thus, given the slow but steady march in changing circumstances of racial and ethnic minorities in the United States, for the foreseeable future, at least, we can say that when we consider the role of racial and ethnic identity in structuring their politics, our conclusions about these groups must now also encompass a new dimension of identity. In the end, greater sensitivity to this identity is, I think, good scientific practice. But I also think that greater attention to PoC is good in a normative sense, because it can help social scientists do greater justice to the complexity and nuance among a growing segment of the American population.

## Acknowledgments

My first book, I had to write. With my back against the wall and a ticking tenure clock in front of me, I had no choice but to put forward my best effort, follow people's advice, close my eyes, and hope for the best. This strategy worked! (At least this time.) But it was a mentally exhausting experience. After picking myself up and looking at all of the emotional debris left in its wake, I promised myself one thing: my next book would be different. I would figure out a way to complete my book on my terms and timetable.

That second book is now in your hands. And while I followed through on my self-promises, I was still unable to shake off the feeling that I also *had to write* this book. What was different this time was the root cause of my malaise. I began *Diversity's Child* during my last year in Vanderbilt University's political science department—a place where my colleagues had coached me to become the scholar I am today. It was an utterly satisfying place to work in. Many of my standards, as a researcher and mentor, stem from those very happy ten years. But as I was growing accustomed to my new intellectual home, my wife was growing increasingly unhappy about us living in the South, particularly its mores and politics. It also did not help that our parents were getting older, with looming responsibilities ahead of us both. An opportunity arose to move back home to Los Angeles by joining UCLA's faculty. I was compelled to act, not because I wanted to leave Vanderbilt but because my sense of obligation as a husband and son demanded it. Despite my nerves, we made the leap and left Nashville.

It was while making this transition that I developed a working paper with one original data collection into the book in front of you. When I sent out this working paper for review, I was told that "this paper should not be an article," that instead, "it should be expanded into a book." And so I wrote a book. This time, however, the drive, focus, and persistence to produce another long slog of a manuscript came from my need to manage all of the emotional baggage that came from making a professional move I was unsure about. To deal with the uncertainty, the anguish, and the isolation of changing departments, I wrote a book by drawing on the standards that my former colleagues had inculcated in me. I built a new intellectual home by paying homage to those who had shaped my thinking and approach to scholarship.

So where did the actual idea for this book come from? Like so much of social science, it arose from accumulating anecdotes. The first of these shards arrived in the early 2000s, before I entered graduate school. For three years, I worked for a Los Angeles–based campaign consulting firm that is still directed by Kerman Maddox (African American) and Rick Taylor (Jewish American): two former Tom Bradley aides who specialized in minority politics. I was one of their early hires—an effort, they said, to better liaise with Los Angeles's minority communities, writ large. While *person of color* was not the label used to describe me at that time, I did sense many of the sentiments that this book uncovers: although I was member of a specific in-group (Mexican Americans), I shared many attributes—historical, affective, physical—that lumped me with other non-Whites.

This evolving sense of "we" continued for me when I enrolled for doctoral study at Duke University. As a grad student, I gravitated toward American politics and the study of race and politics. I was welcomed with open arms by Paula McClain, my dissertation advisor, and the larger BLiPS crew (Blacks and Latinos in Political Science). These were the doctoral students who fostered an intellectual space for me: Jessica Carew Johnson, Niambi Carter, Vicky DeFrancesco Soto, Monique Lyle, Shayla Nunnally, Eugene Walton, and Candis Watts Smith. It was one of the first times I was explicitly called a *person of color*, and upon hearing it, I thought to myself: hell, yeah!

But after grad school, when I arrived at Vanderbilt, I sometimes found myself feeling that this welcome into a larger circle of non-Whites was tepid, at best. It was in Nashville that I was first told that being a PoC really meant *Black*. The lesson I took was not that I was unworthy of this label but that other individuals reflected it better than I did. This is when it clicked for me: if a PoC ID exists, it must be broadly inclusive, with some people identifying more strongly as PoC than others, and with some PoC as better reflections of this category.

I took these lessons and plowed ahead. But I did not plow alone. Several individuals helped me carry this intellectual load and I am pleased to publicly acknowledge them here. First among them is Cindy Kam, who adroitly played the roles of mentor, colleague, and friend, modeling how to be a researcher as well as an active parent, and how to be both without compromising either. Cindy offered crucial advice on the "bigger picture" of this project when it was little more than a handful of intuitions with some data to back them. Indeed, she incubated this idea by inviting me back—twice!—to present early versions of book chapters to members of the Research on Individuals, Politics & Society Lab. I don't think she will ever understand how essential those invitations were, both to my book's development and to my personal well-being. Each time I visited, I left with a blueprint of what a strong book needed. And so, I would return to UCLA each time and implemented each blueprint.

In addition to Cindy, I relied on the advice and camaraderie of Liz Zechmeister and Allison Anoll. Liz was my suitemate at Vanderbilt, always willing to listen to my rantings, offer advice, and crack a funny joke for good cheer. I really miss the times when I would just knock on her door and have a brief chat. Allison was the most junior addition to the political behavior group at Vanderbilt while I was there. But there was nothing junior about her. She has always been an intellectually sharp and imaginative colleague, and I was all the better for having her on our team. To this list of individuals, I also add Larry Bartels, Josh Clinton, David Lewis, Noam Lupu, and Alan Wiseman, who, in their own ways, provided feedback when my project needed it most.

At UCLA, I am especially grateful to Matt Barreto, Lorrie Frasure, and Natalie Masuoka, each of whom has worked hard to integrate me into my new department. I am also thankful for members of the Race, Ethnicity, Politics & Society Lab, which I started when I joined UCLA, especially Enya Kuo, Jason Chin, Rodolfo Solís, Bianca Vicuña, Nico Studen, Jessica Bushman, Cindy Berganza, Lauren Saliz, Kaumron Eidgahy, and Alondra Serrano, who broadly share interests with me in group identity. I also owe a debt of gratitude to the Intergroup Relations Lab (IRL) in UCLA's psychology department, which has embraced my work and efforts to further blend political science and psychology. I am specifically indebted to Tiffany Brannon, Yuen Huo, David Sears, Pete Fisher, and Dan Rosenfeld for prompting me to consider my project from other angles. Outside of UCLA, I am also indebted to Lauren Davenport, Justin Grimmer, and Hakeem Jefferson at Stanford University for inviting me to present this project in early form. I also wish to acknowledge Marisa Abrajano at University of California, San Diego, for being a generous colleague with her time and advice. My book is all the better for it.

Book writing can be a lonely endeavor. For keeping me company during this time, I thank my parents, Efrén and Maricela Pérez. I am sometimes asked by colleagues *why* and *how* I still remain intellectually productive, posttenure. My answer is my mom and dad. Parental socialization is no subtle thing; certainly not for me. As immigrants, my parents arrived to this country like many of their peers: they traded the Mexican countryside, where they barely subsisted, for the urban landscape of Los Angeles, where they subsisted a little more. The lessons I drew from them were many, but a crucial one is that work is a badge of honor: you do it because you need to eat, and you do it well because there is no other way, really. While my parents' work ethic was impressively scary to me at times, I realize now that they modeled for me one of the greatest advantages I enjoy as a researcher. For this and so many other things, I thank them.

I also appreciate the company that my cousin, Carlos Covarrubias, continues to provide me. When we were young, we were the starry-eyed kids in our families who dared to dream beyond high school. We followed through on those visions, even if we have fumbled around to find an exit to a better life. Now older, we conspire to ensure that, like each of us, our kids retain a positive sense of being Mexican, even as they establish new beachheads on our family's halting incorporation into this new country of ours.

Of course, I would be remiss if I did not thank my wife, Tammy. She suspended many of her own preferences for the sake of my early academic career, which I really cannot repay but can only gratefully acknowledge. Despite some of the challenges we faced together, she gave me three wonderful gifts that are the Pérez boys. My young sons have taught me so much about what is essential in life and what is important for parents to (not) do. But the thing that is, perhaps, most gratifying to me as a father is that they maintain a healthier balance than me in managing their identities as Mexican and American. For this reason, and so many others, I dedicate this book to each of them: Efrén Osvaldo Pérez III, Emiliano Antonio Pérez, and Enrique Valentín Pérez—three unique reminders of my family's continued legacy in this country as people of color.

# References

Abascal, Maria. 2015. "Us and Them: Black-White Relations in the Wake of Hispanic Population Growth." *American Sociological Review* 80 (4): 789–813.
Abrajano, Marisa A., and R. Michael Alvarez. 2010. *New Faces, New Voices: The Hispanic Electorate in America*. Princeton, NJ: Princeton University Press.
Abrajano, Marisa A., and Zoltan Hajnal. 2015. *White Backlash: Immigration, Race, and American Politics*. Princeton: Princeton University Press.
Alba, Richard, and Victor Nee. 2003. *Remaking the American Mainstream: Assimilation and Contemporary Immigration*. Cambridge: Harvard University Press.
Allen, Richard L., Michael C. Dawson, and Ronald E. Brown. 1989. "A Schema-Based Approach to Modeling an African-American Racial Belief System." *American Political Science Review* 83 (2): 421–41.
American Community Survey. 2019. US Census Bureau.
Anderson, Benedict. 1983. *Imagined Communities: Reflections on the Origin and Spread of Nationalism*. New York: Verso.
Anoll, Allison. 2018. "What Makes a Good Neighbor? Race, Place, and Norms of Political Participation." *American Political Science Review* 112 (3): 494–508.
Anoll, Allison. 2021. *The Obligation Mosaic: Race and Social Norms in US Political Participation*. Chicago: University of Chicago Press.
Anoll, Allison, and Mackenzie Israel-Trummel. 2019. "Do Felony Disenfranchisement Laws (De)Mobilize? A Case of Surrogate Participation." *Journal of Politics* 81 (4): 1523–27.
Ashmore, Richard D., Kay Deaux, and Tracy McLaughlin-Volpe. 2004. "An Organizing Framework for Collective Identity: Articulation and Significance of Multidimensionality." *Psychological Bulletin* 130 (1): 80–114.
Barreto, Matt A. 2005. "Si Se Puede! Latino Candidates and the Mobilization of Latino Voters." *American Political Science Review* 101 (3): 425–41.
Barreto, Matt A., and Gabriel R. Sanchez. 2014. "A 'Southern Exception' in Black-Latino Attitudes?" In *Latino Politics in Ciencia Politica*, edited by T. Affigne, E. Hu-Dehart, and M. Orr. New York: New York University Press.
Barreto, Matt A., Gary M. Segura, and Nathan D. Woods. 2003. "The Mobilizing Effect of Majority-Minority Districts on Latino Turnout." *American Political Science Review* 98 (1): 65–75.

Barth, Frederik. 1969. *Ethnic Groups and Boundaries*. Boston: Little, Brown.
Baugh, John. 2000. *Beyond Ebonics: Linguistic and Racial Prejudice*. New York: Oxford University Press.
Beltrán, Cristina. 2010. *The Trouble with Unity: Latino Politics and the Creation of Identity*. New York: Oxford University Press.
Benjamin, Andrea. 2017. *Racial Coalition Building in Local Elections: Elite Cues and Cross-Ethnic Voting*. New York: Cambridge University Press.
Billig, Michael, and Henri Tajfel. 1973. "Social Categorization and Similarity in Intergroup Behaviour." *European Journal of Social Psychology* 3 (1): 27–52.
Block, Ray. 2011. "What about Disillusionment? Exploring the Pathways to Black Nationalism." *Political Behavior* 33 (1): 27–51.
Bobo, Lawrence, and Vincent L. Hutchings. 1996. "Perceptions of Racial Group Competition: Extending Blumer's Theory of Group Position to a Multiracial Context." *American Sociological Review* 61 (6): 951–72.
Bobo, Lawrence D., and Devon Johnson. 2000. "Racial Attitudes in a Prismatic Metropolis: Mapping Identity, Stereotypes, Competition, and Views on Affirmative Action." In *Prismatic Metropolis: Inequality in Los Angeles*, edited by L.D. Bobo, M.L. Oliver, JJH Johnson, and A. Valenzuela. New York: Russell Sage Foundation.
Bollen, Kenneth A. 1989. *Structural Equations with Latent Variables*. Hoboken, NJ: Wiley & Sons.
Branscombe, Nyla R., Michael T. Schmitt, and Richard D. Harvey. 1999. "Perceiving Pervasive Discrimination Among African Americans: Implications for Group Identification and Well-Being." *Journal of Personality and Social Psychology* 77 (1): 135–49.
Branscombe, Nyla R., and Daniel L. Wann. 1994. "Collective Self-Esteem Consequences of Outgroup Derogation When a Valued Social Identity Is on Trial." *European Journal of Social Psychology* 24 (6): 641–57.
Brass, Paul R. 1997. *Theft of an Idol: Text and Context in the Representation of Collective Violence*. Princeton, NJ: Princeton University Press.
Brewer, Marilynn B. 1991. "The Social Self: On Being the Same and Different at the Same Time." *Personality and Social Psychology Bulletin* 17 (5): 475–82.
Brewer, Marilynn B. 1999. "The Psychology of Prejudice: Ingroup Love or Outgroup Hate?" *Journal of Social Issues* 55 (3): 429–44.
Brewer, Marilynn B. 2007. "The Importance of Being We: Human Nature and Intergroup Relations." *American Psychologist* 62 (8): 728–38.
Brown, Rupert. 2020. *Henri Tajfel: Explorer of Identity and Difference*. New York: Routledge Press.
Brown, Timothy A. 2007. *Confirmatory Factor Analysis for Applied Research*. New York: The Guilford Press.
Browning, Rufus, Dale Rogers Marshall, and David H. Tabb. 1984. *Protest Is Not Enough: The Struggle of Blacks and Hispanics for Equality in Urban Politics*. Berkeley: University of California Press.
Carey, Tony E., Valerie Martinez-Ebers, Tetsuya Matsubayashi, and Phillip Paolino. 2015. "Eres Amigo Enemigo? Contextual Determinants of Latinos' Perceived Competition with African-Americans." *Urban Affairs Review* 52 (2): 155–81.
Carter, Niambi M. 2019. *American While Black: African Americans, Immigration, and the Limits of Citizenship*. New York: Oxford University Press.

REFERENCES

Carter, Niambi, and Efrén O. Pérez. 2016. "Race and Nation: How Racial Hierarchy Shapes National Attachments." *Political Psychology* 37 (4): 497–513.
Census Bureau. 2017. Annual Estimates of the Resident Population. Washington, DC: Population Division.
Chandra, Kanchan. 2005. "Ethnic Parties and Democratic Stability." *Perspective on Politics* 3 (2): 235–52.
Chandra, Kanchan. 2012. *Constructivist Theories of Ethnic Politics*. New York: Oxford University Press.
Chandra, Kanchan and Cilanne Boulet. 2012. "A Baseline Model of Change in an Activated Demography." In *Constructivist Theories of Ethnic Politics*, edited by K. Chandra. New York: Oxford University Press.
Charmaz, Kathy. 2014. *Constructing Grounded Theory*. Thousand Oaks, CA: SAGE Publications.
Chong, Dennis, and Reuel Rogers. 2005. "Racial Solidarity and Political Participation." *Political Behavior* 27 (4): 347–74.
Chudy, Jennifer. 2019. "Racial Sympathy and its Political Consequences." *Journal of Politics*. https://doi.org/10.1086/708953.
Citrin, Jack, and David O. Sears. 2014. *American Identity and the Politics of Multiculturalism*. New York: Cambridge University Press.
Cohen, Cathy J. 1999. *The Boundaries of Blackness: AIDS and the Breakdown of Black Politics*. Chicago: University of Chicago Press.
Cohen, Jacob. 1992. "A Power Primer." *Psychological Bulletin* 112 (1): 155–59.
Collingwood, Loren, Nazita Lajevardi, and Kassra A.R. Oskooii. 2018. "A Change of Heart? Why Individual-Level Public Opinion Shifted against Trump's 'Muslim Ban.'" *Political Behavior* 40 (4): 1035–72.
Collins, Allan M., and Elizabeth F. Loftus. 1975. "A Spreading-Activation Theory of Semantic Processing." *Psychological Review* 82 (6): 407–28.
Conover, Pamela J. 1984. "The Influence of Group Identifications on Political Perception and Evaluation." *Journal of Politics* 46 (3): 760–85.
Converse, Phillip E. 1964. "The Nature of Belief Systems in Mass Publics." In *Ideology and Its Discontents*, edited by D. E. Apter. New York: Free Press.
Cortland, Clarissa, Maureen A. Craig, Jenessa R. Shapiro, Jennifer A. Richeson, Rebecca Neel, and Noah Goldstein. 2017. "Solidarity through Shared Disadvantage: Highlighting Shared Experiences of Discrimination Improves Relations between Stigmatized Groups." *Journal of Personality and Social Psychology* 113 (4): 547–67.
Craig, Maureen A., and Jennifer A. Richeson. 2012. "Coalition or Derogation? How Perceived Discrimination Influences Intraminority Intergroup Relations." *Journal of Personality and Social Psychology* 102 (4): 759–77.
Craig, Maureen A., and Jennifer A. Richeson. 2014a. "On the Precipice of a 'Majority-Minority' America: Perceived Status Threat from the Racial Demographic Shift Affects White Americans' Political Ideology." *Psychological Science* 25 (6): 1189–197.
Craig, Maureen A., and Jennifer A. Richeson. 2014b. "More Diverse Yet Less Tolerant? How the Increasingly-Diverse Racial Landscape Affects White Americans' Racial Attitudes." *Personality and Social Psychology Bulletin* 40 (6): 750–61.
Craig, Maureen A., and Jennifer A. Richeson. 2016. "Stigma-Based Solidarity: Understanding the Psychological Foundations of Conflict and Coalition Among Members of Different Stigmatized Groups." *Current Directions in Psychological* Science 25 (1): 21–27.

Craig, Maureen A., and Jennifer A. Richeson. 2017. "Hispanic Population Growth Engenders Conservative Shift Among Non-Hispanic Racial Minorities." *Social Psychological and Personality Science* 9 (4): 383–92.

Craig, Maureen A., Julian M. Rucker, and Jennifer A. Richeson. 2018. "The Pitfalls and Promise of Increasing Racial Diversity: Threat, Contact, and Race Relations in the 21st Century." *Current Directions in Psychological Science* 27 (3): 188–93.

Crowne, Douglas P., and David Marlowe. 1960. "A New Scale of Social Desirability Independent of Psychopathology." *Journal of Consulting Psychology* 24 (4): 349–54.

Cutaia Wilkinson, Betina. 2015. *Partners or Rivals? Power and Latino, Black, and White Relations in the 21st Century*. Charlottesville: University of Virginia Press.

Dana, Karam, Bryan Wilcox-Archuleta, and Matt Barreto. 2017. "The Political Incorporation of Muslims in the United States: The Mobilizing Role of Religiosity in Islam." *Journal of Race, Ethnicity, and Politics* 2 (2): 170–200.

Danbold, Felix, and Yuen J. Huo. 2015. "No Longer 'All-American'? Whites' Defensive Reactions to Their Numerical Decline." *Social Psychological and Personality Science* 6 (2): 210–18.

Davenport, Lauren D. 2018. *Politics Beyond Black and White: Biracial Identity and Attitudes in America*. New York: Cambridge University Press.

Davis, Darren W., and Ronald E. Brown. 2002. "The Antipathy of Black Nationalism: Behavioral and Attitudinal Implications of an African American Ideology." *American Journal of Political Science* 46 (2): 239–52.

Dawson, Michael C. 1994. *Behind the Mule: Race and Class in African-American Politics*. Princeton, NJ: Princeton University Press.

Dawson, Michael C. 2000. "Slowly Coming to Grips with the Effects of the American Racial Order on American Policy Preferences." In *Racialized Politics: The Debate about Racism in America*, edited by D. O. Sears, J. Sidanius, and L. Bobo. Chicago: University of Chicago Press.

Dawson, Michael C. 2001. *Black Visions: The Roots of Contemporary African-American Political Ideologies*. Chicago: University of Chicago Press.

de Figueiredo, Rui J. P., and Zachary Elkins. 2003. "Are Patriots Bigots? An Inquiry into the Vices of In-Group Pride." *American Journal of Political Science* 47 (1): 171–88.

de la Garza, Rodolfo, Louis DeSipio, F. Chris Garcia, John Garcia, and Angelo Falcon. 1992. *Latino Voices: Mexican, Puerto Rican, and Cuban Perspectives on American Politics*. Boulder, CO: Westview Press.

de la Garza, Rodolfo O., Angelo Falcon, and F. Chris Garcia. 1996. "Will the Real Americans Please Stand Up: Anglo and Mexican American Support of Core American Political Values." *American Journal of Political Science* 40 (2): 335–51.

Devos, Thierry, and Mahzarin R. Banaji. 2005. "American = White?" *Journal of Personality and Social Psychology* 88 (3): 447–66.

Doosje, Bertjan, Naomi Ellemers, and Russell Spears. 1995. "Perceived Intragroup Variability as a Function of Group Status and Identification." *Journal of Experimental Social Psychology* 31: 410–36.

Doosje, Bertjan, Russell Spears, and Naomi Ellemers. 2002. "Social Identity as Both Cause and Effect: The Development of Group Identification in Response to Anticipated and Actual Changes in the Intergroup Status Hierarchy." *British Journal of Social Psychology* 41:57–76.

Druckman, James N., and Thomas J. Leeper. 2012. "Learning More from Political Communication Experiments: Pretreatment and Its Effects." *American Journal of Political Science* 56 (4): 875–96.

DuBois, W. E. B. 1903. *The Souls of Black Folk: Essays and Sketches*. Chicago: A.C. McClurg & Company.

Duff, Brian, Michael J. Hanmer, Won-Ho Park, and Ismail K. White. 2007. "Good Excuses: Understanding Who Votes with an Improved Turnout Question." *Public Opinion Quarterly* 71 (1): 67–90.

Dunbar Nelson, Alice. 1917. "People of Color in Louisiana." *Journal of Negro History* 2 (1): 51–78.

Eberhardt, Jennifer L. *Biased: Uncovering the Hidden Prejudice That Shapes What We See, Think, and Do*. New York: Viking Press.

Ellemers, Naomi. 2001. "Individual Upward Mobility and the Perceived Legitimacy of Intergroup Relations." In *The Psychology of Legitimacy: Emerging Perspectives on Ideology, Justice, and Intergroup Relations*, edited by J. T. Jost and B. Major. New York: Cambridge University Press.

Ellemers, Naomi, and Jolanda Jetten. 2012. "The Many Ways to Be Marginal in a Group." *Personality and Social Psychology Review* 17 (1): 3–21.

Ellemers, Naomi, Russell Spears, and Bertjan Doosje. 1997. "Sticking Together or Falling Apart: In-Group Identification as a Psychological Determinant of Group Commitment versus Individual Mobility." *Journal of Personality and Social Psychology* 72 (3): 617–26.

Ellemers, Naomi, Russell Spears, and Bertjan Doosje. 2002. Self and Social Identity. *Annual Review of Psychology* 53: 161–86.

Ellemers, Naomi, Ad van Knippenberg, and Henk Wilke. 1990. "The Influence of Permeability of Group Boundaries and Stability of Group Status on Strategies of Individual Mobility and Social Change." *British Journal of Social Psychology* 29 (3): 233–46.

Ellemers, Naomi, Henk Wilke, and Ad van Knippenberg. 1993. "Effects of Legitimacy of Low Group or Individual Status on Individual and Collective Status-Enforcement Strategies." *Journal of Personality and Social Psychology* 64 (5): 766–78.

Elster, Jon. 1989. *Nuts and Bolts for the Social Sciences*. New York: Cambridge University Press.

Ethier, Kathleen A., and Kay Deaux. 1994. "Negotiating Social Identity When Contexts Change: Maintaining Identification and Responding to Threat." *Journal of Personality and Social Psychology* 67 (2): 243–51.

Farris, Emily M., and Heather Silber Mohammed. 2018. "Picturing Immigration: How the Media Criminalizes Immigrants." *Politics, Groups, and Identities* 6 (4): 818–24.

Fazio, Russell H., and Tamara Towles-Schwen. 1999. "The MODE Model of Attitude-Behavior Processes." In *Dual-Process Theories in Social Psychology*, edited by S. Chaiken and Y. Trope. New York: Guilford Press.

Ferree, Karen. 2012. "How Fluid Is Fluid? The Mutability of Ethnic Identities and Electoral Volatility in Africa." In *Constructivist Theories of Ethnic Politics*, edited by K. Chandra. New York: Oxford University Press.

Fowler, James H., and Cindy D. Kam. 2007. "Beyond the Self: Social Identity, Altruism, and Political Participation." *Journal of Politics* 69 (3): 813–27.

Fraga, Bernard L. 2018. *The Turnout Gap: Race, Ethnicity, and Political Inequality in a Diversifying America*. New York: Cambridge University Press.

Franklin, John Hope. 1947. *From Slavery to Freedom: A History of Negro Americans*. New York: Alfred A. Knopf.

Frey, William H. 2018. *Diversity Explosion: How New Racial Demographics are Remaking America*. Washington, DC: Brookings Press.

Gaertner, Samuel L., John F. Dovidio, Jason A. Nier, Christine M. Ward, and Brenda S. Banker. 1999. "Across Cultural Divides: The Value of a Superordinate Identity." In *Cultural Divides:*

*Understanding and Overcoming Group Conflict*, edited by D. A. Prentice and D. T. Miller. New York: Russell Sage Foundation.

Gaertner, Samuel, Jeffrey Mann, Audrey Murrell, and John F. Dovidio. 1989. "Reducing Intergroup Bias: The Benefits of Recategorization." *Journal of Personality and Social Psychology* 57 (2): 239–49.

García, John A. 2012. *Latino Politics in America: Community, Culture, and Interests*. Lanham, MD: Rowman & Littlefield Publishers, Inc.

Garcia Bedolla, Lisa. 2005. *Fluid Borders: Latino Power, Identity, and Politics in Los Angeles*. Berkeley: University of California Press.

García-Ríos, Sergio I., and Matt A. Barreto. 2016. "Politicized Immigrant Identity, Spanish-Language Media, and Political Mobilization in 2012." *RSF: The Russell Sage Foundation Journal of the Social Sciences* 2 (3): 78–96.

García-Ríos, Sergio I., Francisco Pedraza, and Bryan Wilcox-Archuleta. 2019. "Direct and Indirect Xenophobic Attacks: Unpacking Portfolios of Identity." *Political Behavior* 41:633–56.

Gay, Claudine. 2006. "Seeing Difference: The Effect of Economic Disparity on Black Attitudes toward Latinos." *American Journal of Political Science* 50 (4): 982–97.

Gay, Claudine, Jennifer Hochschild, and Ariel White. 2016. "Americans Belief in Linked Fate: Does the Measure Capture the Concept?" *Journal of Race, Ethnicity, and Politics* 1 (1): 117–44.

Gerring, John. 2001. *Social Science Methodology: A Criterial Framework*. New York: Cambridge University Press.

Gerring, John. 2004. "What Is a Case Study and What Is It Good For?" *American Political Science Review* 98 (2): 341–54.

Gilens, Martin. 1999. *Why Americans Hate Welfare: Race, Media, and the Politics of Antipoverty Policy*. Chicago: University of Chicago Press.

Goh, Jin X., Judith A. Hall, and Robert Rosenthal. 2016. "Mini-Meta Analysis of Your Own Studies: Some Arguments on Why and a Primer on How." *Social and Personality Compass* 10:535–49.

Green, Donald P., Robert P. Abelson, and Margaret Garnett. 1999. "The Distinctive Political Views of Hate-Crime Perpetrators and White Supremacists." In *Cultural Divides: Understanding and Overcoming Group Conflict*, edited by D. A. Prentice and D. T. Miller. New York: Russell Sage Foundation.

Greer, Christina M. 2013. *Black Ethnics: Race, Immigration, and the Pursuit of the American Dream*. New York: Oxford University Press.

Gurin, Patricia, Arthur H. Miller, and Gerald Gurin. 1980. "Stratum Identification and Consciousness." *Social Psychology Quarterly* 43 (1): 30–47.

Hainmueller, Jens, and Daniel J. Hopkins. 2014. "Public Attitudes toward Immigration." *Annual Review of Political Science* 17: 225–49.

Hajnal, Zoltan L. 2007. "Black Class Exceptionalism: Insights from Direct Democracy on the Race Versus Class Debate." *Public Opinion Quarterly* 71 (4): 560–87.

Hajnal, Zoltan, and Taeku Lee. 2011. *Why Americans Don't Join the Party: Race, Immigration, and the Failure (of Political Parties) to Engage the Electorate*. Princeton, NJ: Princeton University Press.

Haney López, Ian. 1996. *White by Law: The Legal Construction of Race*. New York: New York University Press.

Hanmer, Michael J., Antoine J. Banks, and Ismail K. White. 2014. "Experiments to Reduce the Over-Reporting of Voting: A Pipeline to the Truth." *Political Analysis* 22 (1): 130–41.

REFERENCES

Haynie, Kerry L. 2019. "Containing the Rainbow Coalition: Political Consequences of Mass Incarceration." *DuBois Review* 16 (1): 243–51.
Heit, Evan, and Stephen P. Nicholson. 2010. "The Opposite of Republican: Polarization and Political Categorization." *Cognitive Science* 34 (8): 1503–16.
Hewstone, Miles, and Rupert Brown. 1986. *Contact and Conflict in Intergroup Encounters*. Oxford: Basil Blackwell.
Higham, John. 1955. *Strangers in the Land: Patterns of American Nativism, 1860–1925*. New Brunswick, NJ: Rutgers University Press.
Ho, Arnold K., Jim Sidanius, Daniel T. Levin, and Mahzarin R. Banaji. 2011. "Evidence for Hypodescent and Racial Hierarchy in the Categorization and Perception of Biracial Individuals." *Journal of Personality and Social Psychology* 100 (3): 492–506.
Hochschild, Jennifer L. 1981. *What's Fair? American Beliefs about Distributive Justice*. Cambridge, MA: Harvard University Press.
Hopkins, Daniel J., Cheryl Kaiser, Efrén O. Pérez, Sara Hagá, Corin Ramos, and Michael Zárate. 2019. "Does Perceiving Discrimination Influence Partisanship among Immigrant Minorities? Evidence from Five Experiments." *Journal of Experimental Political Science* 7 (2): 112–36.
Huddy, Leonie. 2001. "From Social to Political Identity: A Critical Examination of Social Identity Theory." *Political Psychology* 22 (1): 127–56.
Huddy, Leonie. 2013. "From Group Identity to Political Cohesion and Commitment." In *Oxford Handbook of Political Psychology*, edited by L. Huddy, D. O. Sears, and J. Levy. New York: Oxford University Press.
Huddy, Leonie, and Nadia Khatib. 2007. "American Patriotism, National Identity, and Political Involvement." *American Journal of Political Science* 51 (1): 63–77.
Huddy, Leonie, and Simo V. Virtanen. 1995. "Subgroup Differentiation and Subgroup Bias Among Latinos as a Function of Familiarity and Positive Distinctiveness." *Journal of Personality and Social Psychology* 68 (1): 97–108.
Hunter, Margaret, Walter Allen, and Edward Telles. 2001. "The Significance of Skin Color among African Americans and Mexicans." *African American Research Perspectives* 7 (1): 174–84.
Jacobson, Matthew Frye. 1998. *Whiteness of a Different Color: European Immigrants and the Alchemy of Race*. Cambridge, MA: Harvard University Press.
Jardina, Ashley. 2019. *White Identity Politics*. New York: Cambridge University Press.
Jiménez, Tomás R. 2010. *Replenished Ethnicity: Mexican Americans, Immigration, and Identity*. Berkeley: University of California Press.
Jiménez, Tomás R., and Marlene Orozco. 2019. "Constructing Better Interview Protocols.: Working Paper. Stanford University Press.
Jones-Correa, Michael, Sophia J. Wallace, and Chris Zepeda-Millán. 2016. "The Impact of Large-Scale Collective Action on Latino Perceptions of Commonality and Competition with African Americans." *Social Science Quarterly* 97 (2): 458–75.
Junn, Jane. 2005. "Mobilizing Group Consciousness: When Does Ethnicity Have Political Consequences?" In *Transforming Politics, Transforming America: The Political and Civic Incorporation of Immigrants in the United States*, edited by T. Lee, S. K. Ramakrishnan, and R. Ramirez. Charlottesville: University of Virginia Press.
Junn, Jane, and Natalie Masuoka. 2008. "Asian American Identity: Shared Racial Status and Political Context." *Perspective on Politics* 6 (4): 729–40.

Kam, Cindy D., and Jennifer M. Ramos. 2008. "Joining and Leaving the Rally: Understanding Surge and Decline in Presidential Approval Following 9/11." *Public Opinion Quarterly* 72 (4): 619–50.

Kam, Cindy D., and Marc J. Trussler. 2016. "At the Nexus of Observational and Experimental Research: Theory, Specification, and Analysis of Experiments with Heterogenous Treatment Effects." *Political Behavior* 39 (4): 789–815.

Kim, Claire Jean. 2003. *Bitter Fruit: The Politics of Black-Korean Conflict in New York City*. New Haven: Yale University Press.

Kinder, Donald R., and Nathan Kalmoe. 2017. *Neither Liberal Nor Conservative: Ideological Innocence in the American Public*. Chicago: University of Chicago Press.

Kinder, Donald R., and Cindy D. Kam. 2009. *Us against Them: Ethnocentric Foundations of American Opinion*. Chicago: University of Chicago Press.

Kinder, Donald R., and Lynn M. Sanders 1996. *Divided by Color: Racial Politics and Democratic Ideals*. Chicago: University of Chicago Press.

King, Desmond. 2000. *Making Americans: Immigration, Race, and the Origins of the Diverse Democracy*. Cambridge, MA: Harvard University Press.

King, Martin L., Jr. 1963. "I Have a Dream." Speech. Lincoln Memorial, Washington, DC (August 28).

Knowles, Eric D., and Brian S. Lowery. 2011. "Meritocracy, Self-Concerns, and Whites' Denial of Racial Inequity." *Self and Identity* 11 (2): 202–20.

Kuo, Alexander, Neil Malhotra, and Cecilia Mo. 2017. "Social Exclusion and Political Identity: The Case of Asian American Partisanship." *Journal of Politics* 79 (1): 17–32.

Leach, Colin Wayne, Patricia M. Rodriguez Mosquera, Michael L. W. Vliek, and Emily Hirt. 2010. "Group Devaluation and Group Identification." *Journal of Social Issues* 66 (3): 535–52.

Leach, Colin Wayne, Martjin van Zomeren, Sven Zebel, Michael L. W. Vliek, Sjoerd F. Pennekamp, and Bertjan Doosje, Jaap W. Ouwerkerk, and Russell Spears. 2008. "Group-Level Self-Definition and Self-Investment: A Hierarchical (Multicomponent) Model of In-Group Identification." *Journal of Personality and Social Psychology* 95 (1): 144–65.

Lee, Jennifer, and Frank D. Bean. 2010. *The Diversity Paradox: Immigration and the Color Line in Twenty-First Century America*. New York: Oxford University Press.

Lee, Nora Kelly. 2016. "President Obama: 'This Is an American Issue That We Should All Care About.'" *The Atlantic* (July 7), https://www.theatlantic.com/politics/archive/2016/07/obama-shootings-minnesota-louisiana/490403/.

Lee, Taeku. 2008. "Race, Immigration, and the Identity-to-Politics Link." *Annual Review of Political Science* 11:457–78.

Lerman, Amy E., and Vesla M. Weaver. 2014. *Arresting Citizenship: The Democratic Consequences of American Crime Control*. Chicago: University of Chicago Press.

Levendusky, Matthew S. 2018. "Americans, Not Partisans: Can Priming American National Identity Reduce Affective Polarization?" *Journal of Politics* 80 (1): 59–70.

Lewin, Kurt. 1948. *Resolving Social Conflicts*. New York: Harper & Row.

Lien, Pei-Te, M. Marget Conway, and Janelle Wong. 2004. *The Politics of Asian Americans: Diversity & Community*. New York: Routledge.

Lippi-Green, Rosina. 2012. *English with an Accent: Language, Ideology, and Discrimination in the United States*. New York: Routledge.

Lodge, Milton, and Charles Taber. 2013. *The Rationalizing Voter*. New York: Cambridge University Press.

REFERENCES

Lowery, Brian S., Eric D. Knowles, and Miguel M. Unzueta. 2007. "Framing Inequity Safely: Whites' Motivated Perceptions of Racial Privilege." *Personality and Social Psychology Bulletin* 33 (9): 1237–50.

Luhtanen, Riia, and Jennifer Crocker. 1992. "A Collective Self-Esteem Scale: Self-Evaluation of One's Social Identity." *Personality and Social Psychology Bulletin* 18 (3): 302–18.

Mackie, Diane M., Eliot R. Smith, and Devin G. Ray. 2008. "Intergroup Emotions and Intergroup Relations." *Social and Personality Compass* 2:1866–80.

Marable, Manning. 1993. "Multicultural Economics: Minority Consumers and White Corporate America." *New York Amsterdam News* (March 27).

Marx, Anthony W. 1998. *Making Race and Nation: A Comparison of South Africa, the United States, and Brazil.* New York: Cambridge University Press.

Massey, Douglas, and Jennifer A. Martin. 2003. "The NIS Skin Color Scale." Office of Population Research, Princeton University.

Masuoka, Natalie. 2006. "Together They Become One: Examining the Predictors of Panethnic Group Consciousness among Asian Americans and Latinos." *Social Science Quarterly* 87 (5): 993–1011.

Masuoka, Natalie. 2017. *Multiracial Identity and Racial Politics in the United States.* New York: Oxford University Press.

Masuoka, Natalie, and Jane Junn. 2013. *The Politics of Belonging: Race, Public Opinion, and Immigration.* New York: Cambridge University Press.

McClain, Paula D. 1993. "The Changing Dynamics of Urban Politics: Black and Municipal Employment—Is There Competition?" *Journal of Politics* 55 (2): 399–414.

McClain, Paula D. 2006. "Racial Intergroup Relations in a Set of Cities: A Twenty-Year Perspective (Presidential Address)." *Journal of Politics* 68 (4): 757–70.

McClain, Paula D., Niambi M. Carter, Victoria M. DeFrancesco Soto, Monique L. Lyle, Jeffrey D. Grynaviski, Shayla C. Nunnally, Thomas J. Scotto, J. Alan Kendrick, Gerald F. Lackey, and Kendra Davenport Cotton. 2005. "Racial Distancing in a Southern City: Latino Immigrants' Views of Black Americans." *Journal of Politics* 68 (3): 571–84.

McClain, Paula D., and Jessica D. Johnson Carew 2017. *"Can We All Get Along?" Racial and Ethnic Minorities in American Politics.* New York: Westview Press.

McClain, Paula D., Jessica Johnson Carew, Eugene Walton, Jr., and Candis S. Watts. 2009. "Group Membership, Group Identity, and Group Consciousness." *Annual Review of Political Science* 12: 471–85.

McClain, Paula D., and Albert K. Karnig. 1990. "Black and Hispanic Socioeconomic and Political Competition." *American Political Science Review* 84 (2): 535–45.

McClain, Paula D., Gerald F. Lackey, Efrén O. Pérez, Niambi M. Carter, Jessica Johnson Carew, Eugene Walton Jr., Candis S. Watts, Monique L. Lyle, and Shayla C. Nunnally. 2011. "Intergroup Relations in Three Southern Cities." In *Just Neighbors? Research on African American and Latino Relations in the United States*, edited by E. Telles, M. Q. Sawyer, and G. Rivera-Salgado. New York: Russell Sage Foundation.

McClain, Paula D, Monique L. Lyle, Niambi M. Carter, Victoria M. DeFrancesco Soto, Gerald F. Lackey, Kendra Davenport Cotton, Shayla C. Nunnally, Thomas J. Scotto, Jeffrey D. Grynaviski, and J. Alan Kendrick. 2007. "Black Americans and Latino Immigrants in a Southern City: Friendly Neighbors or Economic Competitors." *DuBois Review: Social Science Research on Race* 4 (1): 97–117.

McClain, Paula D., and Steven C. Tauber. 1998. "Black and Latino Socioeconomic and Political Competition: Has a Decade Made a Difference?" *American Politics Quarterly* 26:101–16.

McDermott, Rose. 2011. "External Validity." In *Cambridge Handbook of Experimental Political Science*, edited by J. N. Druckman, D. P. Green, J. H. Kuklinski, and A. Lupia. New York: Cambridge University Press.

McGarty, Craig, John C. Turner, Michael A. Hogg, Barbara David, and Margaret S. Wetherell. 1992. "Group Polarization as Conformity to the Prototypical Group Members." *British Journal of Social Psychology* 31 (1): 1–19.

Meier, Kenneth J., Paula D. McClain, J. L. Polinard, and Robert D. Wrinkle. 2004. "Divided or Together? Conflict and Cooperation between African Americans and Latinos." *Political Research Quarterly* 57 (3): 399–409.

Merseth, Julie Lee. 2018. "Race-ing Solidarity: Asian Americans and Support for Black Lives Matter." *Politics, Groups, and Identities* 6 (3): 337–56.

Michelson, Melissa R., and Ali A. Valenzuela. 2016. "Turnout, Status, and Identity: Mobilizing Latinos to Vote with Group Appeals." *American Political Science Review* 110 (4): 615–30.

Miller, Arthur H., Patricia Gurin, Gerald Gurin, and Oksana Malanchuk. 1981. "Group Consciousness and Political Participation." *American Journal of Political Science* 25 (3): 494–511.

Mora, G. Cristina. 2014. *Making Hispanics: How Activists, Bureaucrats, and Media Constructed a New American*. Chicago: University of Chicago Press.

Moseley, Mariya. 2017. "Obama's Record-High Diverse Cabinet Compared to Trump's Majority White, Male Cabinet." *Essence Magazine* (January 20), https://www.essence.com/news/politics/obamas-record-high-diverse-cabinet/.

Myrdal, Gunnar. 1944. *An American Dilemma: The Negro Problem and Modern Democracy*. New York: Harper and Row.

NAACP. 2018. *Criminal Justice Fact Sheet*. Washington, DC: National Association for the Advancement of Colored People.

Nagel, Joane. 1996. *American Indian Ethnic Renewal: Red Power and the Resurgence of Identity and Culture*. New York: Oxford University Press.

Newman, Benjamin. 2012. "Acculturating Contexts and Anglo Opposition to Immigration in the U.S." *American Journal of Political Science* 57 (2): 374–90.

Newman, Benjamin J., and Neil Malhotra. 2019. "Economic Reasoning with a Racial Hue: Is the Immigration Consensus Purely Race Neutral?" *Journal of Politics* 81 (1): 153–66.

Ngai, Mae M. 2004. *Impossible Subjects: Illegal Aliens and the Making of Modern America*. Princeton, NJ: Princeton University Press.

Oakes, Penelope J., S. Alexander Haslam, and John C. Turner. 1994. *Stereotyping and Social Reality*. Hoboken, NJ: Blackwell Publishing.

Ocampo, Angela X., Karam Dana, and Matt A. Barreto. 2018. "The American *Muslim* Voter: Community Belonging and Political Participation." *Social Science Research* 72:84–99.

Olson, Mancur. 1965. *The Logic of Collective Action: Public Goods and the Theory of Groups*. Cambridge, MA: Harvard University Press.

Omi, Michael, and Howard Winant. 1986. *Racial Formation in the United States*. New York: Routledge.

Ortiz, Vilma, and Edward Telles. 2012. "Racial Identity and Racial Treatment of Mexican Americans." *Race and Social Problems*. 4 (1): 41–56.

Osgood, Charles E. 1962. "Studies on the Generality of Affective Meaning Systems." *American Psychologist* 17 (1): 10–28.

# REFERENCES

Oskooii, Kassra, Nazita Lajevardi, and Loren Collingwood. 2019. "Opinion Shift and Stability: The Information Environment and Long-Lasting Opposition to Trump's Muslim Ban." *Political Behavior* (published electronically), https://link.springer.com/article/10.1007/s11109-019-09555-8#citeas.

Ostfeld, Mara, and Nicole Yadon. n.d. "The Content of Our Color: The Politics of Skin Color in America." Unpublished manuscript. University of Michigan.

Pantoja, Adrian D., Ricardo Ramirez, and Gary M. Segura. 2001. "Citizens by Choice, Voters by Necessity: Patterns in Political Mobilization by Naturalized Latinos." *Political Research Quarterly* 54 (4): 729–50.

Parker, Christopher S. 2009. *Fighting for Democracy: Black Veterans and the Struggle against White Supremacy in the Postwar South*. Princeton, NJ: Princeton University Press.

Parker, Christopher S., and Matt A. Barreto. 2013. *Change They Can't Believe In: The Tea Party and Reactionary Politics in America*. Princeton, NJ: Princeton University Press.

Pérez, Efrén O. 2015a. "Ricochet: How Elite Discourse Politicizes Racial and Ethnic Identities." *Political Behavior* 37 (1): 155–80.

Pérez, Efrén O. 2015b. "Xenophobic Rhetoric and Its Political Effects on Immigrants and Their Co-Ethnics." *American Journal of Political Science* 59 (3): 549–64.

Pérez, Efrén O. 2016. *Unspoken Politics: Implicit Attitudes and Political Thinking*. New York: Cambridge University Press.

Pérez, Efrén O., Maggie Deichert, and Andrew M. Engelhardt. 2019. "E Pluribus Unum? How Ethnic and National Identity Motivate Reactions to a Political Ideal." *Journal of Politics* 81 (4): 1420–33.

Pérez, Efrén O., and Enya Kuo. Forthcoming. *Racial Order, Racialized Responses: Interminority Politics in a Diverse Nation*. New York: Cambridge University Press.

Pérez, Efrén O., and Margit Tavits. 2019. "Language Heightens the Political Salience of Ethnic Divisions." *Journal of Experimental Political Science* 6 (2): 131–40.

Pew Research Center. 2015. "Modern Immigration Wave Brings 59 Million to U.S., Driving Population Growth and Change through 2065: Views of Immigrations' Impact on U.S. Society Mixed." Washington, DC (September).

Pew Research Center. 2018. "Wider Gender Gap, Growing Educational Divide in Voters' Party Identification." Washington, DC (March).

Philpot, Tasha S. 2007. *Race, Republicans, and the Return of the Party of Lincoln*. Ann Arbor: University of Michigan Press.

Philpot, Tahsa S. 2017. *Conservative but Not Republican: The Paradox of Party Identification and Ideology Among African Americans*. New York: Cambridge University Press.

Portes, Alejandro, and Rubén Rumbaut. 2014. *Immigrant America: A Portrait*. Berkeley: University of California Press.

Posner, Daniel N. 2005. *Institutions and Ethnic Politics in Africa*. New York: Cambridge University Press.

Rainey, Carlisle. 2014. "Arguing for a Negligible Effect." *American Journal of Political Science* 58 (4): 1083–91.

Ramirez, Mark D. 2013a. "Americans' Changing Views toward Crime and Punishment." *Public Opinion Quarterly* 77 (4): 1006–31.

Ramirez, Mark D. 2013b. "Punitive Sentiment." *Criminology* 52 (2): 329–64.

Ranganath, Kate A., Colin Tucker Smith, and Brian A. Nosek. 2008. "Distinguishing Automatic and Controlled Components of Attitudes from Direct and Indirect Measurement Methods." *Journal of Experimental Social Psychology* 44 (2): 386–96.

Reid, Scott A., and Michael A. Hogg. 2005. "Uncertainty Reduction, Self-Enhancement, and In-group Identification." *Personality and Social Psychology Bulletin* 31 (6): 804–17.

Reny, Tyler, Ali Valenzuela, and Loren Collingwood. 2019. "'No, You're Playing the Race Card': Testing the Effects of Anti-Black, Anti-Latino, and Anti-Immigration Appeals in the Post-Obama Era." *Political Psychology* 41 (2): 283–302.

Reyna, Christine, Amanda Tucker, William Korfmacher, and P. J. Henry. 2005. "Searching for Common Ground between Supporters and Opponents of Affirmative Action." *Political Psychology* 26 (5): 667–82.

Rogers, Reuel. 2006. *Afro-Caribbean Immigrants and the Politics of Incorporation: Ethnicity, Exception, or Exit*. New York: Cambridge University Press.

Rubin, Herbert J., and Irene S. Rubin. 2012. *Qualitative Interviewing: The Art of Hearing Data*. Thousand Oaks, CA: SAGE Publications.

Safire, William. 1988. "People of Color." *The New York Times Magazine* (November 20).

Sanchez, Gabriel R. 2006a. "The Role of Group Consciousness in Political Participation among Latinos in the United States." *American Politics Research* 34 (4): 427–51.

Sanchez, Gabriel R. 2006b. "The Role of Group Consciousness in Latino Public Opinion." *Political Research Quarterly* 59 (3): 435–46.

Sanchez, Gabriel R., and Natalie Masuoka. 2010. "Brown Utility Heuristic? The Presence and Contributing Factors of Latino Linked Fate." *Hispanic Journal of Behavioral Sciences* 32 (4): 519–31.

Sawyer, Mark Q. 2005. *Racial Politics in Post-Revolutionary Cuba*. New York: Cambridge University Press.

Schwarz, Norbert. 2007. "Attitude Construction: Evaluation in Context." *Social Cognition* 25 (5): 638–56.

Sears, David O. 1986. "College Sophomores in the Laboratory: Influences of a Narrow Data Base on Social Psychology's View of Human Nature." *Journal of Personality and Social Psychology* 51 (3): 515–30.

Seger, Charles R., Eliot R. Smith, and Diane M. Mackie. 2009. "Subtle Activation of a Social Categorization Triggers Group-Level Emotions." *Journal of Experimental Social Psychology* 45 (3): 460–67.

Sellers, Robert M., and J. Nicole Shelton. 2003. "The Role of Racial Identity in Perceived Racial Discrimination." *Journal of Personality and Social Psychology* 84 (5): 1079–92.

Sen, Maya, and Omar Wasow. 2016. "Race as a Bundle of Sticks: Designs the Estimate Effects of Seemingly Immutable Characteristics." *Annual Review of Political Science* 19: 499–522.

Shadish, William R., Thomas D. Cook, and Donald T. Campbell. 2002. *Experimental and Quasi-Experimental Designs for Generalized Causal Inference*. Hoboken, NJ: Blackwell.

Shapiro, Jenessa R., and Steven L. Neuberg. 2008. "When Do the Stigmatized Stigmatize? The Ironic Effects of Being Accountable to Perceived Majority Group Prejudice-Expression Norms." *Journal of Personality and Social Psychology* 95 (4): 877–98.

Shapiro, Thomas. 2017. *State of the Union 2017: Wealth*. Palo Alto, CA: Stanford Center on Poverty and Inequality.

Shear, Michael D. 2014. "Obama, Daring Congress, Acts to Overhaul Immigration." *New York Times* (November 20), https://www.nytimes.com/2014/11/21/us/obama-immigration-speech.html.

Sherif, Muzafer, O. J. Harvey, B. Jack White, William R. Hood, and Carolyn R. Sherif. 1961. *Intergroup Conflict and Cooperation: The Robbers Cave Experiment*. Norman: University of Oklahoma Book Exchange.

Shingles, Richard D. 1981. "Black Consciousness and Political Participation: The Missing Link." *American Political Science Review* 75 (1): 76–91.

Sidanius, Jim, Seymour Feshbach, Shana Levin, and Felicia Pratto. 1997. "The Interface between Ethnic and National Attachment: Ethnic Pluralism or Ethnic Dominance?" *Public Opinion Quarterly* 61 (1): 102–33.

Sidanius, Jim, and Robert Kurzban. 2013. "Toward an Evolutionarily Informed Political Psychology." In *Oxford Handbook of Political Psychology*, edited by L. Huddy, D. O. Sears, and J. S. Levy. New York: Oxford University Press.

Sidanius, Jim, and John R. Petrocik. 2001. "Communal and National Identity in a Multiethnic State: A Comparison of Three Perspectives." In *Social Identity, Intergroup Conflict, and Conflict Reduction*, edited by R. D. Ashmore, L. Jussim, and D. Wilder. New York Oxford University Press.

Sidanius, Jim, and Felicia Pratto. 1999. *Social Dominance: An Intergroup Theory of Social Hierarchy and Oppression*. New York: Cambridge University Press.

Silber Mohammed, Heather. 2017. *The New Americans? Immigration, Protest, and the Politics of Latino Identity*. Lawrence: University of Kansas Press.

Silber Mohammed, Heather, and Emily M. Farris. 2019. "'Bad Hombres'? An Examination of Identities in U.S. Media Coverage of Immigration." *Journal of Ethnic and Migration Studies* 46 (1): 158–76.

Sirin, Cigdem V., Nicholas A. Valentino, and José D. Villalobos. 2016a. "Group Empathy in Response to Nonverbal Racial/Ethnic Cues: A National Experiment on Immigration Policy Attitudes." *American Behavioral Scientist* 60 (14): 1676–97.

Sirin, Cigdem V., Nicholas A. Valentino, and José D. Villalobos. 2016b. "The Social Causes and Political Consequences of Group Empathy." *Political Psychology* 38 (3): 427–48.

Skrentny, John D. 2002. *The Minority Rights Revolution*. Cambridge, MA: Harvard University Press.

Smith, Rogers M. 1997. *Civic Ideals: Conflicting Visions of Citizenship in U.S. History*. New Haven, CT: Yale University Press.

Sniderman, Paul M. 2011. "The Logic and Design of the Survey Experiment: An Autobiography of a Methodological Innovation." In *Cambridge Handbook of Experimental Political Science*, edited by J. N. Druckman, D. P. Green, J. H. Kuklinski, and A. Lupia. New York: Cambridge University Press.

Sniderman, Paul M., and Edward G. Carmines. 1997. *Reaching Beyond Race*. Cambridge, MA: Harvard University Press.

Sniderman, Paul M., Louk Hagendoorn, and Markus Prior. 2004. "Predisposing Factors and Situational Triggers: Exclusionary Reactions to Immigrant Minorities." *American Political Science Review* 98 (1): 35–49.

Sniderman, Paul M., and Thomas Piazza. 1993. *The Scar of Race*. Cambridge, MA: Harvard University Press.

Sonenshein, Raphael J. 1993. *Politics in Black and White: Race and Power in Los Angeles*. Princeton: Princeton University Press.

Southern Poverty and Law Center. 2019. *The Year in Hate and Extremism*. Montgomery, AL: SPLC.

Spears, Russell, Bertjan Doosje, and Naomi Ellemers. 1997. "Self-Stereotyping in the Face of Threats to Group Status and Distinctiveness: The Role of Group Identification." *Personality and Social Psychology Bulletin* 23 (5): 538–53.

Staerkle, Christian, Jim Sidanius, Eva G. T. Green, and Ludwin Molina. 2010. "Ethnic

Minority-Majority Asymmetry in National Attitudes around the World: A Multilevel Analysis." *Political Psychology* 31 (4): 491–519.
Stimson, James A. 1991. *Public Opinion in America: Moods, Cycles, and Swings*. Boulder, CO: Westview Press.
Sue, Derald Wing. 2010. *Microaggressions in Everyday Life: Race, Gender, and Sexual Orientation*. Hoboken, NJ: John Wiley & Sons.
Sullivan, Patricia. 2009. *Lift Every Voice: The NAACP and the Making of the Civil Rights Movement*. New York: New Press.
Tajfel, Henri. 1978. *The Social Psychology of Minorities*. New York: Minority Rights Group.
Tajfel, Henri. 1981. *Human Groups and Social Categories: Studies in Social Psychology*. New York: Cambridge University Press.
Tajfel, Henri, M. G. Billig, R .P. Bundy, and Claude Flament. 1971. "Social Categorization and Intergroup Behaviour." *European Journal of Social Psychology* 1 (2): 149–78.
Tajfel, Henri, and John C. Turner. 1986. "An Integrative Theory of Intergroup Relations." In *The Social Psychology of Intergroup Relations*, edited by W. G. Austin and S. Worchel. Monterey, CA: Brooks Cole.
Takaki, Ronald. 1989. *Strangers from a Different Shore: A History of Asian Americans*. Boston: Little, Brown and Company.
Tate, Katherine. 1991. "Black Political Participation in the 1984 and 1988 Presidential Elections." *American Political Science Review* 85 (4): 1159–176.
Telles, Edward, Mark Sawyer, and Gaspar Rivera-Salgado. 2011. *Just Neighbors? Research on African American and Latino Relations in the United States*. New York: Russell Sage Foundation.
Tesler, Michael. 2016. *Post-Racial or Most-Racial? Race and Politics in the Obama Era*. Chicago: University of Chicago Press.
Tesler, Michael, and David O. Sears. 2010. *Obama's Race: The 2008 Election and the Dream of a Post-Racial America*. Chicago: University of Chicago Press.
Theiss-Morse, Elizabeth. 2009. *Who Counts as an American? The Boundaries of National Identity*. New York: Cambridge University Press.
Todd, Andrew, Karlene Hanko, Adam D. Galinsky, and Thomas Mussweiler. 2011. "When Focusing on Differences Leads to Similar Perspectives." *Psychological Science* 22 (1): 134–41.
Tourangeau, Roger, Lance J. Rips, and Kenneth Rasinski. 2000. *The Psychology of Survey Response*. New York: Cambridge University Press.
Transue, John E. 2007. "Identity Salience, Identity Acceptance, and Racial Policy Attitudes: American National Identity as a Uniting Force." *American Journal of Political Science* 51 (1): 78–91.
Trounstine, Jessica. 2018. *Segregation by Design: Local Politics and Inequality in American Cities*. New York: Cambridge University Press.
Turner, John C., Michael A. Hogg, Penelope J. Oakes, Stephen D. Reicher, and Margaret S. Wetherell. 1987. *Rediscovering the Social Group: A Self-Categorization Theory*. New York: Basil Blackwell.
Turner, John C., Penelope J. Oakes, S. Alexander Haslam, and Craig McGarty. 1994. "Self and Collective: Cognition and Social Context." *Personality and Social Psychology Bulletin* 20 (5): 454–63.
Unzueta, Miguel M., and Brian S. Lowery. 2008. "Defining Racism Safely: The Role of Self-Image Maintenance on White Americans' Conceptions of Racism." *Journal of Experimental Social Psychology* 44 (6): 1491–97.
US Census Bureau. 1903. *Annual Estimates of the Resident Population*. Washington, DC: Population Division.

REFERENCES

US Census Bureau. 2018. *Annual Estimates of the Resident Population*. Washington, DC: Population Division.

Vaca, Nicholas C. 2004. *The Presumed Alliance: The Unspoken Conflict between Latinos and Blacks and What It Means for America*. New York: HarperCollins.

Vidal-Ortiz, Salvador. 2008. "People of Color." In *Encyclopedia of Race, Ethnicity, and Society*, edited by R. T. Schaefer. Thousand Oaks, CA: SAGE Publications.

Waldzus, Sven, Amélie Mummendey, Michael Wenzel, and Franziska Boettcher. 2004. "Of Bikers, Teachers, and Germans: Groups' Diverging Views about Their Prototypicality." *British Journal of Social Psychology* 43 (3): 385–400.

Walker, Hannah L. 2020. *Mobilized by Injustice: Criminal Justice Contact, Political Participation, and Race*. New York: Oxford University Press.

Walsh, Katherine J. 2016. *The Politics of Resentment: Rural Consciousness in Wisconsin and the Rise of Scott Walker*. New York: Cambridge University Press.

Watts Smith, Candice. 2014. *Black Mosaic: The Politics of Black Pan-Ethnicity*. New York: New York University Press.

Weaver, Vesla. 2007. "Frontlash: Race and the Development of Punitive Crime Policy." *Studies in American Political Development* 21: 230–65.

Weaver, Vesla M., and Amy E. Lerman. 2010. "Political Consequences of the Carceral State." *American Political Science Review* 104 (4): 817–33.

Weiss, Robert S. 1994. *Learning from Strangers: The Art and Method of Qualitative Interview Studies*. New York: Free Press.

Wenzel, Michael, Amélie Mummendey, and Sven Waldzus. 2007. "Superordinate Identities and Intergroup Conflict: The Ingroup Projection Model." *European Review of Social Psychology* 18 (1): 331–72.

White, Ismail K. 2007. "When Race Matters and When It Doesn't: Racial Group Differences in Response to Racial Cues." *American Political Science Review* 101 (2): 339–54.

White, Ismail K., and Chryl N. Laird. 2020. *Steadfast Democrats: How Social Forces Shape Black Political Behavior*. Princeton, NJ: Princeton University Press.

White, Ismail K., Chryl Laird, and Troy D. Allen. 2014. "Selling Out? The Politics of Navigating Conflicts between Racial Group Interest and Self-Interest." *American Political Science Review* 108 (4): 783–800.

Wilkins, David E., and Heidi Kiiwetinepinesiik Stark. 2018. *American Indian Politics and the American Political System*. Lanham, MD: Rowman & Littlefield.

Winter, Nicholas J. G. 2008. *Dangerous Frames: How Ideas about Race and Gender Shape Public Opinion*. Chicago: University of Chicago Press.

Wong, Cara. 2010. *Boundaries of Obligation in American Politics: Geographic, National, and Racial Communities*. New York: Cambridge University Press.

Wong, Janelle, S. Karthick Ramakrishnan, Taeku Lee, and Jane Junn. 2011. *Asian American Political Participation: Emerging Constituents and Their Political Identities*. New York: Russell Sage Foundation.

Yuen, Edward. 1997. "Social Movements, Identity Politics and the Genealogy of the Term 'People of Color.'" *New Political Science* 19:97–107.

Zaller, John. 1992. *The Nature and Origins of Mass Opinion*. New York: Cambridge University Press.

Zou, Linda X., and Sapna Cheryan. 2017. "Two Axes of Subordination: A New Model of Racial Position." *Journal of Personality and Social Psychology* 112 (5): 696–717.

# Index

Page numbers in italics refer to tables.

affirmation hypothesis, 27, 73, 85
African Americans: #BlackLivesMatter and, 6–7, 27, 31, 77, 86, 88, *91*, 123–24, 128–29, 132, 141, *143–45*, 165–70, 180; citizens of color and, 3; classification and, 33–38, 40–42, 44, 48–49, 52–55, 58–62, *63*; coherence and, 147–71, *174–78*; conceptual issues and, 25–27, 29, 31, 75–79, *83*, 84–87, *89–91*; demographics of, 1–2; disenfranchisement and, 33; distinctiveness and, 163, 165–67, *175*, *177–78*; diversity and, 180–82, 185; hostility toward Latinos, 2; "I Feel Your Pain" experiments and, 99–116, *117–20*; immigrants and, 27, 87; Jim Crow system and, 3, 33; King, 3; Ku Klux Klan and, 33; median incomes of, 93; NAACP and, 3, 92; Obama and, 133–34, 136, 138; as panracial category, 4; police brutality and, 27, 33, 55, 86, 133; political galvanization and, 122–23, 126–38, 141, *142*, *146*; political opinions and, 72–73, 77, 84; poverty rates and, 93; power and, 9, 16, 67, 155, 180; sense of identity and, 1–12, 15–17; shared experiences and, 92–95, 99–116, *117–20*; slavery and, 2–3, 12, 44, 53, 147, 160, 163; social identity theory (SIT) and, 25, 29; Trump and, 132
American ID, 77–79, 81, *83*, 85, *89–91*, 140, *143–45*
American National Election Study (ANES), 4–5, 134, 138
Aquino, James, 40, 44
Asian Americans: classification and, 34–63; coherence and, 148–85; conceptual issues and, 23–31; demographics of, 1; distinctiveness and, *169*, 170, *176–78*; "I Feel Your Pain" experiments and, 99–116, *117–20*; immigrants and, 2, 12, 54, 62, 77, 82, 87, 92, 147, 168; median incomes of, 93; police brutality and, 27, 86, 92; political galvanization and, 123, 126–42, *144*, *146*; political opinions and, 67, 69, 72–87, *89–91*; poverty rates and, 93; power and, 9, 12, 16, 26, 31, 33, 40, 67, 93, 155, 164, 180, 185; predominate condition and, 12, *153*, 154, *156–57*, *174*, *177*; sense of identity and, 1–12, 16–21; shared experiences and, 92–95, 99–116, *117–20*; social identity theory (SIT) and, 26–29

Bello, Karina, 40, 47, 50, 150–51
Beltrán, Cristina, 21, 147–48, 183
Benin, 184
Benjamin, Andrea, 15–16
bias, 5, 98–100, *121*
Black Distinctiveness, 163, 165–67, *175*, *177–78*
#BlackLivesMatter: African Americans and, 6–7, 27, 31, 77, 86, 88, *91*, 123–24, 128–29, 132, 141, *143–45*, 165–70, 180; coherence and, 165–70; conceptual issues and, 27, 31, 77, 86, 88, *91*; diversity and, 180; political galvanization and, 123–24, 128–29, 132, 141, *143–45*; sense of identity and, 6–7
Blaxicans, 55
Brewer, Marilynn, 25, 30, 71
Brown, Aliyah, 47, 52, 55, 58

Carter, Ebony, 50–51, 150–51, 160
Carter, Isabel, 36
Carter, Isaiah, 40, 52, 56
centrality, 9, 70, 96–97, 99, 102, 105
Chandra, Kanchan, 184
Cheryan, Sapna, 38, 181
Cheung, Christina, 37, 50

Chewas, 184
Chile, 55
Chinese: classification and, 34, 37, 40, 43, 49–50, 56–57; coherence and, *153*, *177–78*; conceptual issues and, 73n1, *83*, *89–91*; sense of identity and, 3, 20; shared experiences and, *117*, *119–20*
citizens of color, 3
civil rights, 45, 122
classification: African Americans and, 33–38, 40–42, 44, 48–49, 52–55, 58–62, *63*; Asian Americans and, 34–63; Chinese and, 34, 37, 40, 43, 49–50, 56–57; color line and, 33, 37–38, 57–58; Common Ingroup Identity Model (CIIM) and, 16, 26; demographics and, 33, *63*; designation worthiness and, 51–57; discrimination and, 38, 40, 44, 50, 55; distinctiveness and, 39, 46; diversity and, 33, 40, 50, 54; education and, 35, 56–58, 65; exclusion and, 46–51; Filipinos and, 36–40, 43–44, 47–49, 55–57; generic IDs and, 11, 23–25, 51, 70–73, 183; Google searches and, 41; hierarchies and, 36; Implicit Association Test (IAT) and, 9, 58–61; inequality and, 37; in-groups and, 39, 42–43, 46, 53, 58–61; internal identity and, 58–61; interview protocols and, 63–65; Latinos and, 33–37, 41–43, 46–49, 52, 54, 56, 59–63; marginalization and, 33, 38, 51, 62; Mexicans and, 34, 36–37, 40, 43, 47, 49, 52, 55, *59*; multiracial, 9, 29; nested identities and, 42–46, 149, 180; newspaper data and, 53–54, 65–66; out-groups and, 39, 58; pan-racial groups, 6, 9–10, 12–13, 22, 31, 46, 58, 96, 128, 131, 133, 158, 183; "People of Color" surveys and, 10, *42*, 73–81, 126, 135; power and, 33, 40, 43; pride and, 38–42; prototypical groups and, 36, 52–53, 55; psychology and, 36; racial disadvantages and, 37–38; racial identity and, 42–43; sense of belonging and, 25, 30, 38–42, 46; skin tone and, 36–37, 46–52, 55–59; social identity theory (SIT) and, 23–29; solidarity and, 38–42; status and, 37, 49–50, 56, 61–62; unity and, 50; Whites and, 34, 36–39, 42, 45, 47–48, 54, 57–61
coherence: African Americans and, 147–71, *174–78*; Asian Americans and, 148–85; #BlackLivesMatter and, 165–70; Chinese and, *153*, *177–78*; competition and, 161, 164–70, 171n4; control groups and, *152*, 155, *177*; demographics and, 152–58, 161–62; discrimination and, 150, 159, 161–69, *172*, *175–76*; "Distinct Experiences" experiment and, 12, 158, 161–65, 170, 173, *175–78*, 182–83; "Distinct Stations" experiment and, 12, 151–54, 157, 164, 173, *177*; diversity and, 147, 151–56, *157*, 160–64; education and, 162; Filipinos and, 159–60; hierarchies and, 150–51, 155, 158; immigrants and, 168, 171; in-groups and, 147–49, 151, 157, 160–65, 167, 171; intergroup, 173; Latinos and, 147–71, *174–78*; marginalization and, 155, 160, 162–63; Mexicans and, 150, *154*, *177–78*; nested identities and, 149; out-groups and, 151, 164, 170–71; pan-racial groups and, 158; parallel positions and, 149–51, 159–61; power and, 151, 155, 164, 171; prototypical groups and, 154–58, *174*; psychology and, 148–50; racial identity and, 148–49, 162, *172*, *173*; reality constraints and, 151–52, 158; skin tone and, 150, 159–60; social identity theory (SIT) and, 149, *173*; solidarity and, 147; status and, 150–52, 157–58; unity and, 147–48, 151, 157, *173*; Whites and, 149–52, 155, 158, 160, 164–66; Widatalla editorial and, 147–48, 159, 171
collective action, 19, 39, 97, 137, 182
color line, 33, 37–38, 57–58
commitment, 18, 75, 106–7
Common Ingroup Identity Model (CIIM), 16, 26
comparative fit indexes (CFIs), 77, *78*
competition: coherence and, 161, 164–70, 171n4; conflict and, 15, 28; interminority, 13, 15, 25; perceived, 161; political, 2; sense of identity and, 2, 13, 15, 21; social, 28–30, 186; zero-sum, 164–65, *166–67*, *169*, 171n4, *175–76*
conceptual issues: African Americans and, 25–27, 29, 31, 75–79, *83*, 84–87, *89–91*; Asian Americans and, 23–31; #BlackLivesMatter and, 77, 86, 88, *91*; Chinese and, 73n1, *83*, *89–91*; confirmatory factor analysis (CFA) and, 77, *78*, 81n3, *146*; demographics and, 81, 84–85, 87; discrimination and, 26, 82; distinctiveness and, 24–32, 72; diversity and, 30, 79; education and, 29, 73, 82–84, *89–91*; generic IDs and, 11, 23–25, 51, 70–73, 183; inequality and, 82, *121*; in-groups and, 24–27, 29, 31, 71–75, 79; Latinos and, 25–31; marginalization and, 31; Mexicans and, 31, 82, *83*, *89–91*; nested identities and, 23, 27–31, 72–73, 78–79; out-groups and, 25–27, 30–31, 72, 76; "People of Color" surveys and, 10, *42*, 73–81, 126, 135; PoC ID criteria and, 68–70; power and, 26, 28, 31n2, 67–68, 85, 88; prototypical groups and, 25, 72, 87; psychology and, 23–26, 29, 69–70, 72; racial identity and, 23, 25–27, 29, 31n2, 68, 72–79, 82–87, *89–91*; skin tone and, 29; social identity theory (SIT) and, 23–29; solidarity and, 30, 75, 85, *86*, 88, *89*; status and, 28–30; unity and, 23–32; voting rights and, 76, 86, 88, *90*; Whites and, 26–30, 76, 79, 82, 85
confirmatory factor analysis (CFA), 77, *78*, 81n3, *146*
conflict: competition and, 15, 28; cooperation and, 180–83; group, 15–17, 24, 26–28, 34, 116, 180–83; interminority, 15–16, 179, 182; perceived, 166; Sherif's Robbers Cave experiment and, 27
*Congressional Record*, 45–46
conservatism, *63*; exclusion and, 50–51; fiscal, 51; immigrants and, 51; Latino population growth

INDEX

and, 16; political views of, 50–51; Republicans and, 1, 51, 57; social, 51; status groups and, 29n1
control groups, 11; coherence and, 152, 155, *177*; distracter task and, 127–28; "I Feel Your Pain" experiments and, 103, 107, 110; manipulation and, 127–28; political galvanization and, 127–29, 131, 142; prototypical groups and, 155; regional diversity and, *152*
cooperation, 15–16, 26–27, 34, 73, 179–83
Craig, Maureen, 16–17, 182
Cubans, 20–21, 82, *83*, *89–91*, *117*, *119–20*, 154, 184

Davis, Alyssa, 39, 43–44, 50, 56
Dawson, Michael, 17–18, 28, 44, 184
Deferred Action for Childhood Arrivals (DACA): coherence and, 165–71, *172*, *175–76*; immigrants and, 86, 87, *91*, 129, 141, *143–45*, 165–71, *172*, *175–76*; political galvanization and, 129, 141, *143–45*
de la Cruz, Josephine, 39, 43, 53, 56
Democrats: "Distinct Stations" experiment and, *177–78*; liberalism and, 46, 82–84, *89–91*; mention of people of color (PoC) by, 45, 46; minorities identifying with, 11, 93, *117–20*, 128, 131; partisanship and, 62, 82, 93; "People of Color" surveys and, 75; political galvanization and, 128, 131, 141, *143–45*; political opinions and, 76, 81–85, *86*, 88, *89–91*
demographics: classification and, 33, *63*; coherence and, 152–58, 161–62; conceptual issues and, 81, 84–85, 87; diversity and, 185; "I Feel Your Pain" experiments and, 103, *117*; political galvanization and, 122, 126, 137; sense of identity and, 1–2, 4, 9, 12, 14; shared experiences and, 103, *117*; US Census Bureau and, 1, 31n2, 33–34, 92, 137, 161–62
devaluation, 4, 150
Diaz, Orlando, 36, 47
discrimination: classification and, 38, 40, 44, 50, 55; coherence and, 150, 159–69, *172*, *175–76*; conceptual issues and, 26, 82; diversity and, 180–81; King speech and, 3; NAACP and, 3, 92; sense of identity and, 3–4, 13, 16–17, 19; shared experiences and, 97, 100–101, *121*
disenfranchisement, 33
"Distinct Experiences" experiment, 12, 158, 161–65, 170, 173, *175–78*, 182–83
distinctiveness: Asian, 169, 170, *176–78*; Black, 163, 165–67, *175*, *177–78*; classification and, 39, 46; coherence and, 148–49, 162–71, *172*, *175–78*; conceptual issues and, 24–32, 72; diversity and, 180, 182; in-groups and, 10, 12, 24–32, 39, 46, 72, 96, 125, 148–49, 162–71, *172*, *175–78*, 180, 182; Latino, *167*, 168, *175*, *177–78*; political galvanization and, 125; positive, 24–25, 27–28, 30, 39, 96, 125; sense of identity and, 10, 12; shared experiences and, 96

"Distinct Stations" experiment, 12, 151–54, 157, 164, 173, *177*
distracter task, 127–28, 161–62
diversity: African Americans and, 180–82, 185; classification and, 33, 40, 50, 54; coherence and, 147, 151–56, *157*, 160–64; color line and, 33; conceptual issues and, 30, 79; control groups and, *152*; demographics and, 185; discrimination and, 180–81; distinctiveness and, 180, 182; group identity and, 183–84; group unity and, 94–97; hierarchies and, 150–51, 155, 158; individual, 94–97; in-group, 183; intergroup, 180–86; Latinos and, 180, 182–83, 185; marginalization and, 184; Mexicans and, 184; Obama and, 133; out-group, 186; pan-racial groups and, 183; political galvanization and, 122, *127*, 133, 137, 139, 182; power and, 180, 185; psychology and, 181–85; regional, 12, *152*, 154, 156, *157*; sense of identity and, 2, 12, 14–15; shared experiences and, 93–97, 107, 115; solidarity and, 180, 182, 186; status and, 181, 183, 185; unity and, 50, 94–97, 115, 151, 186; voting rights and, 180; Whites and, 180–82, 185
Dominicans, 20, *154*
Doosje, Bertjan, 25, 149
Dovidio, Jack, 16, 26
Druckman, Jamie, 133
drugs, 132
DuBois, W. E. B., 33–34

education: classification and, 35, 56–58, 65; coherence and, 162; conceptual issues and, 29, 73, 82–84, *89–91*; demographic data and, 162; sense of identity and, 15; shared experiences and, *121*
Ellemers, Naomi, 25, 36, 149
empathy, 17, 40, 93
Espejo, Mariana, 37, 43, 57
ethnocentrism, 71
exclusion, 43, 46–51, 132, 160–63

favoritism, 5, 24–27, 31, 73, 95, 99–100, 115, 149, 183
feeling thermometer, 4, 75, 134, 141
fertility rates, 2
Filipinos: classification and, 36–40, 43–44, 47–49, 55–57; coherence and, 159–60; sense of identity and, 1–2, 5, 20; shared experiences and, 92–93, *117*, *119–20*

Gaertner, Samuel, 16, 26
Garay, Jessica, 49
García, José, 37, 40–41, 149–50
Gay, Claudine, 18, 69
gender, 6n1, *63*, 73, 84, 122
generic IDs, 11, 23–25, 51, 70–73, 183
Google, 41
group closeness, 20, 67–69
group consciousness, 19–20, 67, 69, 97

Haley, J. L., *121*
hate crimes, 44; combating, 86, *90*, 124, 128, 140, *143–45*, 180; harsher penalties for, 76, 140; reporting, 11, 140; social identity theory (SIT) and, 124
hierarchies: classification and, 36; coherence and, 150–51, 155, 158, 184–86; de-escalation of PoC ID effects and, 27–31; diversity and, 150–51, 155, 158; pecking order and, 28, 57, 150, 158; political galvanization and, 124; racial, 4, 28, 30, 82, 124, 151, 182, 184; social identity theory (SIT) and, 27–31
Hochschild, Jennifer, 18, 35, 69
homogeneity: "I Feel Your Pain" experiments and, 99, 102, 104–12, *113*; in-group, 96, 99, 102, 104–12, *113*, 132; perceived, 102, *105*, 108, 111–12
Hopkins, Dan, 100n1
Huddy, Leonie, 181

"I Feel Your Pain" experiments: African Americans and, 99–116, *117–20*; Asian Americans and, 99–116, *117–20*; centrality and, 99, 102, 105; control group for, 103, 107, 110; demographics and, 103, *117*; homogeneity and, 99, 102, 104–12, *113*; implications for, 115–16; in-groups and, 99–107, 110–11, 115–16; Latinos and, 99–116, *117–20*; methodology of, 99–102; out-groups and, 10, 100, 106–7, 109–10; patterns in, 111–15; political galvanization and, 123–25, 127, 129, *143–45*; research design of, 101–2; self-stereotyping and, 99, 102–4, *107*, 108–9, 111, *112–13*; shared experiences and, 10, 99–115, *117–20*, 149, 182; social identity theory (SIT) and, 99; Whites and, 93, 97, 100–101, 115–16
"I Have a Dream" (King), 3
immigrants, 44; African Americans and, 27, 87; Asian Americans and, 2, 12, 54, 62, 77, 82, 87, 92, 147, 168; children of, 62; coherence and, 171; conservatism and, 51; DACA support and, 86, 87, *91*, 129, 141, *143–45*, 165–71, *172*, *175–76*; differing experiences of, 12; ethnocentrism and, 71; fertility rates and, 2; high-skilled, 11; Latino, 2, 12, 54, 62, 77, 82, 87, 92, 132, 147, 168; legal, 77, 123, 128–29; Muslim, 2, 132; Proposition 187 and, 54; stricter controls over, 27; undocumented, 77, 123, 128, 133, 141, 180; unnaturalized, 92; visas and, 11, 77, 86, 87, *91*, 129, 141, *143–45*, 165–71
Implicit Association Test (IAT), 9, 58–61
incarceration, 2, 33, 92
inclusion, 6n1, 57, 95, 101
Indians, 1, 20, 73, 153
individual mobility, 28–29
inequality: classification and, 37; coherence and, 147; conceptual issues and, 82, *121*; favoritism and, 5, 24–27, 31, 73, 95, 99–100, 115, 149, 183; marginalization and, 4, 31, 33, 38, 51, 62, 101, 155, 160, 162–63, 184; sense of identity and, 3–4

in-group homogeneity, 96, 99, 102, 104–12, *113*, 132
in-group projection, 53, 79
in-groups: acting White and, 47–50; affirmation hypothesis and, 27, 73, 85; classification and, 39, 42–43, 46, 53, 58–61; coherence and, 147–49, 151, 157, 160–65, 167, 171; Common Ingroup Identity Model (CIIM) and, 16, 26; conceptual issues and, 24–27, 29, 31, 71–75, 79; conflict and, 116; distinctiveness of, 10, 12, 24–32, 39, 46, 72, 96, 125, 148–49, 162–71, *172*, *175–78*, 180, 182; diversity and, 183; favoritism and, 5, 24–27, 31, 73, 95, 99–100, 115, 149, 183; "I Feel Your Pain" experiments and, 99–107, 110–11, 115–16; Implicit Association Test (IAT) and, 9, 58–61; political galvanization and, 10–11, 123–25, 127, 129, *143–45*; positive distinctiveness and, 24–25, 27–28, 30, 39, 96, 125; power and, 12, 26; sense of identity and, 5, 8, 10–12, 18–19; shared experiences and, 93–107, 110–11, 115–16; Sherif's Robbers Cave experiment and, 27
Instagram, 148n1
intergroup politics: coherence and, 148–51, 173; diversity and, 180–86; political galvanization and, 125; shared experiences and, 97–98, 116
interminority coalitions, 15–17
intimidation, 11, 124, *127*

Jackson, Jesse, 54
Jackson, Kisha, 42–43, 47–48, 52, 55
Japanese, 20, 73n1, 83, *89–91*, 153
Jim Crow system, 3, 33

Kaiser, Cheryl, 100n1
Kam, Cindy D., 129, 142
Khoudry, Miriam, 37, 47, 151
King, Martin Luther, Jr., 3
King, Rodney, 54
Koreans, 20–21, 73n1, 153
Ku Klux Klan, 33

labor markets: classification and, 45, 55–56, 65; sense of identity and, 2, 11, 15; visas and, 11, 77, 86, 87, *91*, 129, 141, *143–45*, 165–71
Latinos: ascending, 12, 154, *156*, 157, *174*, *177*; bias against, *121*; classification and, 33–37, 41–43, 46–49, 52, 54, 56, 59–63; coherence and, 147–71, *174–78*; conceptual issues and, 25–31, 68, 71–88, *89–91*; demographics of, 1–2; distinctiveness and, *167*, 168, *175*, *177–78*; diversity and, 180, 182–83, 185; as fastest growing minority, 2; hostility toward African Americans, 2; "I Feel Your Pain" experiments and, 99–116, *117–20*; immigrant, 2, 12, 54, 62, 77, 82, 87, 92, 132, 147, 168; median incomes of, 93; as pan-racial category, 4; police brutality and, 33, 86; political galvanization and, 122–23, 126–41, *142*, *145*; poverty rates and, 93;

INDEX

power and, 9, 12, 16, 26, 31, 33, 67, 155, 164, 180, 185; sense of identity and, 1–12, 15–21; shared experiences and, 92–95, 99–116, *117–21*; Trump and, 132; "wetbacks" slur and, *121*
Leach, Colin Wayne, 18
Leeper, Thomas, 133
liberalism, 6n1, 50; American identity and, 82, 85–86, 142; Democrats and, 46, 82–84, *89–91*; demographics on, 62, *63*, *175–76*; impact of, 44, 46; political galvanization and, 142, *143–45*; structural inequities and, 44
Likert scales, 74–75, 126
linked fate, 17–19, 21, 67, 69
Los Angeles riots, 54
*Los Angeles Times*, 147

Mackie, Diane M., 93
Maddox, Nadia, 39–40, 49, 52, 94
majority-minority nation, 1, 185
manipulation, 11–12, 101–2, 111, 127–28, 162
Marable, Manning, 1–3, 122–24, 137–38
marginalization: classification and, 33, 38, 51, 62; coherence and, 155, 160, 162–63; conceptual issues and, 31; diversity and, 184; sense of identity and, 4; shared experiences and, 101
McClain, Paula D., 15–16, 19, 67–69, 97
measurement error, 81, 135
Mexicans: Blaxicans and, 55; classification and, 34, 36–37, 40, 43, 47, 49, 52, 55, *59*; coherence and, 150, *154*, *177–78*; conceptual issues and, 31, 82, *83*, *89–91*; diversity and, 184; identifying as Latino, 20–21, 47, 52; national origin group and, 31; political galvanization and, 132; poverty rates for, 93; sense of identity and, 3, 20–21; shared experiences and, 92–93, *117*, *119–20*; Trump and, 132; White-passing behavior and, 49
multiracial individuals, 9, 29, 35, 63
Muslims, 2, 132, 185

National Association for the Advancement of Colored People (NAACP), 3, 92
national origins, 20–21, 31, 73n1, 82
Native Americans, 1–2, 27, 34, 62, 107, 162, 164, 185
nested identities: classification and, 43; coherence and, 149; conceptual issues and, 23, 27–31, 72–73, 78–79; hypothesis of, 27, 42–46, 149, 180; sense of identity and, 8; shared experiences and, 95–96, 98–99, 101, 115
newspapers, 53–54, 65–66
Nguyen, Ngoc, 40, 49, 51, 93, 159

Obama, Barack, 133–34, 136, 138
Ocampo, Joanna, 160
Omi, Michael, 29
ordinary least squares (OLS) regression, *7*, 81, 83, *91*

out-groups: classification and, 39, 58; coherence and, 151, 164, 170–71; conceptual issues and, 25, 27, 30, 72, 76; conflict and, 17, 26; diversity and, 186; feeling thermometer and, 4; "I Feel Your Pain" experiment and, 10, 100, 106–7, 109–10; political galvanization and, 123–29, *143–45*; sense of identity and, 4–5, 10–11, 16–17; shared experiences and, 94, 96, 100, 106–7, 109–10

pan-ethnic identity, 20–21, 30–31, 183
pan-racial groups: classification and, 6, 9–10, 12–13, 22, 31, 46, 58, 96, 128, 131, 133, 158, 183; coherence and, 158; diversity and, 183; political galvanization and, 128, 131, 133; sense of identity and, 6, 9–10, 12–13, 22; shared experiences and, 96
partisanship, 62, 73, 82, 93, 100
pecking orders, 28, 57, 150, 158
people of color (PoC): acting White and, 47–50; conversing with, 34–36; free, 3; growth of, 1, 16, 122; internal identity and, 58–61; label of, 3; newspapers' use of term, 53–54, 65–66; parallel positions and, 149–51, 159–61; persuasion of term, 3; racial disadvantages and, 37–38; Republicans'/Democrats' use of term, 45–46; shifting society and, 2; skin tone and, 36–37, 46–52, 55–59; Widatalla editorial and, 147–48, 159, 171
people of color identity (PoC ID): access to, 3, 32, 46, 131–33, 136–38, *142*; citizens of color and, 3; classification and, 34–62, 66; coherence and, 147–51, 155–73, *174–78*; conceptual issues and, 23–32, 67–88, *89–91*; confirmatory factor analysis (CFA) and, *77*, *78*, 81n3, *146*; criteria for, 68–70; delineating, 68–70; demographics of, 1; differentiating from other IDs and, 77–84; diversity and, 179–86; empirical issues and, 67–71, 74–75, 87–89; generic IDs and, 11, 23–25, 51, 70–73, 183; impact of, 4; as new identification, 3; political galvanization and, 122–38, *142–46*; political/social influences of, 84–87, *89–91*; racial ID bond and, 25–29; relevance of, 4, 73, 77, 129, 134, 138, 149, 164; resurgent racial politics and, 132–37; salience of, 4, 31, 75, *78*, 116; sense of belonging and, 25, 30, 38–42, 46; sense of identity and, 1–22; shared experiences and, 92–99, 102–16; social identity theory (SIT) and, 23–29; sociopolitical influence of, 4
"People of Color" surveys, 10, *42*, 73–81, 84, 126, 135
Phan, Brandon, 53
photo identification laws, 33
Pierce, Iris, 56, 58
police brutality, 44; African Americans and, 27, 33, 55, 86, 133; Asian Americans and, 27, 86, 92; curbing, 11, 86, *90*, 124, 128, 140, *143–45*; deadly force and, 76, 133, 140; Latinos and, 33, 86; racial profiling and, 76, 140; social identity theory (SIT) and, 124

political galvanization: African Americans and, 122–23, 126–38, 141, *142*, *146*; Asian Americans and, 123, 126–42, *144*, *146*; #BlackLivesMatter and, 123–24, 128–29, 132, 141, *143–45*; control groups and, 127–29, 131, 142; Democrats and, 128, 131, 141, *143–45*; demographics and, 122, 126, 137; distinctiveness and, 125; distracter task and, 127–28; diversity and, 122, *127*, 133, 137, 139; hierarchies and, 124; in-groups and, 10–11, 123–25, 127, 129, *143–45*; intergroup, 125, 148–51; Latinos and, 122–23, 126–41, *142*, *145*; lessons from, 137–39; liberalism and, 142, *143–45*; manipulation and, 127–28; Marable and, 1–3, 122–24, 137–38; Mexicans and, 132; Obama and, 133–34, 136, 138; out-groups and, 123–29, *143–45*; pan-racial groups and, 128, 131, 133; power and, 122, 138; racial identity and, 124–29, 139, 142, *143–45*; Republicans and, 128, 141; resurgent racial politics and, 132–37; social creativity and, 125; social identity theory (SIT) and, 8, 123–25, 128; solidarity and, 125–26, 128, 131, 142, *143–45*; status and, 125; threats and, 123–32, 142; Trump and, 51, 132–34, 136, 138; unity and, 123, 138; voting rights and, 124, 128, 132, 140, *143–45*; Whites and, 124, 127–28, 134–35, 141

"Political Galvanization" experiment: bolstering people of color identity (PoC ID) and, 128–29; diversity and, 182; lessons learned from, 137–39; methodology of, 126–28; question wordings for, *127*, 139–42; Trump and, 132, 134

political opinions: African Americans and, 72–73, 77, 84; Asian Americans and, 67, 69, 72–87, *89–91*; collective action and, 19, 39, 97, 137, 182; *Congressional Record* and, 45–46; conservatism and, 1 (*see also* conservatism); DACA support and, 86, 87, *91*, 129, 141, *143–45*, 165–71, *172*, *175–76*; Democrats and, 76, 81–85, *86*, 88, *89–91*; ethnic identity and, 17–21; group consciousness and, 19–20, 67, 69, 97; influences on, 84–87, *89–91*; intergroup, 97–98, 116, 125, 148–51, 173, 180–86; interminority coalitions and, 15–17; liberalism and, 44 (*see also* liberalism); partisanship and, 62, 73, 82, 93, 100; racial identity and, 17–21; Republicans and, 76, *83*, 84–85, 88, *89–91*; social identity theory (SIT) and, 23–29; Widatalla editorial and, 147–48, 159, 171

Polynesians, 55

positive distinctiveness, 24–25, 27–28, 30, 39, 96, 125

poverty, 33, 93

power: access to, 1, 28, 138; African Americans and, 9, 16, 67, 155, 180; Asian Americans and, 9, 12, 16, 26, 31, 33, 40, 67, 93, 155, 164, 180, 185; classification and, 33, 40, 43; coherence and, 151, 155, 164, 171; conceptual issues and, 26, 28, 31n2, 67–68, 85, 88; diversity and, 180, 185; in-groups and, 12, 26; Latinos and, 9, 12, 16, 26, 31, 33, 67, 155, 164, 180, 185; political galvanization and, 122, 138; sense of identity and, 1, 9, 12, 16; shared experiences and, 93; Whites and, 1, 9, 16, 26, 151, 185

pride, 38–42, 46, 125

profiling, 76, 140

Prolific, 110, 161

Proposition 187, 54

prototypical groups: classification and, 36, 52–53, 55; coherence and, 154–58, *174*; conceptual issues and, 25, 72, 87; control groups and, 155; sense of identity and, 12; shared experiences and, 95; shifting, 154–58

psychology: classification and, 36; coherence and, 148–50; conceptual issues and, 23–26, 29, 69–70, 72; Craig and, 16–17, 182; diversity and, 181–85; group, 24–25; heightened similarity perceptions and, 17; "I Feel Your Pain" experiments and, 10, 99–115, *117–20*, 149, 182; Implicit Association Test (IAT) and, 9, 58–61; Richeson and, 16, 182; sense of identity and, 9, 16–18, 21; shared experiences and, 94–95, 97, 99–100; social identity theory (SIT) and, 24–25

Puerto Ricans, 20, 55, 82, *83*, *91*, *117*, 119–20, 154, 184

Race, Ethnicity, Politics & Society (REPS) Lab, 153

racial identity: classification and, 42–43; coherence and, 148–49, 162, *172*, *173*; conceptual issues and, 23, 25–27, 29, 31n2, 68, 72–79, 82–87, *89–91*; people of color identity (PoC ID) bond and, 27–29; political galvanization and, 124–29, 139, 142, *143–45*; sense of identity and, 7, 9, 11, 13, 16, 20; shared experiences and, 109–11, 116. *See also specific races*

racial profiling, 76, 140

racial uniqueness hypothesis, 30–31

racism, 3, 33, *121*, 127, 131–33, 147, 150, 160

Ramírez, Lupe, 43, 47, 150

Ramos, Alejandra, 57–58

reality constraints, 151–52, 158

Republicans, 63; conservatism and, 1, 51, 57; mention of people of color (PoC) by, 45–46; minorities identifying with, 93; minority opinion on, 11; partisanship and, 93; "People of Color" surveys and, 75; political galvanization and, 128, 141; political opinions and, 76, *83*, 84–85, 88, *89–91*; White supremacy and, 51

resources, 1, 15, 26, 28, 37, 116, 185

Reyes, Sara, 38, 47–49, 53, 55, 159

Richeson, Jennifer, 16, 182

root mean square error of approximation (RMSEA), *77*, *78*, *146*

rudeness, 10, 110–11, 113–14

salience, 4, 31, 75, *78*, 116
Salvadorans, 20, 55, *154*
Sanchez, Gabriel R., 19
Sanchez, Linda, 37, 40–41, 92–93, 150–51
Santos, David, 37, 39, 43–45, 48–49, 51, 55, 92
school, 2, 12
Seger, Charles R., 93
self-stereotyping, 95–96, 99, 102–4, *107*, 108–9, 111, *112–13*, 121
self-worth, 24, 46, 125
sense of belonging, 25, 30, 38–42, 46
sense of identity: African Americans and, 1–12, 15–17; Asian Americans and, 1–12, 16–21; #BlackLivesMatter and, 6–7; Chinese and, 3, 20; competition and, 2, 13, 15, 21; demographics and, 1–2, 4, 9, 12, 14; discrimination and, 3–4, 13, 16–17, 19; distinctiveness and, 10, 12; diversity and, 2, 12, 14–15; education and, 15; ethnic, 17–21; Filipinos and, 20; group closeness and, 20, 67–69; Implicit Association Test (IAT) and, 9, 58–61; inequality and, 3–4; in-groups and, 5, 8, 10–12, 18–19; interminority coalitions and, 15–17; internal, 58–61; Latinos and, 1–12, 15–21; linked fate and, 17–19, 21, 67, 69; marginalization and, 4; Mexicans and, 3, 20–21; national origins and, 20–21, 31, 73n1, 82; nested identities and, 8; out-groups and, 4–5, 10–11, 16–17; pan-ethnic, 20–21, 30–31, 183; pan-racial groups and, 6, 9–10, 12–13, 22; "People of Color" surveys and, 10, *42*, 73–81, 126, 135; power and, 1, 9, 12, 16; prototypical groups and, 12; psychology and, 9, 16–18, 21; racial identity and, 7, 9, 11, 13, 16–21; self-worth and, 24, 46, 125; social identity theory (SIT) and, 8; solidarity and, 1–2, 6, 9, 16, 18; status and, 1–2, 6, 16, 19; unity and, 11, 21
shared experiences: African Americans and, 92–95, 99–116, *117–21*; Asian Americans and, 92–95, 99–116, *117–20*; bias and, 5, 98–100, *121*; centrality and, 96–97, 99, 102, 105; Chinese and, *117*, *119–20*; demographics and, 103, *117*; discrimination and, 97, 100–101, *121*; "Distinct Experiences" experiment and, 162; diversity and, 93–97, 107, 115; education and, *121*; Filipinos and, 92–93, *117*, *119–20*; group unity and, 94–97; homogeneity and, 96, 99, 102, 104–12, *113*, 132; "I Feel Your Pain" experiments and, 10, 99–115, *117–20*, 149, 182; incarceration and, 92; income inequality and, 92–93; in-groups and, 93–111, 115–16; intergroup, 97–98, 116; Latinos and, 92–95, 99–116, *117–21*; linked fate and, 17–19, 21, 67, 69; marginalization and, 101; Mexicans and, 92–93, *117*, *119–20*; nested identities and, 95–99, 101, 115; new insights for, 111–15; out-groups and, 94, 96, 100, 106–7, 109–10; pan-racial groups and, 96; patterns in, 111–15; poverty rates and, 93; power and, 93; prototypical groups and, 95; psychology and, 94–95, 97, 99–100; racial identity and, 109–11, 116; rudeness and, 10, 110–11, 113–14; self-stereotyping and, 95–96, 99, 102–4, *107*, 108–9, 111, *112–13*, *121*; social identity theory (SIT) and, 30, 94–97; status and, 97, 101; Whites and, 92–93, 97, 100–101, 115–16, *121*
Sherif's Robbers Cave experiment, 27
Sidanius, Jim, 29, 150
Sirin, Cigdem V., 17, 92–93, 95, 182
skin tone: classification and, 36–37, 46–52, 55–59; coherence and, 150, 159–60; conceptual issues and, 29; darker, 37, 47, 52, 55, 57–58, 150, 160; exclusion and, 46–47; lighter, 29, 46–48, 55, 60
slavery, 2–3, 12, 44, 53, 147, 160, 163
slurs, *121*
Smith, Eliot R., 93
social competition, 28–30, 186
social creativity, 28–30, 39, 125, 186
social identity theory (SIT): affirmation hypothesis and, 27, 73, 85; African Americans and, 25, 29; Asian Americans and, 26–29; centrality and, 9, 70, 96–97, 99, 102, 105; coherence and, 149, 173; Common Ingroup Identity Model (CIIM) and, 26; conceptual issues and, 23–29; group unity and, 94–97; hate crimes and, 124; hierarchies and, 27–31; "I Feel Your Pain" experiments and, 99; individual mobility and, 28–29; in-group favoritism and, 24–27, 31; minimal group experiments and, 24; nested identities hypothesis and, 27; normal distributions and, 51; police brutality and, 124; political galvanization and, 8, 123–25, 128; positive distinctiveness and, 24–25, 27–28, 30, 39, 96, 125; psychology of groups and, 24–25; racial ID/PoC ID bond and, 25–27; sense of identity and, 8; shared experiences and, 30, 94–97; Tajfel and, 24–28; unity and, 23–29
social media, 148n1
social scientists, 1, 15–16, 88, 134, 186
solidarity: as by-product, 18–19; classification and, 38–42; coherence and, 147; commitment and, 18–19; common identity and, 2; conceptual issues and, 30, 75, 85, *86*, 88, *89*; diversity and, 180, 182, 186; hypothesis for, 1–2; "People of Color" surveys and, 75; political galvanization and, 125–26, 128, 131, 142, *143–45*; pride and, 38–42; sense of belonging and, 25, 30, 38–42, 46; sense of identity and, 1–2, 6, 9, 16, 18
Spears, Russell, 25, 149
status: classification and, 37, 49–50, 56, 61–62; coherence and, 150–52, 157–58; conceptual issues and, 28–30; disadvantages and, 16, 37; diversity and, 181, 183, 185; hierarchies and, 29 (*see also* hierarchies); political galvanization and, 125;

status (cont.)
  sense of identity and, 1–2, 6, 16, 19; shared experiences and, 97, 101
Stimson, James A., 65
subordinate identities, 28, 43, 72, 95, 150–51, 173
superordinate identities, 43–44, 58, 72, 95, 149, 171, 173, 183
Survey Sampling International (SSI), 73, 103, 107
sympathy, 5, 20, 135

Tajfel, Henri, 24–28, 30, 70, 186
"Term *People of Color* Erases Black People, The. Let's Retire It" (Widatalla), 147
test-retest correlation, 80–81
Transue, John E., 27
*Trouble with Unity, The* (Beltrán), 21
Trump, Donald, 51, 132–34, 136, 138
Trussler, Marc J., 129, 142
Tucker-Lewis index (TLI), 77, 78, 146
Tumbukas, 184
Turner, John, 28, 30, 36, 70, 96, 186
Twitter, 148n1

uniqueness, 21, 30–31, 148, 160, 162, 164–65, 168, 170
unity: classification and, 50; coherence and, 147–48, 151, 157, 173; conceptual issues and, 23–32, 85; diversity and, 50, 94–97, 115, 151, 186; group, 94–97; political galvanization and, 123, 138; sense of identity and, 11, 21; shared experiences and, 94–97; social identity theory (SIT) and, 23–29
University of California, Los Angeles (UCLA), 35, 57–59, 62–64, 151–58
US Census Bureau, 1, 31n2, 33–34, 92, 137, 161–62

Valentino, Nicholas A., 17, 92–93, 95, 182
vandalism, 11, 124, *127*
variance-covariance matrix, 77
verbal abuse, 94, 110
Vietnamese, 37, 40, 49, 51, 53, 73n1, 93, *153*, 159

Villalobos, José, 17, 92–93, 95, 182
violence, 11, 33, 54, 124, *127*
visas, 11, 77, *86*, 87, *91*, 129, 141, *143–45*, 165–71
voting rights: conceptual issues and, 76, 86, 88, *90*; diversity and, 180; impact of, 76; "People of Color" surveys and, 75; political galvanization and, 124, 128, 132, 140, *143–45*; strengthening, 75, 86, 88, *90*, 128, 132, 140, *143–45*, 180, 214

wealth, 29, 92
"wetbacks" slur, *121*
White, Ariel, 18, 69
White-passing behavior, 47–50
Whites: classification and, 34, 36–39, 42, 45, 47–48, 54, 57–61; coherence and, 149–52, 155, 158, 160, 164–66; conceptual issues and, 26–30, 76, 79, 82, 85; diversity and, 180–82, 185; growth of people of color (PoC) and, 1, 16, 122; "I Feel Your Pain" experiments and, 93, 97, 100–101, 115–16; median incomes of, 93; minority sense of identity and, 1–5, 8–9, 11, 16; political galvanization and, 124, 127–28, 134–35, 141; resistance by, 1–2; shared experiences and, 92–93, 97, 100–101, 115–16, *121*; shifting society and, 2; Trump and, 51, 132–34, 136, 138; wealth of, 92
White supremacists, 51, 57, 124, 127–28
Widatalla, Nadra, 147–48, 159, 171
Winant, Howard, 29
Winters, Ingrid, 52–53
Wong, Cara, 20
Wu, Avery, 40, 57

xenophobia, 25, 71

Yoruba-Nagot, 184

Zambia, 184
zero-sum games, 164–65, *166–67*, *169*, 171n4, *175–76*
Zou, Linda X., 38, 181

www.ingramcontent.com/pod-product-compliance
Lightning Source LLC
Chambersburg PA
CBHW051357290426
44108CB00015B/2047